Insatiable
Is Not Sustainable

Doug Brown

Westport, Connecticut
London

Library of Congress Cataloging-in-Publication Data

Brown, Douglas M., 1947–
    Insatiable is not sustainable / Doug Brown.
        p.   cm.
    Includes bibliographical references and index.
    ISBN 0–275–96848–0 (alk. paper)—ISBN 0–275–97416–2 (pbk. : alk. paper)
        1. Sustainable development.   I.   Title.
    HC79.E5B758   2002
    338.9′27—dc21   2001032905

British Library Cataloguing in Publication Data is available.

Library of Congress Catalog Card Number: 2001032905
ISBN: 0–275–96848–0
        0–275–97416–2 (pbk.)

First published in 2002

Praeger Publishers, 88 Post Road West, Westport, CT 06881
An imprint of Greenwood Publishing Group, Inc.
www.praeger.com

Printed in the United States of America

The paper used in this book complies with the
Permanent Paper Standard issued by the National
Information Standards Organization (Z39.48–1984).

10 9 8 7 6 5 4 3 2 1

Copyright Acknowledgments

The author and publisher gratefully acknowledge permission for use of the following:

Excerpted with permission from Marshall Sahlins. STONE AGE ECONOMICS (New York: Aldine de Gruyter). Copyright © 1972 by Marshall Sahlins.

Reprinted by permission of the publishers and the Trustees of the Loeb Classical Library from SENECA: EPISTLES, VOLUMES IV and VI, Loeb Classical Library Volume #L075 and #L077, translated by Richard M. Gummere, Cambridge, Mass.: Harvard University Press, 1917. The Loeb Classical Library ® is a registered trademark of the President and Fellows of Harvard College.

Regarding the verse on page 198 by Ansel Adams and Nancy Newhall (San Fransisco: Sierra Club, 1968) every effort has been made to trace the owners of the copyright materials but it has proven impossible. The author and publisher will be glad to receive information leading to more complete acknowledgments in subsequent printings of the book and in the meantime apologize for any omissions.

For Beth, my wife:

my companion,

my soul mate,

whose presence in my life inspires

love and compassion

and a fundamental desire,

as yet still unsatisfied:

a satiable world of social justice

at peace with humanity and nature.

Contents

Illustrations

Acknowledgments

The ideas in this book have been stewing about in my mind for twenty years at least, and therefore they have a history connected to the many friends and colleagues who have contributed to their formulation and clarification. One of the most important people in this process is Ron Stanfield, who directed my Ph.D. dissertation at Colorado State University in 1984–1985. Ron initially turned me on to Karl Polanyi, whose influence in this book is paramount. Although Polanyi did not take up environmental or sustainability issues, as he died in 1964, before the public became sensitized to these problems, he has provided me with a framework in which to situate today's crisis of sustainability. I owe Ron a tremendous debt of gratitude for his keen understanding of Polanyi and his ability to communicate that to me.

I also want to thank the College of Business at Northern Arizona University for its support of this project. Our dean, Patricia Meyers, has been generous in both her financial support and encouraging words, and for both I am very thankful and appreciative.

Additionally, I owe Theresa Stacy-Ryan a huge thank-you for her reading of the manuscript, her helpful suggestions, and, most of all, her superior skills in doing the hard-core formatting for the book. She is a master of desktop publishing in the College of Business with capabilities in using Word software that I could never imagine achieving. Without her friendly association and diligence this book would not have been published. Thank you so much, Theresa.

Finally, I want to thank my wife, Beth, and my son and daughter, Mathieu and Sierra. Beth not only read the manuscript and gave me excellent advice but, most importantly, introduced me to Thich Nhat Hanh and Buddhist ways of satiable living. Not only do I thank her for this, but she took me to Plum Village in France, tolerated my grumpiness, and has given me a richer understanding of love and simplicity. Her love is something that I can never be too thankful for. Mathieu, Sierra, Beth, and I have lived and talked the ideas in this book for the past two years. Without their kind support, helpful insights, and suggestions this wouldn't have been a book at all. All three have listened to me over the years, offered their critical, deep, and careful opinions, and have been a truly enriching force for this book. They have both supported and challenged my ideas, and our conversations about what it means to be a human and whether or not Be All You Can Be is the ultimate end-all of life, have been assimilated into much of the text of this book and have deepened it significantly. We have spent untold hours talking about what it means to be a satiable self in an insatiable world—not that any us have accomplished this. I want to thank them especially for their optimism and faith in the ability of people to change the world. I have enormous admiration for not only their belief in people but their practice of this faith in daily life.

Introduction: Is Sustainability a New Cultural Paradigm? *The Three Cultures Approach*

How often have you heard: "That's very good, but you know, you can always do better"? It usually starts when you're a kid. Of course, it's merely one example in what for many is a fundamental theme of life: Be All You Can Be! It's time to question this theme.

Be All You Can Be is now a moral and social imperative. It is what we use to judge one another. But it wasn't always this way, although it has a long history at least as far back as the Agricultural Revolution 10,000 years ago (when settled farming began). We have, as a modern culture in the industrial parts of the world, assimilated this maxim to such an extent that to challenge the idea that humans are genetically engineered to "actualize our potential" seems absurd.

For some, the childhood stress arising from this imperative never ceases. Their parents always told them that they could be more. Of course, their parents loved them dearly. It has nothing to do with that. Several generations of parents have been simply stating that what counts is giving your best shot at becoming more tomorrow than you are today. There is always more that one can be. Some rebel against the imperative, others fail at it, and some suffer the stress of mastering it.

For decades we have failed to see that this imperative, Be All You Can Be, is not universal or eternal. Only now with the looming environmental crisis have I begun to understand that our modern fixation with "self-actualizing our potential" is *the defining feature of our culture*. The concept that humans are unique among life forms because they have unlimited and thus insatiable potential is so deeply embedded that we should not expect otherwise. We assume it, we embrace it, we try to escape it, we suffer from it, but it is us, and we are it.

It is, for sure, more of a white, European, modern, and industrial notion. Indigenous people and those who have not encountered our culture of insatiable improvers are more likely to be miffed or puzzled by this, and not everyone has had to struggle with measuring up, succeeding at life, or accomplishing goals. For many, Being All You Can Be has been exciting, fun, and gratifying without being scary, stressful, or anxiety-provoking. So be it. This is fine, except for one thing: anyone can see that our insatiable desire to "have more" is directly related to the potential destruction of our earthly habitat. What most do not recognize and is therefore the central argument of this book is that *the insatiable desire to HAVE more is a result of the insatiable desire to BE more.* But "being more," we believe, is the meaning of humankind itself! Humans, so the conventional wisdom goes, are the "insatiable improvers." If it's good, then it can and should be improved upon. That was all our parents really wanted to tell us as kids.

But their view was still only an expression of what had been evolving for 10,000 years: *the Culture of Insatiable Freedom.* As kids, many of us subconsciously searched for an escape from the Be All You Can Be treadmill. It seemed to get harder and harder to stay ahead of the accomplishment-driven competitive process. What is clear is that we did judge each other by our achievements and successes. Many tried to avoid competition and stay out of the loop of "succeed or fail." Most of us didn't want to fail. But to try to succeed risked that outcome, and there is only one way to "succeed," and that is to try to BE MORE tomorrow than you are today. For many then and now, this is stressful. Constantly having to BE MORE can make some folks into winners, but for many others it can mean giving up and being judged a "loser" or a "slacker."

But this is not just self-imposed stress. It is our culture. We assimilate and hope for the best, that is, to be winners at "being more." Or we resist and suffer other consequences like failure, alienation, and economic hardship. Drop out? The hippie movement appealed to some for this reason. Here was a movement that suggested implicitly that to just BE was all right. So there were those who wanted off the productivist treadmill and who were disaffected with the mainstream cultural insatiability of "having more." What was wrong with a simple life based upon "being" rather than the treadmill of "becoming"?

Dropping out is an effort at creating a "noncareer lifestyle." In a new Culture of Sustainability there will be room for such a lifestyle, and moreover it will become a socially acceptable way of living. As anticipated by folks in the 1960s like Theodore Roszak (*The Making of a Counter Culture* 1969), the noncareer lifestyle would then be part of the dominant culture rather than the "counterculture."

What follows is not simply a critique of our cultural fixation with self-realization. The fundamental concern is environmental and human sustainability for the next century. If we want to assure the sustainability of humankind, we need to rethink our cultural value of Be All You Can Be. We need to go beyond our present Culture of Insatiable Freedom and create a new Culture of Sustainability. Why? The following verse explains it.

Sustainability means
Living simply, harmoniously, and justly
With humans and nature.
BUT
To be human is
To Be...
ALL YOU CAN BE
How much is that?
It's insatiable
BUT
Insatiable is NOT Sustainable

Our Culture of Insatiable Freedom is at odds with that of Sustainability. To get sustainable, we have to give up our view of what we believe is our "human nature," the insatiable self. Yet most get very defensive about any suggestion that there might be more to life than actualizing our potential. Rightly so, maybe. *But the fact is that there have been only two cultures in human history up to this point: (1) our present Culture of Insatiable Freedom, which began with Capitalism in the sixteenth century and (2) the Culture of Security.* This earlier culture lasted for 2 to 3 million years. It was sustainable, and it worked. More importantly, it was *not* premised upon an imperative of Be All You Can Be. It was not driven by insatiable improvement. It was not about "getting ahead." It was not about either having more or being more. It was not about self-actualization, self- and social development, self-realization, or self- or social improvement.

In his classic statement *The Ascent of Man,* Jacob Bronowski said that he used the word *ascent* in a very precise fashion: "Man is distinguished from other animals by his imaginative gifts. He makes plans, inventions, new discoveries, by putting different talents together" (Bronowski 1973, 20). Bronowski argues that humans are different because they are clever and quick learners. Improvements happened; they weren't the thematic and driving force that motivated the hunter-gatherers. It is true that "imaginative gifts" associated with human intelligence make it possible for humans not only to improve their lives but to perceive themselves as insatiable improvers.

It would be a misinterpretation of Bronowski to equate "imaginative gifts" with "driven by improvement." In the course of history, to shift our notion of the essence of humans from that of beings who are unique because of their "imaginative gifts" to beings who must continuously improve is more than a semantic twist. It is a culturally induced shift, because with the Neolithic (Agricultural) Revolution, we began to redefine what it means to be a human and eventually made ourselves into the beings who must Be All You Can Be. "Imaginative gifts" do not imply this. So over the past 10,000 years we have evolved an entire culture constituted by our self-imposed definition that To Be is to Be More. Moreover, Be All You Can Be has become a *cultural imperative.*

If we are to save ourselves, we need to understand both the Culture of Security and the Culture of Insatiable Freedom and then glean from them what is necessary to create a third culture: the Culture of Sustainability. The point is, of course, not to go back but "to improve." This suggests that, paradoxically, if we are to improve our chances at human sustainability, we should focus on something other than improvement. In other words, perhaps to improve at this historic juncture means to give up the improvement fixation. But we should not misinterpret what this means. *The elimination of human suffering—most, but not all of it, needless—is different from "improvement for its own sake." To go beyond our current culture, which is driven by improvement, does not mean that we should give up the struggle to end suffering in all of its forms.* The Culture of Sustainability still calls us to create a just and secure world in which the end to suffering continues to be a worthy goal that demands our vigilance and attention throughout the future.

The goal of ending human suffering has both objective and subjective dimensions, of course. Subjectively, it is obviously difficult to quantify someone's "emotional pain." Yet it is frequently observable. On the other hand, there are many objective indicators of human suffering like depression, despair, physical starvation, and such. Each of us has our own sense for what suffering is.

The point is that a sustainable culture that is not driven by improvement can still task itself with ending human suffering. The character of this culture would be much different from ours today. Ending human suffering suggests limits. We know when we've progressed toward achievement of this goal. Today's culture, driven by insatiable self-actualizing, knows no limits. You can always be more tomorrow than you are today. Its premise is insatiability. Ending human suffering, by comparison, is a measurable and satiable goal. Ending human suffering can be sustainable. The realization of unlimited potential, *as a cultural imperative*, is not.

Clearly, human potential is insatiable, at least insofar as psychologists and anthropologists have been able to determine. But to make this *the* driving force of a culture is now unhealthy.

We should recall Marx's famous quote that to be radical is to go to the root of the problem. For humans, the root of the problem is humans themselves. In this case the root of the problem is humans' *perception* of themselves. How we perceive who we are is jeopardizing our future. The notion that we are meant to always go beyond ourselves, to be more, and to actualize our potential is a cultural artifact.

Consider the Culture Pyramid. These are the "three Cs," and each has to do with control. At the top of the pyramid are corporations. They are at the peak only because they are the most visible and wield tremendous power in today's global economy. Most would agree that they are the biggest and most influential players in the economic arena, notwithstanding the nation-state. Yet many would argue that the nations of the world today are the corporations. Their preoccupation is with controlling people and markets. They want to shape workers in their image and clearly want to shape consumers likewise. They need to exercise as much control over all markets as they possibly can. Their ticket to "improvement" of their institutional and economic life lies in the process of shaping, molding, and influencing both consumer and worker behavior.

Culture Pyramid

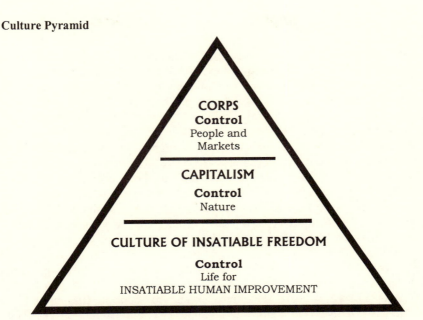

But we can't understand business behavior without looking at what lies underneath it: the competitive market economy itself. The climate that shapes and molds corporations' efforts at control, that constrains and governs them is the global system of capitalism. To understand the corporate world and what drives it, we need to understand the system in which business operates. Capitalism itself is also a "driven" system, as competition forces much of corporate behavior. This is not a new idea, as Marx was one of the first to make this case.

So the system of capitalism, viewed as a "system," is bent on controlling the natural world. On behalf of the corporate players, it plows, drives, pirates, and pushes all that surrounds it. With the title of Martin O'Connor's book, he asks, *Is Capitalism Sustainable?* (O'Connor 1994). We should ask, "Is humankind sustainable *on the basis of capitalism?*" Left-wing environmentalists and economists have been arguing for years that capitalism is doing us in, that is, doing in our biosphere and earthly home. Our economic system prides itself on its insatiable drive and its insatiable ability to "improve" our lives. The case for capitalism as made by classical and neo-classical economists is that it is the "best of all possible worlds," precisely because it can do the most with our insatiable freedom and can infinitely grow, making life bigger and better for more and more folks. Improvement is what capitalism has always been about. Marx would have agreed, except to add that the improvements accrued mostly to the business owners at the expense of workers. But he and the classicals took as an article of faith that its purpose was to maximize material wealth. It is the freedom-driven, wealth-maximizing machine. So corporations are about "more," and capitalism is about "more": more of everything that is deemed good—more profits, more growth, more productivity, more markets, more wealth, more stuff for everyone.

But again, we can't understand the Economy of Insatiable Improvers (capitalism) unless we look lower on the pyramid. At the base is the basic "C": the Culture of Insatiable Freedom. Corporations and capitalism are merely the most recent development in a 10,000-year-old evolution. It is the notion that humans are, in their essence, genetically engineered to Be All You Can Be. Today's culture is that of freedom and insatiability. Our perception of ourselves as having the freedom to actualize our unlimited potential grounds both capitalism and corporations. Consumers are driven to want more. Workers want more. Corporations want more. What's unique about capitalism is that it channels "more" into "having more." This is assumed in all principles of economics textbooks: human wants are unlimited. But the Culture of Insatiable Freedom is about "being more." To insatiably actualize our potential, we think it necessary to control the life process itself.

Corporations want to control people and markets; capitalism is premised upon control of the natural world; and, finally, our entire culture is premised upon the control of life itself. How else can humans continuously and relentlessly improve their condition except to control life in all its multidimensionality? Our argument is simply that our Culture of Insatiable Freedom is doing us in, not capitalism or corporations. They are cultural expressions; they are effects rather than causes.

Today's culture is that of the "insatiable self." But to understand how we got here and what we can do about it, we have to look to the earliest humans— those of the pre-Neolithic period. For almost 3 million years people lived with a much different concept of themselves than we do today. They lived in the Culture of Security, and whether they were aware of it or not, they were "Satiable Selves." This does not mean that they failed to appreciate an improvement. The Eolithic people had tools made from chipped flint. But they were not in a culture that was "driven by improvement."

But the Agricultural Revolution marked the beginning of a new definition of the self. Yet this occurred in the context of the existing Culture of Security. In other words, there was no dramatic change in culture with the gradual emergence of the "insatiable self." This was, in part, a consequence of the fact that these early sedentary societies, both slave and feudal in character, were still "embedded" economies like their predecessors. Additionally, they were "no-growth" economies. So, with ancient Greece, for example, the economy of slavery was one in which people were not free to buy and sell at will. Economic activity, as Karl Polanyi argued, was "embedded," because it was governed by social norms, customs, and traditions (Polanyi [1944] 1957). There was not a separate economic sphere that resulted from individual economic freedom. Because these were embedded economies, people were taken care of whether they were slaves or serfs or peasants. The notion of economic growth had yet to surface.

Aristotle's work is an example, on the other hand, of the early idea that people have the potential to be more tomorrow than they are today. As we will see, although he understood that humans are transcendent beings, he didn't suggest that they should actualize their insatiable potential. Yet art, music, poetry, and literature, among other activities, are Aristotle's evidence that people can be more. Freedom in this early view is the ability to change what one is today to something more tomorrow! Freedom is the awareness of the gap between where we are and where we could be. Presumably, the purpose of life is to narrow this gap. Because our potential is insatiable, we assume that the gap can never be closed.

Before capitalism's emergence in the sixteenth century, the notion that humans should realize their potential was rather restricted. For lack of material means, it had to be restricted to the members of privileged classes. Consequently, "certain" humans should Be All You Can Be. But this could not be universalized without two essential conditions: (1) everyone had to have the individual freedom to pursue self-actualization and (2) everyone would have to have access to the material requisites for this, such as education, tools, property, and the instruments of culture.

So before capitalism, the universalizing of the insatiable self was constrained by (1) the continuation of the Culture of Security, until A.D. 1500, (2) the limits imposed by the otherworldly focus of the Judeo-Christian tradition, and (3) lack of economic growth awareness. The Culture of Security created barriers that kept average people from pursuing self-actualization. There was little freedom to buy and sell, to pursue economic and political self-interest, and to achieve more in life. Additionally, the religious norms of feudal Europe were not favorable to acquisitive behavior and self-realization. The focus on salvation and faith did not require that people should try to be more. It is hard for anyone to be more when there are few cultural resources available (like musical instruments, art tools, formal education, and a standard of living that created a measure of free time).

The sixteenth century changed all of this. People were free to pursue their destiny, to buy and sell, to "get ahead," and to be more. People could not only be more but have more. Economic growth created the material means for anyone in general to have more. By allowing this, commoners could then be more. The Culture of Security was giving way to the new Culture of Insatiable Freedom. Everyone in the Western world, except slaves and indigenous people, was formally free to pursue economic and political self-interest. The erosion of church influence, secularization of life, individual freedom, and economic growth spelled an end to the exclusivity of Be All You Can Be. The privileged classes were no longer the only ones who could be more. Everyone was "freed up" to actualize his or her potential.

This became the new fundamental value and moral imperative. By the nineteenth century both John Stuart Mill and Karl Marx had assimilated the value that what humans are about is Be All You Can Be. Everyone *should* have the equal right to pursue his or her self-actualization. Everyone *should* have the equal opportunity to have more. Being more and having more also capture the essence of the Enlightenment.

Be All You Can Be not only became the identifying feature of our culture but did so as a result of capitalist and market logic. Capitalism itself compels this. Because it is a "disembedded economy" as Karl Polanyi argued in *The Great Transformation*, insecurity is a basic condition. People must "achieve" security by developing themselves if they are to have a decent life. The ticket to survival and the good life in this system is to pursue one's actualization through the channels of the market system. If one doesn't, there is real risk of economic hardship and social disrepute. Ambition becomes essential.

Thorstein Veblen realized that capitalism channels the need for self- and social esteem into being more, and, more importantly, it channels being more into having more. One of the peculiarities of capitalism is that it causes us to produce and consume for reasons other than satisfying basic material needs. Veblen understood that "you need to feel good" at some emotional and psychological level. A key way to feel good about yourself is to impress others by what you have become, and an easy way to do this is to become financially successful. Veblen's concepts of invidious distinction, conspicuous consumption, pecuniary prowess, and status emulation, among others, are excellent examples of how Be All You Can Be not only has become the social and moral imperative of our age but has been steered into have all you can have.

Three years after Veblen's death in 1929, Lionel Robbins' *Essay on the Nature and Significance of Economic Science* defined economics as the science of scarcity and choice. Robbins' definition of economics was merely the culmination of a century of the social assimilation of "unlimited wants." Accordingly, as Robbins said, economics analyzed "human behavior as a relationship between given ends and scarce means which have alternative uses." What he meant by "given ends" is insatiable wants.

Then in 1962 we hear Abraham Maslow say that our highest needs are those for "self-actualization." By this time, Be All You Can Be was a cultural cliché, and that's why the U.S. Army has used it so effectively.

However, in the European nations and the Pacific Rim nations, there are more observable remnants of the Culture of Security. Social democracy and the corporate paternalist (Pacific Rim) economies have maintained a greater degree of institutionalized security for their populations. Is it possible, for this reason, that a new Culture of Sustainability might take hold here before anywhere else? Then there are the new capitalist economies in the former Soviet Union, Eastern Europe, and, to a lesser extent, China. These are folks who are clearly having to consider the trade-offs between insatiable freedom and security. Their choices are not yet clear. Also, there are the Southern Hemisphere nations in Africa, Latin America, and the Indian subcontinent that have been mostly victims of the Economy of Insatiable Improvers. They are having to decide whether or not the global market system is "the best of all possible worlds" or "the only possible world."

Finally, what might a culture of the Satiable Self look like, and what is implied in a transition to the Culture of Sustainability? Consider Mahatma Gandhi and Zorba the Greek (as characterized by Nikos Kazantzakis). They are individuals with whom many readers have some familiarity, and by their lives, they can be viewed as role models for the Satiable Self. Surprisingly, they offer a realistic picture of what a Culture of Sustainability would look like. What does it mean for us to no longer be driven by the imperative of Be All You Can Be? Is there an acceptance for those who want to self-actualize, even though they would be living in a culture that has chosen to subordinate this norm? Of course, the answer is yes. But this needs to be spelled out.

What about "improvements"? They would happen, but by conscious intention and public policy rather than by the inherent logic of the system. Ending as much human suffering as is sustainable and as is humanly caused is another improvement challenge.

This points to the economic reforms that might be implemented to institutionalize a new culture. For the most part, these reforms will be outlined, but most are ones that many progressives have already advocated. I've sketched the cultural landscape in which familiar reform agendas would be positioned.

There is a path that might get us to the Culture of Sustainability: the "movement of movements." Again this is not novel. The idea that a cultural shift will organically evolve makes sense, and that this might happen as a result of coalition building between the many diverse social movements that now exist (labor, environmental, human rights, feminist, etc.) also makes sense. The quality of relationships between people is the one commonality among our social movements today. Just, equitable, fair, and democratic relationships are what these groups can agree upon. What has to be realized is that we can choose to limit our becoming and our insatiable self-actualizing to the requirements of sustainability. Clearly, global redistribution of power and resources is a prerequisite for this. A world that is more equitable is the only way that "quality of relationships" can be institutionalized. This goes without saying once it is understood that to solve our problems, economic growth can't possibly work.

If we don't change directions, we may be headed for a bifurcated world of haves and have-nots with feudalism in the southern half while global capitalism churns away in the northern half. It is not obvious that a shift to a Culture of Sustainability, the Satiable Self, and an Economy of Sufficiency will happen. We have a world that is "driven," and it is driven by "getting ahead" in all of its diverse expressions. We need to choose to subordinate the productivist value of Be All You Can Be to the imperative of sustainability. Sustainability requires a new set of values and a new culture of simplicity, justice, and equality. These three values are not new. Many like the American transcendentalists (Emerson, Thoreau, Whitman, etc.) have given serious consideration to the notion of reconciling limited wants with environmental sustainability.

We have evolved for 10,000 years toward a world driven by "more"—not just by the principle of "having more" but by the principle of "being more." There is every likelihood that the Insatiable Freedom Culture is going to cause more suffering, rather than less, in the next century. To subordinate "more" as well as Be All You Can Be is possible, and suffering can be reduced.

What about the title of this book, *Insatiable Is Not Sustainable*? The pivotal word is "sustainable." The question is not, Is insatiable good, ethical, moral, or just? The question is that of sustainability itself. The word has entered our discourse over the last decade. Since the publication of the *Bruntland Commission Report* in 1987, "sustainable development" has become a household word. Sustainability is, in many respects, a new cultural paradigm. We see it everywhere and hear about it in all political circles, whether left, liberal, or right. Corporations discuss it; the United Nations (UN) discusses it; Republicans and Democrats do likewise, and, of course, environmentalists and social justice activists discuss it.

Does the word have enough definitive meaning to be a new twenty-first-century cultural paradigm going beyond the "isms" of the last century? Some would argue that it is too diluted. Yet it has radical potential and, more importantly, subversive potential. The fact that it is a word that can infiltrate the vernacular of corporate boardrooms, hometown America, CNN, and Greenpeace says something about its character.

First, sustainability has replaced environmentalism in many public debates and in much of the media presentation of these issues. What happened is that environmentalism became, after the 1960s, associated with single-issue politics. That is, environmentalism began to mean "putting the environment first." This not only implied a narrow focus linked to interest-group politics but, moreover, suggested that the environmental movement might frequently clash with other movements' interests, for example, the labor movement's concern for jobs. Rather than forging new alliances and coalitions, the public perception of environmentalism was its willingness to prioritize the green cause above the causes of other progressive movements.

But the notion of sustainability is different, as it suggests a broader scope and can incorporate a wider range of issues and movements. So in this respect we hear that nothing is really sustainable unless it takes into account the full spectrum of social issues, including the environment, jobs, social justice, equal rights, and other dimensions of social and political life. The idea and cause associated with sustainability are beginning to broaden beyond environmentalism. For example, now one can ask, How socially sustainable is the world if it provides a clean environment without addressing inequality, employment security, racism, and sexism, among others? Consequently, a green world without social justice is likely to be an unstable world riddled with terrorism, street violence, wars, and social conflict.

This is where sustainability has radical potential. It leads to questions like, Does capitalism reconcile with a socially and environmentally sustainable world? We can examine issues with respect to whether or not their solutions are consistent with the requirements of a sustainable world.

Sustainability has the potential to attract far more people than environmentalism. It can broaden the debate about our future, and it is politically neutral. Much of the coming debate around sustainability will not be about whether or not it is "good" and is a socially worthy objective but will be about how it is defined. It will be a discourse issue. This is where progressive movements must play an active role. Its radical potential and ability to become the cultural paradigm for the next century will be determined by who shapes and influences its definition. There is already ample evidence that the people in the corporate world are attempting to shape "sustainable development" in their own image. But the point is that they have been unable to ignore it and have felt compelled to address it directly. If they are unable to influence its meaning and definition, they might risk the loss of their sacred freedom to make profits anywhere in the world. The global corporate class hopes to co-opt and assimilate the definition of sustainable development so that it can be reconciled with the logic of profits-first. This effort is challenged by a host of opposing groups, including the Worldwatch Institute, Greenpeace, and some Third World governments.

The radical potential of sustainability and its capacity to be a new cultural paradigm is premised upon two factors. The first is that a substantial majority of humankind comes to accept it as a yardstick by which to measure everything suggestive of social change, in which case it would be comparable to the role that the words "democracy and equal rights" have played in social change for the last several centuries. They have become rallying cries that legitimate movements for social justice and progress. Movements that are perceived as expressions of particular interests get nowhere today. But like democracy and equal rights, sustainability speaks to the common and general interests of humankind. It needs to become a universal value.

Additionally, to become a new cultural paradigm, sustainability must present itself directly as a value that not only is universal but leaves the door open to the comprehensive critique of capitalism. It must subordinate capitalism to its own requirements and logic. For this reason the vested interests in the global economy seek to define it in their image. If they can, they will neutralize its radical potential and subordinate sustainability to today's cultural paradigm of individual freedom.

If the case can be made that individual freedom is paramount over sustainability, then the logic of profits-first will persist. But there is evidence that many would prefer to subordinate individual freedom to the necessities of sustainability. By doing this, sustainability can be the yardstick by which to critique capitalism, the global economy, and much else.

So given the broad appeal of the concept of sustainability, the coming debate will be more about what it means than whether it is worthy or not. The clash between the vested interests of a growth- and profit-driven world and those of its victims will be about whose interests are served by a particular definition of this concept.

Yet the question is whether or not a third culture, that of Sustainability, may emerge, remembering at the same time that in the pre-Neolithic Culture of Security, there were tremendous improvements. These occurred within a culture that was not driven by this logic. These were hunter-gatherer societies that, for all of their harsh living, worked, were successful, and were sustainable. They are, by virtue of their longevity, our most successful and sustainable experience.

In our present freedom culture, improvement is the driving force. Again, much of this has had little to do with ending human suffering. We have accumulated more wealth in the last century than all of the combined wealth that preceded it for 3 million years. Our fixation on "more" is not just about having more. It's about being more in an endless chain of self-actualizing accomplishments. This may well be our undoing.

The extent to which humankind changes directions and subordinates Be All You Can Be will have a lot to do with how the have-nots of the world decide to play out their destinies in the global economy. If they realize in sufficiently mobilized numbers that insatiability for both having and being more is what is victimizing them, then they will grope for alternatives that are fair and sustainable. They will demand redistribution rather than growth. They may use the redistributed power and resources to carve out a more simple, comfortable life based upon sustainable practices.

In the have part of the world, there are those who are beginning to yearn for a simpler and less stressful economy. The pressures of Be All You Can Be are evidenced in the host of emotional and psychological problems that the insatiable treadmill of performance and production is causing. Living simply and harmoniously with humans and nature may be something that stressed-out folks decide to put first. As a result, they may realize that Be All You Can Be is only a personal choice and should not be a cultural imperative. Humans will always exist as potentiality, but to become aware of this as a cultural imperative and choose to subordinate it to a simpler life based upon equality and justice are the way out. The point is that we can work to end human suffering and live a good life without making "more" the defining feature of our culture.

PART ONE

Where We've Been—
The Culture of Security

Chapter 1

A History of the Satiable
Human Self

Humans have not always been "insatiable improvers." They lived sustainably
for close to 3 million years without conceiving of themselves and their purpose
in life as "driven by improvement." They lived within the Culture of Security.
Early humans were more "driven by survival" than by a notion of
self-actualization, self-realization, or self-development.

Clearly, a vast number of tool-related improvements occurred the world
over before the Neolithic Revolution. Yet it's clear from our anthropological
knowledge that improvements were gradual, contingent, and accidental in
character. With little division of labor, there is no evidence that social
organization and culture were based upon the moral and cultural norm of "being
more," that is, of Be All You Can Be. These were not "driven" societies. This is
largely the result of the fact that there was no identifiable concept of the "self."

The "individual" had not surfaced from within the social structure of life.
No individual was free to develop himself or herself in a particular direction.
Each individual was cared for within the social unit. These were societies in
which "improvement" was not an individual motive, nor a social motive. The
Culture of Security ruled, as Marshall Sahlins argues in *Stone Age Economics*
(1972). As satiable, these were sustainable societies. Our roots as humans lie
in this culture. The notion of "more" was limited as well as the notion of
"more is better." Security and satiability define these hunter-gatherers, for
whom "self-realization" was a foreign concept.

There are two important considerations to recognize before we examine our
human ancestry in more detail. First, what motivated early humans, what they
thought about, and how they conceived of themselves are drawn from inference
and extrapolation. As we know, these hunters and gatherers left no written

record, and their ability to communicate about how they *felt* about anything is negligible. So to say anything more about our ancestors than to describe something of what they *did* is speculative and interpretive. There is clearly a great difference between describing what they *did* versus what they *thought* and *felt.*

We have to make inferences about their thoughts and feelings based upon what we know they did. Yet some explanations for what they thought and felt are better than others. Given what we know about their lifestyles, behaviors, and activities, it makes sense to say that they were not motivated by a notion of unlimited improvement, but we can't scientifically prove this. We have to settle for reasonable inferences.

It is not traditional science, because there are no objective facts to convince us about what early humans were thinking. Our approach is similar to Jacob Bronowski's (*The Ascent of Man* 1973). Are we on dangerous ground? Not necessarily. What our ancestors *did* suggests that they didn't think and feel the way that we do today, at least with respect to how they must have conceived of themselves. It is worth considering in an inferential manner what early humans must have thought if it can help us find solutions to the pressing problems of our time.

There's a second concern. The sweep of this study is as broad as we can get. It is historical, and this conjectural history covers all of humankind's experience on earth. Our human ancestors began to diverge from apes between 8 and 5 million years ago in Africa (Wyse and Winkleman [1988] 1997, 51). We call them hominids. Between 5 and 4 million years B.P. (Before Present), archeologists argue that the bipedal hominids, or *Australopithecines*, emerged. Finally, about 2.5 million years B.P. our first real "human" ancestor, *Homo habilis*, enter the world and begin to use stone tools. Another million years goes by before *Homo erectus* evolves and begins using hand axes and cleavers that have been shaped on both sides of their edges. The time span is huge!

The time that it took for humans to emerge from apes and then begin their incredible migration around the entire planet spans several million years, and yet this is but a speck in the evolution of earth itself. Lester Milbrath's analogy illustrates this. Earth is approximately 4.6 billion years old. He suggests that if we tried to capture the entire history of earth on a 16mm film, where each frame is the equivalent of one year, we would have to run the film continuously at six times its normal speed to fit earth's history into one calendar year. Doing this, humans would not show up in the film for 364 days, and finally they would appear in the early evening on New Year's Eve. "The genus *Homo* does not develop until five hours before midnight on December 31. *Homo sapiens sapiens* (modern humans) developed only 100,000 years ago; eleven minutes before midnight. Civilization does not appear until one minute before midnight. A lifetime of a modern human would be only one-half of a second" (Milbrath 1989, 2).

So we have viewed ourselves as "insatiable improvers" only for about four-tenths of a percent of our history (10,000 years since the Neolithic Revolution divided by 2.5 million years since the emergence of *Homo habilis*), and for over 99 percent of our lives as humans we not only lived much differently but conceived of ourselves much differently, that is, if our ancestors had the ability to conceive of themselves at all. Our experience as the modern, civilized, industrialized improvers is but a speck in our history and essentially minuscule in the history of earth itself.

The magnitude of these numbers and the depth of the history that they represent are astounding. "For all but the last few thousand years of their two million years existence humans have obtained their subsistence by a combination of gathering foodstuffs and hunting animals. In nearly every case people lived in small, mobile groups. It was without doubt the most successful and flexible way of life adopted by humans and the one that caused the least damage to natural ecosystems" (Ponting 1991, 18). Yet although we didn't show up until early evening on New Year's Eve, it was just in the last few minutes that we began to say that to be human is to Be All You Can Be. Perhaps this should give us a deeper appreciation for what our history is really about.

WHAT OUR ANCESTORS DID

Ponting argues that there are four essential traits to being a "human." First is the brain size. "A bigger brain seems to have been important in achieving the power of abstract thought so vital in the development of technology" (Ponting 1991, 24). Second is the ability to stand on two feet, beginning about 3.5 million years ago. Next is the use of speech, and we don't know exactly when this began. Finally, there is the ability to adapt to harsh environments. In this regard we should remember that humans are the only creatures to actually make tools, which we figure began about 2 million B.P.

With respect to basic archeological types, we begin with *Homo habilis* in Africa 2.5 million years ago. Then comes *Homo erectus* about 1.5 million B.P., then *Homo sapiens* dating to 100,000 years ago, and lastly *Homo sapiens sapiens*, our present selves, emerging 30,000 B.P. *Homo erectus* not only used flint stones to make cleavers and hand axes but with this technology was able to use fire, make clothes, and build shelters. The ability to adapt to harsher climates allowed these humans to leave Africa and begin a migration that lasted over a million years and eventually covered the entire earth. During this time there was but one technology, the stone-cutting tool, and this lasted and served these humans well for over 1 million years. Given the way that we currently upgrade and improve our computer technology, this is a phenomenal achievement. No invention has ever lasted so long without an improvement to replace it.

Then between 400,000 and 120,000 B.P. in Europe, the "prepared-core" toolmaking technique was invented. With this method the flint was shaped so that the tools that were then struck could have their shape more closely controlled (Wyse and Winkleman [1988] 1997, 62). For tools to improve as they then did, this could be possible only if hands and fingers evolved with greater dexterity and better eye–hand coordination (Bronowski 1973, 41–42).

Although these tools were essential to the success of the hunting-and-gathering lifestyle, there is evidence of the settled life. From within the Olduvai Gorge

(Tanzania) archeologists have concluded that hunters and gatherers 1.8 million years ago had "home bases" that they occupied and to which they would bring food after excursions in the region (Wyse and Winkleman [1988] 1997, 56). Since many of them died before the age of twenty, many children were left orphaned. Therefore, others in the group had to care for the orphaned children. Bronowski argues that this was important, because it engendered the idea of family and community (Bronowski 1973, 40), and this, moreover, suggests the early roots of the Culture of Security.

All of this occurs within the period of *Homo erectus*, between 1.5 million and 100,000 years ago. With the one amazing technology of stone-cutting tools, these people combed the planet, began to build a sense for community, and also began to eat meat. Eating meat may seem irrelevant, but, as Bronowski maintains, it reduced the time spent getting and eating food by two-thirds. As we know, meat contains a more concentrated form of protein than plants, and by switching from vegetarian to omnivore, *Homo erectus* had more disposable time. But, according to Bronowski, switching to a meat diet meant that collective and cooperative labor became pivotal. The hunt was a group affair requiring teamwork and communication, planning, and organization on a more refined scale. "The hunt is a communal undertaking of which the climax, but only the climax, is the kill" (Bronowski 1973, 45). Thus, meat-eating, too, is instrumental in the creation of the Culture of Security.

Moreover, with the development of the prepared-core technique, meat-eating, and orphan-caring, by 120,000 B.P. in China archeologists have found that early modern peoples had advanced to the point of having more sophisticated stone tools, burials, and animal-tooth beads for personal adornment. They were still hunters and gatherers, but evidence indicates that their social organization had grown complex enough to actually have "work groups" to which certain tasks might be assigned (Wyse and Winkleman [1988] 1997, 60). The Neanderthals enter the scene in Eurasia at about this time (between 120,000 and 35,000 B.P.). They are the first known humans to bury their dead; they used ritual behavior, and it is accepted by archeologists that they probably cared for their invalids and disabled (64). The Culture of Security became more embedded.

WHERE THEY WENT

Our human ancestors were, above all, premier trekkers. They walked out of Africa beginning 1.5 million B.P. These were our *Homo erectus* relatives. The first wave of migration spread around the world (excluding the Western Hemisphere and Australia), and with one toolmaking invention they populated the Middle East, Eurasia, and the Indian subcontinent. They were the Neanderthalers in Europe. This took over 1 million years. They didn't invent much, and they didn't seek improvements in their lifestyle as we might have done; they walked. But then a second wave of migration began with the Middle Stone Age around 100,000 B.P. Eventually, the Neanderthalers were replaced by *Homo sapiens sapiens,* beginning 35,000 B.P., and with their migration out of Africa and into all of the world, they mark 'the beginning of the Upper Paleolithic Period (35,000–12,000 B.P.).

With this second migration from Africa *Homo sapiens sapiens* populated both the Western Hemisphere and Australia. They, too, walked the distance of the entire earth, including the trek across the Bering Strait (Beringia) sometime around 20,000–15,000 B.P. There is no known occupation of North America before 15,000 B.P. Yet fossil remains discovered and dated at Monte Verde in southern Chile suggest its colonization as early as 32,000 B.P. Although this site's date is controversial, there is ample evidence of humans in South America as early as 12,000 B.P. The early trekking of *Homo sapiens sapiens* also suggests that they crossed from Southeast Asia onto the Australian continent between 50,000 and 30,000 B.P. But this is not totally a walk; they had to have crossed at least sixty kilometers of open ocean, suggesting that some manner of oceanworthy vessel was needed (Wyse and Winkleman [1988] 1997, 68). Consequently, our most immediate ancestors, *Homo sapiens sapiens*, started in Africa and explored the entire earth in approximately 100,000 years. This is their major accomplishment and one that evidence suggests was not "driven by improvement" nor by the insatiable desire to Be All You Can Be.

With fire, clothing, shelters, and the prepared-core technique, they traversed approximately 100,000 square miles in 100,000 years. Their population growth was never out of control. It is hard to say what the original population of *Homo sapiens* was in Africa as they began to leave that continent 100,000 years ago. There were probably about 1 million (Bronowski 1973), and then by the time of the Neolithic (Agricultural) Revolution 10,000 years ago, estimates are that we numbered about 10 million (see Bronowski 1973, 45; Quinn 1996, 288). Therefore, in 100,000 years our population increased ten times. That's an annual growth rate of about two-thousandths of a percent. That also means that it took close to 30,000 years to double the world's population (between the Middle Stone Age and the Neolithic Revolution).

As Daniel Quinn argues, "That's growth. Undeniable growth, definite growth, even substantial growth, but growth at an *infinitesimal* rate. At the end of this period, which is to say ten thousand years ago, this began to change very dramatically. Growth at an infinitesimal rate became growth at a rapid rate. Starting at ten million, our population doubled not in nineteen thousand years but in five thousand years, bringing it to twenty million. The next doubling— doubling and a bit—took only two thousand years, bringing us to fifty million" (Quinn 1996, 288). Amazingly, in my lifetime and since the 1940s, we have doubled the world's population again in only fifty years, from 2.5 billion to 6 billion people.

So with very few people and a 100,000 years, our ancestors covered a lot of territory. They were survivors for sure. They witnessed improvements in technology. But life changed very little, of course. Were they "driven by improvement" or by the idea of "more is better"? It's not likely. Bronowski adds that humans surmounted the challenges of the Ice Ages because they had the "flexibility of mind" to notice their inventions and make them "community property" (Bronowski 1973, 46). Bronowski's mention of "community property" suggests also that in this long migratory trek, a Culture of Security was evolving as well.

The last Ice Age was between 20,000 and 16,000 B.P., during the Upper Paleolithic Period (35,000–12,000 B.P.). *Homo sapiens sapiens* had evolved by 35,000 B.P., and so technological change became less glacial. It was a period of more rapid innovation that included the development of the pressure flaking technique for making more complex shaped tools, spear throwers, bows, fish nets, and hooks (Wyse and Winkleman [1988] 1997, 72). They had art, complex social structures, personal ornaments, cave paintings, and communal graves. Yet these developments were "rapid" only in a relative sense and were spread over 20,000 or more years leading up to the Neolithic Revolution.

WHO WERE THEY?

Between 1.5 million and 10,000 years ago, our human ancestors evolved anatomically into what we are today. They increased their numbers only slowly, invented a variety of stone tools, created a sense of community and sociality, and walked. We can document some of the changes in technology as well as the landscape that they traversed. Their economy was one of "sufficiency," rather than one of "continuous improvement" and insatiable wants. There is no evidence for the existence of what we today call economic growth.

Improvements happened not because these folks were looking for them but because the improvements were accidents that our ancestors didn't fail to recognize and then take advantage of. Did they conceive of themselves as the "insatiable improvers," much as we would say of ourselves today? It is doubtful. Bronowski makes an excellent case for their identifying characteristics to be imagination and creativity. Ponting suggests that "problem solving" may be a significant motive. Improvements occurred, but what caused them? Bronowski says that the "ability to improve" has been due to creativity and imagination, both of which can clearly work together to help solve problems. He adds that although all animals leave traces of what they were, humans are the only ones to leave traces of what they've actually created (Bronowski 1973, 42).

With respect to *Homo sapiens* and their early cave paintings during the Upper Paleolithic Period, Bronowski adds that these artists' works suggest that what we call cultural evolution is "essentially a constant growing and widening of the human imagination" (Bronowski 1973, 56). Creativity, imagination, problem solving—these are characteristics that can account much better for what motivated early people than our modern notion that humans are all about Be All You Can Be. Our ancestors don't demonstrate "driven" behavior. If they were driven at all, they were "driven to walk."

But "drivenness" does not explain their accomplishments. Yes, they did accomplish a great deal, but they did it very slowly and very incrementally. They survived, evolved, invented, created, imagined, and problem-solved. We do these things today as well. But our reasons for doing them are so different. A key operative word that explains much of why we accomplish so much in such little time is the word "more." Yet "more," as an operative and motivating factor, does not gel with the hunter-gatherers. Improvements were helpful, and their lives benefited. But any argument that they lived and organized their lives around this principle is weak. It makes more sense to say that "more" or "more is better" played little role in the success of their *Economies of Sufficiency*.

Bronowski mentions that today's Lapplanders are the only surviving culture that "follows" herds, in this case, herds of reindeer. This is a transhumance lifestyle. They are not herders, as they adjust to reindeer's ways and behavior patterns. The Lapps, says Bronowski, are sustainable not due to "biological adaptation" but due to invention: "by the imaginative use of the reindeer's habits and all its products, by turning it into a draught animal, by artifacts and the sledge" (Bronowski 1973, 50). Surely, fire was a key invention but also a discovery and a problem-solver that humans accidentally happened onto. Imagination is the pivotal feature that constituted our ancestors rather than today's cultural norm of Be All You Can Be—a norm that we too often and mistakenly try to universalize.

Thus, innovations and improvements were more likely to be accidental rather than intentional. Before the Agricultural Revolution there was little innovation, in part, because people were on the move almost all of the time. They walked, gathered, hunted, and walked some more. They did not have the sedentary kind of lifestyle that is needed to reflect, experiment, and come back to the problem the next day. The old habits work and are not quickly replaced by new ones. "The only ambition of the son is to be like the father," and this is "a life without features" (Bronowski 1973, 62). It is not based upon, or driven by, the acculturation of "more is better" or the moral imperative of Be All You Can Be. Unlike today, this is not what the fathers were imparting to their sons 10,000 years ago. It's unlikely that the fathers were imparting to their sons, or mothers to their daughters, that what counts is "getting ahead" and endlessly improving one's life.

What about the emergence of the Culture of Security? There is evidence that collective, cooperative, and communal behavior was essential to their success, but they also understood something about this. A sense that security required certain social and communal behaviors seems evident from these facts. The Culture of Security had to emerge and evolve along with the evolution of our human ancestors, and the antecedents are found in the archeological evidence of caring for their orphans and invalids and burying their dead. That security was far more important in informing their lives than the pursuit of insatiable improvement and freedom is a logical extrapolation from their existence itself. Security and survival go hand in hand. In a sense this is still true today, but now we rely on the results of our freedom in order to *achieve* our security. In other words, we use our freedom as a means to achieve our security, whereas for our ancestors security was more direct and immediate and the means for survival. It didn't have to be *achieved*, as it was assured to each member of the group by virtue of being in the group itself. The tribe may wrestle with insecurity, but not the individual. Insecurity was not a motivating force for individual members of the group or tribe. Security was synonymous with the group itself.

We have to make a distinction between the collective and the individual. As a tribe *Homo sapiens* did make choices, like whether to move now or wait until later in the season. They did have freedom and exercised it in making these decisions. They did so in order to assure their survival and therefore their security. But within the collectivity of the tribe, each individual, as an individual, was secure. These people had little individual freedom to become more and actualize themselves, of course. The personal or individual freedom that we value so much today they had little experience with, except to the extent that they were aware of the choices made by the group as a whole. The group exercised freedom; the individual experienced security. The Culture of Security had to have been built in this manner.

THE AGRICULTURAL REVOLUTION

The end of the last Ice Age occurred about 12,000 years ago. As a result, glaciers began to retreat, and this created a new set of conditions for early humans. The shift from hunting and gathering to settled farming, that is, the Neolithic or Agricultural Revolution, took place at several locations throughout the world. Each was an independent development, but both occurred almost simultaneously. One was in the Near East around 8000 B.C., another in China around 6000 B.C., and finally in Mesoamerica at about 7000 B.C. (Wyse and Winkleman [1988] 1997, 78). Farming was not adopted everywhere or in a similar fashion. There were places like Northwestern Europe where food sources were abundant enough to accommodate population growth without resort to farming. This was also the case in Japan and parts of Africa. Even village-type settlements were in existence before agriculture was necessary. But eventually, population pressures affected these regions as well. Only sites like the Kalahari and Australia, where farming could not be sustainable, were immune to this revolution (77).

Many lowland areas in Europe and Asia were flooded, and new types of plant and animal life prospered with climatic warming. These conditions spawned a variety of innovations and new opportunities for *Homo sapiens sapiens*. Bronowski calls it a biological revolution. He suggests that there was a type of "leapfrog" that occurred between settled farming and domestication of animals, and along with this there was a "crucial realization that man dominates his environment in its most important aspect, not physically but at the level of living things—plants and animals" (Bronowski 1973, 60). So the Agricultural Revolution changed us from hunter-gatherers to sedentary farmers, able to settle down, build permanent cities, begin writing, and create "civilization."

What caused this change from successful hunter-gatherers to farmers? Why did it happen? For our purposes, it is critical to ask whether or not it was an "improvement" that was driven by a cultural understanding and conception of humans as insatiable improvers. Was the Agricultural Revolution, which clearly lasted thousands of years, a change in lifestyle motivated by early humans' view that they are supposed to Be All You Can Be? Was it the result of the internalization of the norm that "to be" is "to be more"? In other words, did these dramatic changes that have shaped who we have become over the last 10,000 years result from an awareness that we have unlimited potential to always be more—and that we should actualize that potential? The archeological and anthropological evidence suggests not.

Ponting as well as most experts argue that the Agricultural Revolution may not have been considered an improvement at all. It was an effort to solve a problem caused by population pressure.

Human societies did not set out to invent "agriculture" and produce permanent settlements. Rather a series of marginal changes were made gradually in existing ways of obtaining food as a result of particular local circumstances. The cumulative effect of the various alterations was important because they acted like a ratchet. Over this long period of time there was no straight line of development from "gathering and hunting" to "agriculture." This long transition can best be understood by abandoning any idea of a clear distinction between gathering and hunting on the one hand and agriculture on the other. They should be seen as parts of a spectrum of human activities of different degrees of intensity designed to exploit ecosystems. (Ponting 1991, 38)

What happened was that as the ice sheets retreated and climate warmed, populations grew. There was an abundance of new food that accommodated this. But previously, people had learned to manage their hunting and gathering to assure propagation. There is evidence that the Aboriginals in Australia would dig yams but also put part of the yam back in the ground so it would reproduce (Wyse and Winkleman [1988] 1997, 78). The combination of growing food and herding animals had great potential for one purpose: such an approach could produce far more output and feed far more people than traditional hunting and gathering. Settled farming was not a laborsaving, productivity-increasing improvement. It did not become revolutionary because it was a better way to live or an easier way to live. Its virtue lay in its ability to feed growing populations. It can be considered an "improvement" only because it could produce what was needed for addressing the population pressures. "Primitive farming made great demands on time and effort: breaking the ground, sowing, weeding and harvesting were all carried out by hand" (78). Hunters and gatherers resorted to agriculture only because they felt that they had to. Thus, the new farming was more "productive." Larger settlements could exist, and even though this lifestyle was more time-consuming than the hunter-gatherer lifestyle, it held the potential for "more."

Agriculture and farming were really a change in the approach to subsistence. But the new approach had major consequences that were clearly unintended. Settled living was the springboard for all kinds of new developments, like written language and class stratification, that none at the time could have predicted (Wyse and Winkleman [1988] 1997, 78). Yet this tremendous change was not "driven by improvement." It was not the result of people's desire to have more, become more, or achieve more. It happened because of the problems of population growth. It was incremental in character. It was a result of problem solving, not the desire to improve life. People didn't decide to become farmers because they wanted more from life or because they understood that "to be" is "to be more." They became farmers in order to solve some very real problems of too many people on the land.

But in this pragmatic approach there were four unintended consequences: (1) it created an awareness that "more" is possible, (2) it meant that "more" is not only possible but "better," (3) this led to the awareness that humans can pursue this insatiably, and (4) finally, what makes humans, as a life form, special and unique is that they have insatiable potential to improve their lives.

Farming spread from the Near East to Europe because it worked. There were contact and trade among the early settlements. Therefore, as Bronowski remarks, the cultural depth that trade enhanced came from the "interplay of inventions," because "a culture is a multiplier of ideas"(Bronowski 1973, 74). For example, 10,000 years ago the hunter-gatherers had sickles, but they lacked serrated edges and were not very efficient. Yet 1,000 years later the early farmers had created the serrated edge so that one could "saw" the wheat stalks. By doing so, the grains of wheat were much less likely to fall out of the ear and chaff and be lost to the ground. The simple technology of the serrated edge is organic and deeply spontaneous, implying that such ideas "*discover man, rather than the other way about*" (74). This again suggests that creativity and imagination, along with problem solving, are more responsible for improvements than an inner drive to improve and Be All You Can Be!

The example of wheat is instructive and supports the inference that the Agricultural Revolution was not caused intentionally by an inner desire to improve and become more. Jericho is the oldest settled farming community and in this part of the Fertile Crescent around 9000 B.C. there was increasing reliance on wild wheat and barley as population pressures mounted. This fostered various efforts to increase food production even more, including "grain scattering" to expand the growing area (Wyse and Winkleman [1988] 1997, 80). It was an incremental type of discovery motivated by the awareness that seeds are what make plants grow. It was a discovery that merely happened. Jericho is a result also of the growing of bread wheat. This type of wheat was larger, and the grains didn't blow off of the grain stalk as easily as did other grains. It stayed in one place, in other words. Jericho's ability to thrive was due to the planting of bread wheat coupled with irrigation techniques for moving water into dry locations.

Consequently, by 4000 B.C. farming was common over all of the Old World. But with more food, there was more population growth, of course. Each reinforced the other in what has become a never-ending spiral. As population grew, it led to efforts to intensify food production (Wyse and Winkleman [1988] 1997, 104). Dams, irrigation canals, and terraced fields were innovations that allowed for agricultural intensification. Yet the motive continued to be population pressure. As in many parts of the world, agriculture spread slowly into Europe, because it had to be adapted to more severe climates, and it took population pressure to bring about this change (106).

Even with the many incremental developments of settled farming, Bronowski continues to argue that imagination and "discovery" caused them. There's a distinction between the molding action of the hand and its splitting action. For example, with the splitting of wood or stone as opposed to the molding of clay, the human hand holding a tool and using it to alter the shape of its object also becomes an *"instrument of discovery"* (Bronowski 1973, 95). The hand is *not* an *instrument of more*, in this case! Early humans made tools by working the stone. The stone might have a natural grain, and the toolmaker might be able to recognize this and take advantage of the grain in shaping the stone. Bronowski argues that this idea probably appeared from splitting wood. Of course, wood has a more observable grain, harder to go against than with, and from this humans pry "open the nature of things and uncover the laws that the structure dictates and reveals." Hands become "an instrument of discovery and pleasure together, in which the tool transcends its immediate use" and illuminates various qualities that "lie hidden in the material" (95).

In all of this there is the beginning awareness that "more" exists and that "more" can be had from the natural world and within one's lifetime. That "more" can be had is itself something that had to be discovered. Bronowski is unambiguous that the power of observation is essential to the Agricultural Revolution's dominance over the hunter-gatherer way of life. For all innovations, the ability of humans to observe and make a mental note of what they observed is pivotal.

With the beginning of settled farming, the power of observation had new meaning. Perhaps as early farmers resided in one place and observed the same landscape over all of the seasons, they observed one key feature: growth happens. We can think of it this way: if people stay in one place throughout an entire year, they can witness how plants start from nothing observable on the landscape and then appear gradually on the ground, rising upward, and then mature, atrophy, and gradually disappear from sight. Growth becomes observable. What they see is "more" occurring, as well as "less." This process is much more visible if one lives in a single area over the course of the changing seasons. Then one sees the same piece of land changing. The landscape is the constant, while what's on it changes. For 2 million years before this, "more" was not as visible, because hunters and gatherers were on the move. They walked. Their landscape was changing along with what was on it. The movement of both foreground and background created a visual that had continuous change. This makes the observation of "more" more difficult.

But as people settled down, the foreground's seasonal changes, the visual experience of "more" growth against a stationary background and landscape, created an awareness that "more" can come from the earth, that is, that "more" is possible. As they learned how to plant seeds and watch them grow into food, again, the message to our early farmers is that "more" can be created. With the visual awareness of more food, there is the subsequent awareness that "more is better." For the hunter-gatherers, their continuous movement obstructed this awareness. The power of observation itself was no doubt sharpened by sedentary living. It is easier to be aware of changes that are seasonally induced. It is easier to see how "more" happens when the landscape is constant. It is true that, although the global migration of both *Homo erectus* and *Homo sapiens* spanned over 1 million years, a generation or more of one group might hunt and gather in a circular movement in one region. They would leave an area when the food sources were used up and then return later when they had regrown. Yet even with this recurring visual landscape, it is harder to see growth take place. It would be more difficult for hunters and gatherers to make the mental link between this same terrain and its ability to host "more" plants and food. It would be harder for them to notice if herds are getting bigger. Also with the domestication of animals, it is then possible to actually observe the size of a goat herd increasing from one season to the next. Growth, whether of plant life or animal life, is something that, to be observed, is best done if one stays in one place. Settled farming allowed this. "More" became an operative concept largely through the observational opportunities that settled living made possible.

THE CULTURE OF SECURITY CONTINUES

First comes the idea of "more," then the idea of "more is better." Along with these notions comes the idea that "more is not only good" but inherently insatiable. Finally, early farmers and their privileged classes of religious leaders and politicians began to realize that "more" arises from the landscape and the natural world only through the efforts of humans themselves. That is, "more" has its origins in human capacities and capabilities. "More" exists within each human as potential and makes itself known in the world through human action. Thus, the Agricultural Revolution implanted a new idea: humans exist as unlimited potential and can insatiably improve.

But the awareness that humans *can be more* came at a time when the culture that had so far evolved was still the Culture of Security. There was no notion that we can detect suggesting that the purpose of humans is to Be All You Can Be. They began to understand that having and being more are possible and that humans have untapped potentiality to create, develop, and actualize more tomorrow than what exists today. But the notion that the "individual" is about exercising freedom in an effort to Be All You Can Be was latent at best. This is largely due to the fact that the individual was still submerged within the Culture of Security.

The Agricultural Revolution occurred within the context of a communal and collective lifestyle. It was itself a social, collective, and communal revolution. Security was still the overriding issue for those who turned to farming as a means to assure their subsistence and address their population growth pressures. The Agricultural Revolution was a means for tribes to stay together, to secure the reproduction of the collectivity. The turn to settled farming was not an expression of individual freedom. It was not the manifestation of the unleashing of the individual, of self-interest, or of economic gain. It did not express a new type of individualism. It was a group effort at problem solving in order to provide security to both the tribe and those within it. For example, in Western Europe by 4000 B.C. "ditched enclosures" existed. This suggests the "communal nature of Neolithic society" (Wyse and Winkleman [1988] 1997, 106). It also signifies the competition between tribes for arable land. As population pressures grew, farmers would gather together in regional groupings and enclose themselves with dug-out ditches in an attempt to protect their farmland.

The communal nature of life is also evidenced by the long barrows or megalith tombs that were common in Europe from 5000 to 3000 B.C. Then came standing stones or "menhirs" and henges, the circular ditched enclosures (Wyse and Winkleman [1988] 1997, 108). The amount of labor involved in constructing such enclosures had to have been so great that forms of collective and cooperative effort were essential. It took "cooperation between communities" as well (108). The labor hours required to build the menhirs, like Stonehenge, apparently increased over time as well. This suggests the continuation of collective activity and the Culture of Security. One of the earliest henges was built at Wessex in southern England during the third millennium B.C. It is estimated that it might have taken 50,000–70,000 labor hours to construct. But 1,000 years later, with Stonehenge, estimates are that it took as many 2 million labor hours to build. Archeologists add that it probably took 1,000 men to haul one stone to this site. So the innovations, the gradual domestication of animals, and the knowledge of how to farm were a shared and collective process that evolved through the improvement of communication.

According to Daniel Quinn:

Undoubtedly the greatest benefit of the ethnic tribal life is that it provides its members cradle-to-grave security. As I must always begin by saying, this isn't the result of the saintliness or unselfishness of tribal peoples. Baboons, gorillas, and chimpanzees enjoy exactly the same sort of security in their social groups. Groups that provide such security are obviously going to hold onto their members much more readily than groups that don't. Once again, it's a matter of natural selection. A group that doesn't take good care of its members is a group that doesn't command much loyalty (and probably won't last long). The fact that ethnic tribes can provide their members with cradle-to-grave security is a true measure of their wealth. (Quinn 1999, 150)

But the most important development with the Agricultural Revolution is the conceptual emergence of "more." Clearly, there were improvements before the Agricultural Revolution, but these were accidents that were shared within the Culture of Security. Improvements happened, but there's little evidence to support the view that they resulted from an inner drive to become more, have more, or insatiably improve. Before the Neolithic Revolution there is no evidence that "improvement" ever applied to the individual, whose being was still embedded in the collective. Tribes might improve but not the individual.

It's also important to clarify what Bronowski meant by "the ascent of man." Because he makes so much of imagination and creativity, it is clear that he does not mean that people "ascended" by virtue of an intrinsic desire to actualize our insatiable potential or that we were primordially driven to ascend to a higher or "new and improved" level of life and being. Yes, there has been an "ascent of man." He is trying to track the "ascent" and suggests that it has resulted not from a need for self-actualization but from a more fundamental human quality of observation and imagination.

ENCLAVES OF OUR FOREBEARS

The pre-Neolithic hunters and gatherers were players in an Economy of Sufficiency. They accepted and benefited from the improvements and innovations. But there is no evidence that they had insatiable wants or that they were driven by anything remotely resembling "insatiability." This, of course, began to change with the Agricultural Revolution. Is there evidence that we might look to today to draw additional conclusions?

If we examine the remnants of hunter-gatherers who continue to live a similar lifestyle today, there are certain noticeable commonalities between the sufficiency orientation of our ancestors and certain indigenous groups that anthropologists currently observe. Marshall Sahlins suggests that, based upon what we see in some of the remaining hunter-gatherers of today, our forebears were not "economic," were not driven by improvement, and did not express a need to actualize their unlimited potential (Sahlins 1972). Sahlins, along with numerous other economic anthropologists, argues that the "struggle for existence" for many early humans was not the struggle that conventional wisdom has maintained. In fact their Economies of Sufficiency displayed a type of underutilization and underuse.

In fact, "The hunter, one is tempted to say, is 'uneconomic man.' At least as concerns nonsubsistence goods, he is the reverse of that standard caricature immortalized in any *General Principles of Economics*, page one. His wants are scarce and his means (in relation) plentiful. Consequently he is 'comparatively free of material pressures,' has 'no sense of possession,' shows 'an undeveloped sense of property,' is 'completely indifferent to any material pressures,' manifests a 'lack of interest' in developing his technological equipment" (Sahlins 1972, 13). Like many indigenous cultures today that have resisted the global market mentality, our ancestors were not maximizers. They were not trying to be more, get more, or have more. "It is not that hunters and gatherers have curbed their materialistic 'impulses'; they simply never made an institution of them" (14).

Thus, underproduction is the key to understanding primitive societies. Based upon current observation, "the domestic mode of production (hunting and gathering and self-sufficient farming) is not organized to give a brilliant performance" (Sahlins 1972, 99). In other words, these economies are not about trying to maximize output or perform up to their potential. They are not driven by a cultural norm based upon insatiable improvement, for if they were, they would be producing at closer to their full potential. If they were driven by "more is better," they wouldn't underutilize their technical potential. Much of Sahlins' argument is drawn from Joseph Spencer's *Shifting Cultivation in Southeastern Asia* (1966), in which Spencer examined early societies based upon slash-and-burn agriculture. Evidence exists that "labor power is underused; technological means are not fully engaged, natural resources are left untapped"; therefore, "social-cultural organization is not designed after the technical limits of production, to maximize output, but rather impedes development of the productive means" (Sahlins 1972, 48).

The domestic mode of production of many of today's indigenous peoples underproduces, in part, because its production is "discontinuous in time" and "discontinuous in space." "And as the former discontinuity accounts for a certain under-use of labor, the latter implies a persistent under-exploitation of resources" (Sahlins 1972, 98). These discontinuities are clearly the by-product of a tribe's movement in the hunting and gathering process. They migrate and change locations on an intermittent basis, and this means that they underuse their labor capacity and technical abilities. They simply don't stay in one place long enough.

Labor power is withheld from production because, for one thing, there is evidence of "immoderate standards of relaxation—or, what is probably a better understanding of the latter, *very moderate standards of 'sufficient work'*" (Sahlins 1972, 52; emphasis added). Also the studies by Douglas and Lee both maintain that labor was underused, in part, because it was not required of teenagers (Douglas 1962; Lee 1968). For example, "hunting and gathering do not demand of !Kung Bushmen that famous 'maximum effort of a maximum number of people.' They manage quite well without the full cooperation of younger men, who are fairly idle sometimes to the age of 25" (Sahlins 1972, 53). Given these features of hunter-gatherer economies, based upon today's enclaves of indigenous peoples, it is hard to view them as either "driven by improvement" or the cultural logic of "more is better."

How hard did they work? "The customary working day is often short; if it is protracted, frequently it is interrupted; if it is both long and unremitting, usually this is only seasonal. Within the community, moreover, some people work much more than others. By the norms of the society, let alone of the Stakhonovite [the Soviet role model of the overachiever popularized by Stalin] considerable labor-power remains underemployed" (Sahlins 1972, 56). These are Economies of Sufficiency based upon the Satiable Self. Rather than being about "more"— getting more, having more, or being more—they are about sufficiency, rest, and relaxation. "Agricultural off-seasons are given over as much to relaxation and diversion, to rest, ceremony and visiting, as they are to other works. Taken over the extended term, therefore, all these modes of livelihood reveal themselves unintensive: they make only fractional demands on the available labor-power" (58).

Sahlins' argument, articulated almost three decades ago, was part of a movement in anthropology to rethink the notion that human history has been mostly about overcoming the "struggle for existence" and that with capitalism, technology, and the Industrial Revolution and high-tech revolution, we should be grateful that so much progress in this eternal struggle has been made. Likewise, this conventional wisdom maintains that people, driven by the "struggle for existence," are also driven by "insatiable improvement." Thus, these two "struggles" are simply two sides of the same coin. But Sahlins and others thirty years ago disputed this. It was also in 1970 that the Tasaday tribe in the rain forests of the Philippines was discovered by the outside world. These people were popularized by *Time* magazine and *National Geographic* as a pristine community of hunter-gatherers who did not face the universal "struggle for existence." Of course, ten years later their actual identities and lifestyle became the subject of much controversy, but at the time of their discovery by Western anthropologists, their existence confirmed Sahlins' argument.

How much of a "struggle" did folks actually face? According to him, not only did many of our forebears not face a "struggle," but the reason that they didn't is that they had limited wants. Sahlins calls this condition "affluence without abundance." Their ability to live sustainably and reasonably well, in other words, was due not to their ability to satisfy insatiable wants but to their ability to limit them. Limited or satiable wants and needs mean that not only is there less of a struggle, but existence becomes easier, less driven, more relaxed. These pre-modern Economies of Sufficiency have their "own cutoff principal: it is an economy of concrete and limited objectives" (Sahlins 1972, 65). In other words, "the system, having thus defined sufficiency, does not realize the surplus of which it is perfectly capable" (68). It stands to reason that if our forebears were driven by Be All You Can Be, they would have realized their potential surplus and performed up to the limits of their capabilities.

OUR ANCESTORS' POINT

It's important to make the distinction between being driven or, more accurately, motivated by survival, on the one hand, and being driven by insatiable improvement, on the other. Our ancestors were highly motivated; they walked; they developed a sense of security-through-community; they reproduced themselves, and social reproduction was done sustainably. Improvements did happen; "man ascended," as Bronowski says, but the improvements were not "driven" by an intrinsic and eternal need to achieve more, nor were they the result of an inner essence of Be All You Can Be. Evidence from today's indigenous peoples suggests that they were more about sufficiency and sustainability than insatiability and the realization of unlimited potential. We can summarize these inferences in this way. Our ancestors' point for us is that they were about:

- Sufficiency
- Limited wants
- The Satiable Self
- Survival and reproduction
- Simplicity
- Community
- Security
- Collective and cooperative production
- Underproduction and underuse
- Minimalism
- Sustainability
- Imagination, creativity, and discovery

Of course, it is vital not to glorify them or romanticize their existence. They were not altruists; they competed with each other; and conflicts over land and resources, brought about by population growth, are, in fact, what led to the Neolithic Revolution.

There was competition, but, as Daniel Quinn argues, it was of a different nature from ours today. Quinn's view is that they practiced the "erratic retaliator" strategy, which is also based upon the principle of "give as good as good as you get," but "don't be too predictable" (Quinn 1997). There was more trust among members of a tribe than between tribes, in other words. Quinn argues that with the Agricultural Revolution there was a qualitative change in the character of human conflicts. We've now decided that it's OK to "wage total war" against our competitors, whereas our ancestors only competed. As Quinn says, with our ancestors, the law of life was that "you may compete, but you may not wage war" (Quinn 1992, 129). The point is that our ancestors were not perfect, nor did they necessarily live enviable lives, but they lived sustainably and successfully without embracing the principle that the unwritten purpose of life is to continuously and insatiably improve and actualize one's full potential.

What our forebears were *not* about:

- Driven by improvement
- Insatiable wants
- Be All You Can Be
- Self-actualization, self-realization, and self-development
- More is better
- Having more, being more, getting more, achieving more
- Maximization of human potential
- Maximization of want satisfaction/minimization of effort
- Drivenness
- Efficiency
- Economic growth and personal growth
- Insatiable freedom
- Individualism

Anthropology teaches us that our ancestors before the Agricultural Revolution were much different from ourselves. After *Homo sapiens sapiens* settled down to farm and build cities, the conditions were created for a new view about what it means to be a human. It makes little sense to argue that pre-Neolithic people conceived of themselves as the one unique and special life form that has the potential to insatiably improve upon its existence, that is, that humans have a special essence to always be more tomorrow than they are today. Yet today we believe that to be human is to give expression to our insatiable potential to be more. We say today that the essence of being human is to actualize our unlimited potential and that our success as a race of beings and a life form actually requires this. There is simply no evidence that our ancestors thought like this. They behaved, from what we can gather, like other life forms around them: to live is to succeed at survival and reproduction, to be, but not always to be more.

And they did succeed. If one dates humankind from 100,000 years ago, that is, with the emergence of *Homo sapiens,* then for only about 10 percent of our history have we acted under the principle that to be is to be more. The Agricultural Revolution initiated a change. "More" became observable and operative. Having more, as well as being more, emerged as meaningful concepts.

How much is enough (see Durning 1992)? It is doubtful that our forebearers before the Neolithic Revolution ever asked this question. Yet today, not only have we gotten used to asking it, but until the environmental crisis began, we were accustomed to answering, Never enough! Yet Aristotle stated: "The wickedness of man is insatiable. For though at first two obols might be sufficient pay, yet when once it has become customary, they continually want something more, until they set no limits to their expectations; for it is the nature of our desires to be boundless, and many live only to gratify them" (Aristotle 1962, 306). It took 6,000–8,000 years for settled civilization to reach Aristotle (384–322 B.C.). During these millennia the Satiable Self was evolving into the insatiable self. Yet all of this happened within the Culture of Security that prevailed with our earliest ancestors.

Chapter 2

The Neolithic Revolution and the Emergence of the Insatiable Self

The Neolithic Revolution marked the beginning of a concept of "more." What about the emergence of the "self," that is, the awareness that humans can be conscious of themselves as "individuals" and be distinguishable from the collectivity in which they live? Even though these feudal or slave societies were a continuation of the Culture of Security, people began to understand that the individual has the capacity and thus the freedom to be more tomorrow than he or she is today. So the self emerges. One explanation for this is that as hunter-gatherers created settled or sedentary civilizations, "more" becomes observable, but because the individual in these societies was taken care of and because economic activity continued to be governed by norms, customs, and traditions, the economy did not emerge as a separable entity.

Economic activity, as Polanyi argues, was "embedded," and, therefore, the individual motive or desire to get more, be more, and have more was seriously constrained by the collective customs of the group. There were not the right or freedom and only limited opportunity to pursue economic self-interest. The group's need for collective security dominated.

Additionally, Daniel Quinn's notion of "totalitarian agriculture" is consistent with the idea of "more" (Quinn 1992). Quinn argues that with settled farming people began not only to see "more" around them as fields and herds grew but understood that by controlling the growth process of plants and animals, they could expand both in an almost limitless fashion. Totalitarian agriculture is what we have continued to practice today in the industrialized world. To get more, we have to continuously expand, and to expand on this basis, we must have control over nature. This type of control takes on a "totalitarian" character, in other words.

Also, the concept of the economic surplus is pivotal, because it allowed a privileged class to begin to develop in a direction beyond that of the laboring class. The economic surplus was the condition for the emergence of the insatiable self. The economic surplus, as Marx and others have argued, was the material foundation for a new kind of personal freedom—the freedom to develop oneself in new ways. So being able to "have more" due to the Agricultural Revolution created a simultaneous idea of the ability to "be more." Those who lived off the economic surplus had more choices about how to spend their time than did the laboring classes. But because these were "embedded" societies in the Culture of Security, their realm of freedom was still narrow.

But "being more" was restricted to members of the dominant classes. The "self" emerged together with the awareness of both individual freedom and the awareness that there is a difference between what the self is and what it can be. Since freedom is the awareness of this gap, it becomes the means to move from what is to what can or should be. The civilizations, their art, and their culture that existed from the Neolithic Revolution until the sixteenth century were premised upon this idea. Aristotle's ideas are early and excellent evidence of the awareness that humans exist as potentiality. Aristotle, after all, stated that "the avarice of mankind is insatiable." Aristotle's concept of *eudaimonia* is an example of how he conceived humans as transcendent and becoming beings, that is, that humans have the capacity to both insatiably have and be more. Yet, Aristotle's view of who were "humans" was limited to the privileged classes.

EARLY CIVILIZATIONS

The Agricultural Revolution was a slow, incremental evolution from hunting and gathering to farming villages and finally to the construction of towns and cities. Between 10,000 B.C. and 4000 B.C. we see the domestication of plants and animals, the building of Jericho—the world's oldest town (9000–8000 B.C.) and farming community—and settled farming in Europe, India, Southeast Asia, China, and Japan. Also by 4000 B.C. the Mesopotamian southern plains were populated, using irrigated agriculture from the Euphrates River. The city of Eridu was said to have as many as 4,000 inhabitants at this time.

Then between 4000 and 1000 B.C. the first cities and states appear. For example, the pyramid age in Egypt occurred between 3250 and 2000 B.C. But these developments sprang up in many parts of the world. The Shang civilization in China is an excellent example. The Shang were the dynastic kings in the middle valley of the Yellow River, which today is in northern and eastern China. The remains of cities, luxury goods, and tombs with accumulated wealth indicates that Shang rulers were sophisticated and relatively urbanized. It's more difficult to get a handle on the quality of life of the commoners. Yet it is clear that a class structure was in place. "The origins of this first Chinese civilization date to about 3000 B.C., when a growing discrepancy between rich and poor burials in the east of the country indicate the rise of a hierarchical society" (Wyse and Winkleman [1988] 1997, 146). The dynasty lasted until the eleventh century B.C., when it collapsed, but it established Chinese culture as we know it today. There were major advances in craftsmanship as the privileged classes had the ability to appropriate the economic surplus for the production of luxury goods. "More" was an operative word by this time. Archeologists have found bronze ritual containers, ceramic molds, jade carvings, and fancy ceilings painted with lacquer (147).

But Western readers are most familiar with the developments in Mesopotamia. This was the first literate, urban civilization (3500 B.C.), often referred to as the "Sumerian" culture, where Hammurabi's Code was written in 1760 B.C. After the Sumerians came Egyptian civilization in 3200 B.C., then the Indus Valley in 2500 B.C., and finally the apex of the Shang dynasty in 1800 B.C. The major development in all of these cases was written language using inscriptions and clay tablets. With written language we can finally understand what they thought about themselves, who they considered themselves to be, and what it might have meant for them to be humans. Although the earliest writing was intended for keeping business accounts, we can go beyond inferential conclusions at this point in history.

CLASSICAL GREECE

Because some of the earliest ideas on what humans are all about originate with the Socratic (and pre-Socratic) philosophers, we need to examine the cultural milieu in which thinkers like Plato and Aristotle wrote and thought. These philosophers are familiar to many of us, and they represent some of the best and most articulate writing about life, being, and being human. Their metaphysics stands as a first historical milepost in the evolution of today's cultural value of insatiable improvement, self-realization, and Be All You Can Be.

The origins of Greek civilization are in Minoan Crete around 2000 B.C. The first palace at Knossos was constructed at this time. It was clearly embedded in the Culture of Security. The Cretan palaces were centers for a "flourishing redistributive economy" (Wyse and Winkleman [1988] 1997, 140). It was a rich culture with elaborate art and decor. The first-floor rooms were the courtrooms with frescoes illustrating dolphins, flying fish, and mass spectator events. But the ground floor and basement storerooms were filled with pots and boxes that clearly contained the surplus output from bountiful harvests and successful farming. There were craftsmen's workrooms adjacent to the palaces, bronze-casting furnaces, along with imported goods and materials like elephant tusks and copper ingots (140). In such a redistributive economy, as in many traditional cultures of the past and present, the rich had an obligation to care for the poor.

They did not have an obligation to give away their riches and become poor themselves but only to assure that those who were in the lower classes were taken care of (see Polanyi [1944] 1957). Redistribution implies a cultural obligation to care for those not part of the ruling or privileged classes and therefore supports the notion that these early civilizations, most of which had redistributive mechanisms and institutions, were part of the Culture of Security. The Minoans are a good example of this.

After the Minoans, leading up to Hellenistic Greece, came the Mycenaean culture. The Mycenaean age extends from 1550 to 1150 B.C. and was established in what is now Greece and Crete. Homer's epics incorporate much of the oral history of Mycenaean civilization, even though these were written much later (900 B.C.). But like most of its contemporary counterparts in the post–Agricultural Revolution era, it was militaristic, with a centralized government structure that presided over workers ranging from herders and oarsmen to bronze craftsmen and priests (Wyse and Winkleman [1988] 1997, 144). Yet by the twelfth century B.C. Mycenaean palaces and towns were sacked and abandoned. But it exemplifies yet another case of the predominant Culture of Security prefiguring Hellenistic Greece.

After the demise of Mycenae there were 200 years of political fragmentation and isolation in the Mediterranean. By 900 B.C. trade with Italy and the Levant resumed, and population growth occurred. There was cultural and linguistic unity in Greece at this time. By 700 B.C. urban centers existed, and the city-state developed. With more wealth and security the Greeks built elegant buildings funded by both state revenues and private donations. There were temples, gymnasiums, theaters, and the agora (market). The Greeks exported pottery, metalwork, and tools to pay for imported food and raw materials, and they had colonies, too. While the average Greek city was approximately 10,000, by 400 B.C. Athens and Corinth may have had as many as 50,000–100,000 inhabitants.

What was the state of technology that the early philosophers observed? Starting about 700 B.C. there was a significant increase in population in Athens, while previously it had been a cluster of farming settlements. Irrigation, drainage, and land reclamation were key innovations that not only increased food production but led to population increases. Eventually, the Greeks developed merchant ships with as much as 1,000-ton carrying capacity for hauling food. With their sophisticated irrigation systems, they even invented siphons for lifting water in certain parts of the water lines. They began to mass-produce pottery, and mining developments occurred. The latifundia—large, regularly laid-out estates—were often operated by slaves, and these frequently involved "ambitious land-improvement schemes such as drainage of the Faiyum Basin in Egypt and parts of the Po plain in Italy" (Wyse and Winkleman [1988] 1997, 179).

The Greeks knew that growth was taking place, as it was visible to everyone. "More" was happening, and the philosophers took note of it. Then, by 400 B.C. Athens reached its peak and became the wealthiest and largest of the Greek city-states, even though it was defeated by Sparta at the end of the Peloponnesian War (404 B.C.). Because Athens was situated within mountains and fertile plains, it accommodated agricultural settlement, growth, and decentralized politics. There were farms, hamlets, and villages surrounding the acropolis (the natural outcropping that fostered peripheral settlement, fortification, and defense).

Greek civilization emphasized communal values more than its Assyrian and Persian predecessors, who were "imperial" (Wyse and Winkleman [1988] 1997, 160). The Greeks were less centralized and autocratic in their power structures. This might also account for their unique artistic achievements. Consequently, with decentralized life, not only was there a greater ability for the individual to emerge from the collectivity, but it allowed for expression of the "self" and the growing awareness that "one can always be more," actualize more, and pursue unlimited improvement in artistic expression. But their economy was never "driven by self-interest" like today's capitalism. The "individual" began to emerge from the collective as an entity that could be contemplated and thought about abstractly but was never allowed to be a driving, motivational force behind the economy. Artistic expression of and by the "individual" was nurtured for those in the privileged class who showed talent, but this notion was not one that was ever generalized or universalized for commoners and folks in general. The individual began to emerge but was still constrained by the Culture of Security.

The agora was the center of life in Athens. The city council met there until 500 B.C. The Acropolis was a separate part of the city, where temples and the Parthenon were constructed (432 B.C.). Most people lived in small houses with dirt floors and central courtyards. Country houses were larger, with fortified stone buildings (Wyse and Winkleman [1988] 1997, 163). With narrow, winding streets, sewage disposal was a problem, and Athens also grew so large that burials in the city were prohibited after 500 B.C.

Although money, merchants, prices, trade, and markets all existed, the merchants were excluded from much of political life and usually were thought of as "resident aliens." Public investments and infrastructure projects were funded with the city-state's silver coinage. But "despite the growth of trade and industry, the economic base remained essentially agricultural" (Wyse and Winkleman [1988] 1997, 164). Although there were the trappings of a market economy—the markets, exchange, and prices, for instance—in Polanyi's terms, it was still an embedded economy in which economic activity was not "free" but subordinated to social customs and traditions.

Aristotle and Plato found themselves in this milieu. There was a host of economic, political, and cultural activity around them. Learning, education, the pursuit of knowledge, and artistic expression were serious priorities. "The Hellenistic monarchs encouraged learning—the famous library of Pergamum was reputed to contain 200,000 works" (Wyse and Winkleman [1988] 1997, 164). This was classical Greece. It was their "Golden Age," of course. There was clear and obvious economic growth. More of all that life had to offer was observable. But it was not driven by the desire of the individual to get rich. Some individuals lived better than others; some benefited more than others from the growth; some individuals began to pursue their self- development and self-realization. But growth was viewed as something that happened for the collectivity, for the group, and for the city-state. Growth and the notion of "more" goods and services were social constructs. They were not, unlike today, seen as something that individuals created or achieved through their own economic activities. Growth was "embedded" in the society's overall Culture of Security. It existed and was observable but was subordinated to broader customs concerning the security of the people and reproduction of the city-state. Growth did not drive the economy as it does for us today. Nor did individual self-interest drive their economy as it does today.

ARISTOTLE AND HIS CONTEMPORARIES

Why look at Greek thought, Aristotle in particular, as we try to come to grips with today's struggle over insatiability? Because our insatiable desire to have more results from our insatiable desire to be more. Where did Be All You Can Be originate? From early Greek philosophers? No. These folks were not philosophers of the insatiable self but of the Satiable Self. Most of them were attempting to go against the grain of the dominant culture. They were *not* into "more is better."

Although this is true of early Western philosophy, it is also true for the East as well. David Korten makes this point in *The Post-Corporate World:* "The ideal of a society grounded in the self-discipline of conscious living has deep historical roots in both Eastern and Western traditions. It was embedded in Chinese culture and philosophy for many centuries before its revival and revitalization by Confucius (551–479 B.C.)" (Korten 1999, 139). Of course, Confucius wrote 200 years before Aristotle, but neither one thought that the good and virtuous life was about insatiable self-realization. The Confucian notion of the "self-discipline of conscious living" is about living satiably with minimal wants, a commonality shared with Aristotle.

The issue concerns what it means "to be," with what it means to be a "human," and with what constitutes our "essence." This is the study of ontology, and if we in the Western industrial culture try to understand how we got be what we are, how we came to view ourselves as insatiable improvers and embrace the value of Be All You Can Be, then we have to look to the early Greeks. "Greek thought traces the building up of a 'capital of ideas' that we have been living on ever since. These ideas, and others like them, have become so much a part of our way of looking at the world today that we can hardly think without them. If 'common sense' means the habits of talking and acting that a culture takes for granted and does not question, our own American common sense can be described as an inheritance from Greek discoveries" (Brumbaugh 1964, 1).

Since the initial question posed in philosophy is, What is Being?, Thales is reputedly the first philosopher of written record, and with him we have the beginning of pre-Socratic philosophy. In fact, he said that "all things are water," but he was trying to discover and articulate an "essence" that grounds the world of appearance. His premise—and this is true of all subsequent philosophical inquiry—is that there is more to life and being human than what we see through our sensory experience alone. That is, that there is something going on behind our backs that would be helpful to know and understand if we are to live well. It makes philosophical inquiry an issue about awareness. More importantly, today we need awareness of the character of our insatiability if we want to get sustainable.

Thales was trying to discover the essence of all things, but our concern here is with the essence of being human. Reexamining our philosophical origins is necessary, because somewhere between Thales and today, we got the idea that the essence of being a human is the unlimited and insatiable quest to Be All You Can Be. Thales was not the originator of this notion. On the other hand, after Thales in the pre-Socratic tradition there's Anaximander (610–546 B.C.), probably a student of Thales, who suggested that, rather than water, all things come from *apeiron* (Brumbaugh 1964, 20; Kahn 1967, 117–118). But *apeiron* translates as "a boundless something." This does connect to our view of being a human today. Whatever is "boundless" is therefore insatiable. Anaximander was onto something—his may be the first philosophical treatment of the concept of infinite potential that later defined human essence. He didn't argue that humans are specifically constituted by *apeiron,* but it is clear that he understood that insatiable potential existed in and around us in the world, if not within each human. He did at some level link being with boundlessness, that being does somehow originate in the infinite or boundless stuff that is common to all things. *Apeiron* meant for Anaximander "limitless" rather than "infinite." *Apeiron* surrounds all things and is the basis for all things. This particular interpretation of *apeiron* led Xenophanes, Aristotle, and the Stoics to the idea of a deity.

There is a truth here: being is unlimited. It is insatiable in a sense. To suggest this is one thing, but to argue that the essence of being human is to continuously actualize it is another. Our sustainability problem today derives from our uncritical acceptance that our essence is not only unlimited but demands actualization. This was not what Anaximander was thinking. With Anaximader and the Milesian school of Natural Philosophers, including Thales and Anaximenes, we identify the earliest articulation of unlimited being. Insatiability exists, in other words. Today's issue of sustainability is grounded in our unlimited/insatiable being. But the unlimitedness of being is a fact that we can't do anything about. It exists. What we can address is our obsession that it must be actualized, realized, and developed in its full magnitude. Why should it be?

Likewise, the early philosophers didn't say that the purpose of being human is to continuously realize this potential. *We can have unlimited being with a Satiable Self.* The infinite potential is real, but we can choose to limit our self-actualization of it. Why? Because not to limit it may drive us over the edge. Everything else in the biosphere has limits. Humans, in their being and essence, do not but should. We need to impose these limits on ourselves rather than adjust to a culture and economy that are unthinkingly driven by this. At least we might rethink what it means to be human and recognize that unlimited being and a Satiable Self can be reconciled.

Between Anaximander and Aristotle there are several other developments worth noting. The Pythagoreans are important because they took the concept of unlimitedness, *apeiron,* and turned it inward. Pythagoras (570–490 B.C.) was a moral philosopher, and his school, more than the Milesians, was concerned with purification of the soul and salvation. The Pythagoreans were less the disinterested intellectuals than the Milesians. They viewed the soul as pure and universal, so they extended the notion of unlimitedness to their construct of the human soul. To gain inner knowledge of the soul and thus the unlimited character of being, one must use self-reflection. More importantly, this effort to look inward was part of what constituted self-realization (Guthrie 1967, 37–39).

Consequently, in the progression of these ideas, there is initially the notion of limitlessness (*apeiron*); then this is conceptualized as the pure and limitless human soul. Finally, this idea is extended to the principle that self-realization is of ultimate importance and takes place through deep inward reflection. Thus, we hear Heraclitus (500 B.C.) admonish: "Know Thyself." Yet it wasn't until Socrates that Greek philosophy turned away from the natural world and focused on the self. Socrates states: "The unexamined life is not worth living."

His student took this to heart, of course, for Plato's ideal was self-realization of the individual (Kahn 1967, 161). Plato suggested that three ingredients constitute the human self: reason, ambition, and appetite. Self-realization occurred, he said, when these three are in harmony. But Plato understood something about insatiability, as he stated that left to their own devices and thus without the tempering effect of reason, "ambition and appetite have no criteria other than a blind urge to have more—more property, more pleasure, more prestige, more power" (Brumbaugh 1964, 167). Clearly, Plato understood the idea of insatiability. But he didn't make a virtue of it. In fact, virtue is Plato's premier value, and the greatest virtue is wisdom, then temperance, justice, and courage (Morrow 1960, 561). Because Plato's supreme virtue is wisdom, he viewed self-realization as an inwardly directed activity. The good life equates with the contemplative life. He believed that to be virtuous, one had to live within a virtuous community, a society itself based upon virtue. He realized that people had the capacity always to be more, have more, and achieve more. He also understood something about self-realization. But he didn't connect the two as we do today. He, like the pre-Socratics, was not a philosopher of Be All You Can Be.

Plato associated Be All You Can Be and probably our contemporary idea of continuous improvement with excess and negative qualities/behaviors. He subscribed to the "ancient doctrine that the real goods are the goods of the soul—i.e., the virtues themselves—whereas the goods of the body and external possessions are of secondary value" (Morrow 1960, 562–563). Plato would have said that self-realization is good and that insatiability and infinite potential exist, but he would not have advocated that the way to self-realization is by actualizing our insatiable potential. In fact, he undoubtedly saw self-realization and insatiable potential as contradictory. Wisdom—inner reflection—was the way to self-realization, and achieving this was possible and satiable and had real limits.

Although it took the right material social conditions, it was not about using the world as means to Be All You Can Be. Plato did not view people as nice. He tended to see humans as puppets whose movements are controlled by strings of pain, pleasure, and the "golden cord" of reason (556). So for Plato, self-realization meant restraining one's insatiability.

In the *Republic* Plato says, "The means by which oligarchy was maintained was excess of wealth. And the insatiable desire of wealth was also the ruin of oligarchy" (Plato 1963, 275). Material wealth was good, in Plato's eyes, only if it was used as a means to facilitate what is most useful—virtue and wisdom. In fact, he says in *Eryxias* that "we now wish for wealth only in order that we may satisfy the desires and needs of the body in respect to our various wants. And therefore if the possession of wealth is useful in ministering to our bodily wants, and bodily wants were unknown to us, we should not need wealth, and possibly there would be no such thing as wealth" (276). So actualizing one's insatiable potential both in the world in general and in pecuniary acquisitiveness in particular can obstruct self-realization. This is clearly at odds with today's cultural norm.

ARISTOTLE: A FIRST PHILOSOPHER OF THE SATIABLE SELF

Aristotle may not be *the* very first philosopher of the Satiable Self, but he stands out as having the best-articulated argument for this, and he is "the last word of Hellenic speculative philosophy" (Brumbaugh 1964, 175). His view is worth greater examination because of its continuity and consistency. Clearly, Aristotle was aware of the insatiability of ambition, as Plato had been, because Aristotle left the Academy and became Alexander the Great's tutor. Alexander would feed Aristotle's curiosity by sending him plants and animals that he discovered on his campaigns, but Aristotle did not share Alexander's embrace of ambition manifested through empire building. Alexander died in 323 B.C., and Aristotle died the next year.

With respect to ambition and insatiability in his *Metaphysics,* Aristotle maintained that "existence is indeed, all active attaining of form, an expression of latent power (material and efficient causes) given direction by an actual form (formal and final causes)" (Brumbaugh 1964, 193). Of course, the prime mover is God. "The efficient cause first gives an appropriate matter its start toward achieving a complete form. It releases a process of growth, at each stage of which there is a power to take on new form, and a desire to reach it. The completed form acts as the goal which is an ideal that makes each thing conserve the actuality it has reached, and reach out toward more" (194). This, for Aristotle, translates into the notion that "all things desire God" and seek perfection. As much as this may sound like Be All You Can Be, it is not. Aristotle did not limit his idea of growth and perfection to humans but said that all living things do this. His understanding that "all things desire God" was that "each thing desires perfection, but in its own specific way. A flatworm strives for self-realization, but its only power and goal are to become a perfect adult flatworm" (196). Aristotle had an organic view about self-development, that within us is this latent power to improve. But he didn't see improvement as insatiable, and clearly not with respect to "having more."

He, like Plato, was aware that people have within themselves always to be more tomorrow than they are today, yet he was confident that they could learn and therefore improve themselves in the direction of greater virtue. It was not the idea of continuously "being more" or "having more" that informed Aristotle. He felt that people have an internal organic growth process, one that is subject to will and freedom. Nature does not dictate our "development of intelligence and excellence," as "to develop these qualities requires free choice by each individual" (Brumbaugh 1964, 197). People can, in other words, veer off the path of virtue.

Aristotle didn't view becoming virtuous as an endless and insatiable quest for ever more virtue, for Be All You Can Be. He valued self-realization, though. "The *Nichomachean Ethics* devotes ten books to the levels and stages of self-realization. In each book, a new level is added, and the 'self' extended further." Additionally, the *Ethics* "gives the reader suggestions for self-improvement, and some techniques for self-evaluation" (Brumbaugh 1964, 203). This may sound like a conversation about Be All You Can Be and insatiability, but it is not. Aristotle understood that (1) people have insatiable appetites in certain dimensions of their being, (2) self-realization can take place, (3) choice and freedom to choose exist, (4) people can improve and develop, and (5) they can be more and have more because they have potential for this.

As much as this strikes us as five ingredients that combine into the insatiable charge to Be All You Can Be, Aristotle didn't make this connection. We can explain this.

Eudaimonia means "the good life," and the good life is "happiness." Yet happiness can be obtained only through "virtue." We have to pursue virtue; thus, as he states in the *Eudaimonian Ethics* (1.2.1214b10), "Not to have one's life organized in view of some end is a mark of much folly" (Sullivan 1977, 160). Freedom and potentiality are isomorphic. They go together. It can't be otherwise. If humans couldn't be anything other than what they are today, there would be no such thing as freedom. If what we are is not changeable, then there are no choices and thus no freedom. There is no such thing, if this were true, as self-realization. There has to be "potentiality" for freedom to have meaning. There wouldn't be any such thing as philosophy if there were no potentiality and freedom. Aristotle knew this, but he didn't see the actualization of insatiable potential by freedom of choice as *the* critical norm or value for humans.

Aristotle felt that all humans share the same basic potentialities and the same kinds of fulfillments (Sullivan 1977, 160). This is significant because he also thought that self-realization was possible and satiable. It was not, for him, a goal that one could spend a lifetime trying to achieve but a goal that would always be elusive, like a moving target that one approximates but never hits. If this were the case, then it would be insatiable; it would always elude us, and we'd be stuck on the self-realization treadmill with the goal of self-realization always ahead of us, always just out of reach. So, for Aristotle, self-realization was simply a set of choices that one made about doing the right thing, and it was achievable—at least for those whose station in life was above that of a slave (167). Aristotle did not view self-realization as something where, no matter how much is realized, there is always more.

The good life is a life consisting of "the best possible activities done in the best possible way" (Sullivan 1977, 160). But this does *not* mean that what is "best" is always beyond our reach and that each day finds us insatiably searching for a "better" way than the day before. It is true that Aristotle used words like *dunameis* (potentialities), *aretai* (excellences), and *hexeis* (abilities), but he did not consider them insatiable or unlimited or endless. In other words, being virtuous, obtaining happiness, doing the right thing, behaving ethically were eminently doable. Yet Sullivan criticizes Aristotle for overlooking the fact that people know no inherent limits to their striving for perfection and enriching their skills. Sullivan adds that Aristotle missed the point that "since we are not perfect beings, we always have new prospects, new possibilities, and new challenges; our limits are not just given, and we can always continue to grow and stretch the present limits" (174–175). But Aristotle didn't overlook this.

He was aware of the unlimited character of being, that we do exist as potentiality that seems insatiable. But Aristotle did not make that *the* essence of what it means to be a human. He didn't make a moral imperative out of it. He didn't say that our purpose is to Be All You Can Be. He said that we can be more, but to live the good and virtuous life, we can get off the self-realization treadmill and simply make ethically rational choices about right and wrong and learn from our mistakes, and that's it. It isn't about the insatiable quest for ever-more human improvement or self-development. It's simply about making the right choices as contingent events confront us.

Aristotle was a philosopher of the *Satiable Self*. He recognized the insatiable potentialities and drives that humans have, and he clearly saw them around him in Athens. Although he believed in self-realization, he argued that the pursuit of anything insatiable is going in the wrong direction. Thus, if it's insatiable, forget it. The key to the good life lies in the pursuit of what is actually satiable and achievable.

For example, Aristotle thought that wealth and the acquisitive behavior that it engendered were the wrong direction. In his *Politics* (1.8) he discusses the role of material wealth in the good life. He concludes that in running a household *(oikonomike,* the root word for "economics"), people must have some wealth as a means to other life activities—like being virtuous. But wealth shouldn't be an end in itself.

Consequently, he says:

There are certain goods that are required for life, and are the sort of thing that can be stored and are of service to civic or household communities. These must either already exist, or they must be supplied by this art [*oikonomike*]. These are the things that make up true wealth. For the amount of such things that one needs, in order to be self-sufficient in regard to the good life, is not unlimited, as it is according to Solon [the Athenian lawgiver who framed the democratic principles of Athens circa 600 B.C.], who wrote, "for men, no bounds to wealth have been established." But such bounds exist, as they do in the case of the other arts. For there is no art that uses an instrument infinite in multitude, and wealth is a plurality of instruments for the use of those managing the household or the city. (Goldin and Kilroe 1997, 28)

Aristotle was a theorist of the Economy of Sufficiency. Maybe we should call him a Buddhist economist after the "Buddhist economics" that E. F. Schumacher discussed in *Small Is Beautiful* (1973).

So, for Aristotle the insatiable pursuit of wealth or too much of it in general gets in the way of living the good life. He says in Book I of the *Nicomachean Ethics* that every art and its associated skills are about achieving some specific good and that, moreover, virtue is the most important good. Therefore, "clearly the good sought is not wealth, for wealth is instrumental and is sought for the sake of something else" (Aristotle 1982, 423). The greatest good is happiness and can be realized only through virtue. We have to make the right choices as situations arise, and for this we don't need wealth. Happiness and the virtue that leads to it can be fulfilled only by living an active life, knowing all along that "all sorts of events caused by chance occur in a lifetime" (432). Happiness, the good life, virtue—these are achievable, satiable, and accessible to most people who are willing to be mindful and focused, "to all those who have not been incapacitated for virtue" (431). More importantly, "if the virtues are neither feelings nor powers, what remains is that they are habits" (443).

Choosing to do the right thing is the key: "[Ethical] virtue, then, is a habit, disposed toward action by deliberate choice" (Aristotle 1982, 445). People must be active, face life's contingencies, and shoot for the mean or moderation between the vices of excess and those of inadequacy. Thus, the "golden mean" of moderation and good habits are a vehicle to virtue, which itself is the basis for happiness. Wealth? It's only a means to these other, more pivotal conditions for the "practice" of virtue and happiness. Freedom, choices, moderation, good habits, minimal wants and needs—it sounds very Buddhist to us today. It's doable and satiable. Although doable, Aristotle would say that it is not easy to obtain the mean, because "excellence is rare and praiseworthy and noble" (450).

We can be virtuous. It is in our power, he says, and "if it is in our power, then, to do what is noble or disgraceful," then it is also in our power to be "good or bad men." "So virtue, too, is in our power, and also vice for a similar reason" (Aristotle 1982, 459). Aristotle is less concerned with actualizing our full and unlimited potential for improvement than he is with using our freedom to make good choices. For him, it's about choice and action as we live each day. The good life does mean striving; it does imply self-realization, too, but it is not about the pursuit of a limitless and ever-greater fulfillment of our human potential. Self-realization and striving are part of a satiable goal: just do the right thing, be aware, find the mean, practice moderation, and make it habitual. Live your life this way. That's it.

What about the problems associated with insatiability, like greed and pleasure? Since the pursuit of anything that is inherently insatiable Aristotle finds loathsome, he feels that people can control their desires. Pleasure and immediate gratification, he admits, have that insatiable quality, but he questions, Why should pleasure be considered any different from health, "which is definite yet admits of degree?" (Aristotle 1982, 535).

Not only is Aristotle a philosopher of the Satiable Self, but he is a philosopher of the "contemplative life," as well. Theoretical activity based on wisdom leads one to "self-sufficiency" (Aristotle 1982, 536). This lifestyle requires the "necessities of life," but the contemplative way "alone is thought to be loved for its own sake; for nothing results from it except contemplation itself" (536). For the gods, Aristotle says that being brave, generous, and just requires more than the simpler contemplative lifestyle (that needs the fewest material possessions). Still, "perfect happiness is contemplative activity" (539). "We must not think that the man who is to be happy will need many and great external goods," as "self-sufficiency and action do not depend on the excess of them" (540). Along with Solon, Aristotle states that Anaxagoras was another great thinker who regarded wealth as the wrong path to happiness (540). In fact, in Book II of *Rhetoric* Aristotle says that wealth is corrupting and "belongs to the character of a happy fool" (628).

He understood that uncontrolled desire drives acquisitive activity, as well. One clearly needs a sufficiency of material goods to live the virtuous and contemplative lifestyle, but moderation is important. The insatiable desire for wealth must be harnessed. Those with the biggest and most insatiable appetites are frequently the young. "They err by doing things in excess or more intensely, they love too much, they hate too much, and likewise with all other things" (Aristotle 1982, 625). Aristotle adds that the reason for their excess is their unfounded arrogance about life and their self-validating attitudes.

Excesses are a serious concern for Aristotle, and he knew that there was a quality of insatiability with many of them. He no doubt saw desire as insatiable. He speaks to us today and admonishes us to get control over it, rather than simply channeling it. Our modern view, based upon the norm of Be All You Can Be, is not to limit our desires so much as to channel and direct them toward socially legitimate improvements of life. We argue today that the self is insatiable and therefore good, because by accepting our insatiable desires and then focusing them in the right direction, we stand to gain the most in both self-realization and human improvement. Today we believe that humans are driven by insatiable greed or desire, and as long as it is pointed in the right direction, we all benefit. Aristotle disagrees in Book VII of *Politics*: "The care of the body must precede the care of the soul, and then the care of desire must follow; for the care of the body is for the sake of the soul, and the care of desire is for the sake of thought" (Aristotle 1982, 602). It's the satiable contemplative life that really counts.

Thus, to get to the good life, humans need to get control over their insatiability. It's a matter of limiting it, according to Aristotle. It gets in the way of the contemplative virtuous and moderate lifestyle that leads one to happiness. The perspective today is that insatiable desire is what makes us human; it simply needs to blossom—the full and free development of the individual, as Marx said—by directing it toward "human improvement."

Clearly, Aristotle, at the high point of Hellenic philosophy and culture, can't be read as an advocate or theorist of Be All You Can Be. He was a philosopher of the Satiable Self in an Economy of Sufficiency rather than a philosopher of insatiable improvement. In many respects, he was a man going against the tide of emerging insatiability. His philosophical position had much to do with challenging the commercial, improvement-driven forces that he witnessed in the high life of Athenian culture.

He was aware of insatiability, as his comments about kids suggest. He was aware that the desire for wealth might be getting out of control. His philosophy disputes the growth, improvement, and development tendencies that most observers of the time saw happening. He was fighting an uphill battle to protect the integrity of what he was sure being a human was all about: virtue, doing the right thing. He was skeptical of the notion that "progress" means getting more, having more, and being more. As David Korten says, "The ruthless pursuit of personal material advantage that modern economists consider normal, Aristotle would have judged pathological and destructive of both self and civility of society" (Korten 1999, 140). For Aristotle, humans would be best served by practicing moderation, good habits, and making good and right choices in their daily life. Such a view makes happiness seem simple, satiable, and achievable. His comments about the gods' behavior, their great valor, and bold conquests and likewise his similar comments aimed at the military leaders of his time suggest that he was not into measuring people by their achievements and accomplishments. "Just go do the right thing and keep it simple," he might say. "It's not that complicated; it takes effort and discipline, but anybody can do it, and it's not an insatiable task." The drift of history was not in his direction, and he knew it. He tried to offer an alternative to Be All You Can Be, and perhaps in the future in a Culture of Sustainability he will be vindicated.

AFTER ARISTOTLE

In the centuries after Aristotle and classical Greek life, there were continued economic growth, technological improvements, population growth, and cultural innovations. But life was still situated within the Culture of Security. The insatiable self was not fully unleashed. But there was continuous behavior expressive of being more, having more, and getting more. The economies of antiquity were not driven by insatiable improvement, because the individual was not free to pursue unbridled economic self-interest and gain. The unlimited pursuit of wealth did not drive these "embedded economies." To be driven by insatiable improvement requires that this be an individual economic motive. This is true today in our modern capitalist economies. Prior to capitalism's slow emergence beginning in the sixteenth century, individual economic motives were based upon obligation and command, and economic activity was suppressed by politics, religion, and culture. There were empire building, economic growth, and improvements, but, as in the earliest civilizations after the Neolithic Revolution, expansion was not "driven" by the internal logic of the culture, nor was it driven by individual motives of "getting ahead." Obligations and commands kept people working.

There was, as Aristotle observed, an awareness that at least some folks could have more and even be more. Having more, getting more, and even being more were notions that the privileged classes began to feel and experience. This was not generalized or universalized to all classes, however. These were political societies rather than economic ones. They had commerce, but they were not, like today, commercial societies. If we examine the Roman Empires and emperors, we do see expansion, growth, development, and such. The Punic Wars between 264 and 146 B.C., when Rome defeated the Carthaginians, brought Rome to the Mediterranean center stage. A century later Julius Caesar crossed the Rubicon with his army and became "dictator for life." Within two years he was assassinated and deemed a "tyrant." Octavian, Caesar's grandnephew, won the subsequent power struggle with Mark Antony, and at this point Rome, formerly a republic, became an empire. The Senate then conferred the title of "Augustus" (revered) on Octavian. Until A.D. 180 the institutional structure put in place by Augustus worked well, and the Roman Empire reached its apex during this period. But the classical epoch of Pax Romana came to an end when Marcus Aurelius died in A.D. 180 (Greer 1972, 77).

Consequently, we have to acknowledge the expansionary character of this period. Although expansion occurred, empire building is much different from the commercial and economic expansion that we both take for granted and promote today. Since these early empires were not fundamentally commercial, their expansionary quality was essentially political. Economic activity was still subordinated to political direction and will. The local economies that were governed by Rome continued to be agricultural and largely self-sufficient. The subjugated peoples continued to live within the Culture of Security, where what counted was taking care of each other rather than "getting ahead."

What drove the emperors? What motivated them and their armies to expand borders and assimilate ever more land and peoples within their domain? It was not to continuously improve the lives of all their subjects. They did not conquer for economic reasons but for political reasons. The patrician class certainly knew that they could be and have more and realized that conquest had its benefits for Rome. There was recognition of the positive effects of redistribution from the vanquished to the conquerors. But the focus was on redistribution rather than economic growth. The purpose of empire building was not to elevate everyone's economic status. Expansion served the powerful and the elites. But their conquests were not driven by a maxim of insatiable improvement for the benefit of all imperial subjects or by the idea that life is about continuous improvement. Empire building by the military and political leaders of the time was more a means to realize a particular vision of how the world should be: it should be a

Roman world. It was not about insatiable improvement but about how the world should look. Their expansionary efforts were not driven by the belief that life itself is about insatiable expansion and growth. On the contrary, the expansionary quality of Roman culture was driven by the vision of realizing a very particular and unique "state of being."

Expansion was to create a "state"—a static state of Roman life, their version of the "good life." Expansion for its own human sake, driven by a cultural definition of what humans are, that is, the insatiable improvers, is not what motivated Roman expansion. This is consistent with Immanuel Wallerstein's distinction between a world economy and a world empire (Wallerstein 1974, 1980). Both are world systems, but a world empire, as in ancient Rome, Egypt, Persia, and Greece, has one "political center" to which the outlying regions "economically relate," like the hub of a wheel whose spokes extend outward to the periphery. A world economy, like capitalism, is economic in character and has no political center that embeds and directs the economic activity. Markets in capitalism serve as the integrating mechanism rather than politics. Rome's expansionary designs were not intended to create new or more wealth. To the extent that the center gained, it came at the redistributive expense of the peripheral regions and subjugated peoples. Yet capitalism is much different because it takes as its purpose the creation of new wealth (although not necessarily for all people).

Roman leaders clearly understood their own personal and political potency and that they could realize and actualize themselves through the mechanism of conquest and expansion. "As my empire expands, so therefore do I." The fact that at some, possibly latent level this was limitless might have been evident to them as well. But they viewed themselves as special in this regard and didn't intend to universalize or generalize the idea of self-development to all individual humans.

Marcus Aurelius had a significant influence on Roman culture as he publicly spread Stoic philosophy and in a sense, popularized it. It appealed to all classes, unlike Epicureanism, which was more aristocratic. Stoicism had its origins with the philosopher Zeno in Athens around 300 B.C. The Stoics shared much with Plato and Aristotle with regard to the importance of virtue. Although the Romans technically imported this philosophy from the Greeks, it dovetailed with their own ideas about living by minimalism, simplicity, and doing the right thing. Emperor Marcus Aurelius was influential in spreading this message throughout the Roman world. It created a legacy, as well. Stoicism made its mark on Roman culture and helped shape the future. It offered a model of the virtuous life that eventually led to early Christian ethics and asceticism (Greer 1972, 67).

In effect, Stoicism is a philosophy of the Satiable Self. The persistence of this cultural view about "being" (ontology) is exemplified in the writings of Seneca, a Stoic philosopher and adviser to Emperor Nero (49 A.D.–62). Seneca was born in Cordoba, Spain, in 4 B.C. and wrote mostly letters (epistles). His thought is less organized and methodical than Aristotle's, but his ideas are parallel. He was not a philosopher of Be All You Can Be, yet he must have been aware of the extent to which various Roman emperors and the privileged class of Roman citizens were actively pursuing having more, getting more, and being more. Like Aristotle, Seneca witnessed growth: growth in the imperial conquests, growth in material possessions, and personal growth as well. It was growth that was restricted to the aristocratic class and growth that "happened" without being a direct result of a growth-driven system like capitalism. Surely, emperors like Caesar Augustus and Marcus Aurelius understood something personally about "being more" and "achieving more."

Seneca cautioned this class against insatiable living. He was an advocate of the contemplative life and "happiness through wisdom" rather than happiness through buying, accumulating, or insatiably becoming more. Seneca admired Epicurus' remark that "if you live according to nature, you will never be poor; if you live according to opinion, you will never be rich" (Seneca 1967a, 107). His point is that nature provides us with an Economy of Sufficiency, while human culture tends to make "being rich" an issue of insatiability motivated by keeping up with the Joneses. Seneca adds that "nature's wants are slight; the demands of opinion are boundless" (Seneca 1967a, 107).

By trying to accumulate wealth, Seneca says that

you will only learn from such things to crave still greater. Natural desires are limited; but those which spring from false opinion can have no stopping-point. The false has no limits. When you are travelling on a road, there must be an end; but when astray, your wanderings are limitless. Recall your steps, therefore, from idle things, and when you would know whether that which you seek is based upon a natural or upon a misleading desire, consider whether it can stop at any definite point. If you find, after having traveled far, that there is a more distant goal always in view, you may be sure that this condition is contrary to nature. (Seneca 1967a, 108–109)

This is an excellent statement of the Satiable Self. Seneca, along with Aristotle, is not saying that the self is, by definition or ontologically, satiable. So, although the self has the character of unlimited being and insatiability, one should not pursue it but stay on the path of wisdom and virtue. Wisdom and virtue are not about insatiability but about using one's freedom of choice correctly. In one sense, Seneca is admitting that we are insatiable but suggesting that we shouldn't act like it.

He believed that wisdom is something that can be completed in one's life— it is not insatiable. Moreover, "riches have shut off many a man from the attainment of wisdom; poverty is unburdened and free from care" (Seneca 1967a, 111). Like Aristotle, this suggests a belief that wealth gets in the way of the good life and that money and riches link one to insatiability, while wisdom and virtue do not. Also "study (contemplation) cannot be helpful unless you take pains to live simply; and living simply is voluntary poverty" (111). This sounds like Buddhism, Gandhi, and the "voluntary simplicity" movement that we hear about today. Seneca says that "nature demands but little, and the wise man suits his needs to nature" (115). He also suggests that "what is enough" or "sufficient" is absolute and not relative to a particular culture: "change the age in which you live [as in previous eras], and you have too much. But in every age, what is enough remains the same" (115). Of course, today we tend to feel that "what's enough" is all relative, and in looking ahead to the future or in looking around us, we'd say that we don't have enough—we can never have "too much"!

Was Seneca an eccentric? He would be if he lived in our world. But in his time, "Seneca is so linked with the age in which he lived that in reading his works we read those of a true representative of the most thrilling period of Roman history" (Gummere 1967, vii). Like Aristotle, Seneca was going against the tide. The privileged classes, his emperor Nero, and the Roman patricians were beginning to value "more is better." Yet Seneca told them that "it is not the man who has little, but he who desires more, that is poor" (Wright 1967, 406).

Seneca was a minimalist: "Turn thyself rather to the true riches. Learn to be content with little, and cry out with courage and with greatness of soul: 'We have water, we have porridge; let us compete in happiness with Jupiter himself.' And why not, I pray thee, make this challenge even without porridge and water? For it is base to make the happy life depend upon silver and gold, and just as base to make it depend upon water and porridge. Do you ask what is the cure for want? It is to make hunger satisfy hunger" (Seneca 1967a, 274, 277). This is extreme. Yet it is reminiscent of both Buddhism and certain subsequent Catholic saints like Augustine and Francis of Assisi.

In Epistle XCIII, "On the Quality, As Contrasted with the Length of Life," Seneca says that "we should strive, not to live long, but to live rightly." Clearly, for him, more is not necessarily better. Then he says, "A life is really long if it is a full life." This could be construed to mean Be All You Can Be, but that's not what he meant. Of a young friend who had recently died, Seneca said: "But he had fulfilled all the duties of a good citizen, a good friend, a good son; in no respect had he fallen short. His age may have been incomplete, but his life was complete" (Seneca 1967b, 5). Consequently, we can infer that a "fulfilled" life did not imply an endless treadmill driven by insatiability and in which total fulfillment is always beyond our reach. Both Seneca and Aristotle had notions of self-realization and fulfillment that were based upon satiability. They would say that there is something within humans (at least those in the dominant classes) that can be realized, developed, and actualized, but, more importantly, that this capacity should be satiable and limited.

Thus, we can be more, but we don't need to Be All You Can Be by means of an insatiable quest. What we are to be, according to both philosophers, is wise and virtuous. Wisdom is not an insatiable goal. "Moreover, the precepts of wisdom should be definite and certain: when things cannot be defined, they are outside the sphere of wisdom; for wisdom knows the proper limits of things" (Seneca 1967b, 21). This is a remarkable comment, given our own modern culture. Surely, virtually every philosopher today would maintain that wisdom knows no limits whatsoever. We can, accordingly, always be wiser tomorrow than we are today—we just have to apply ourselves, our faculties, and capabilities. Of course, many today might agree with the notion that achieving wisdom is more vital and worthy than achieving wealth. In this respect they might embrace the classical philosophers. But still our contemporaries would argue that the potential to realize ever more wisdom is insatiable. Not only is it insatiable, but our real mission as humans is to realize as much of it as possible every day that we live. This was not Seneca's view. He was a philosopher of the Satiable Self.

THE CHRISTIAN TRADITION IN THE MEDIEVAL ERA

The Roman Empire embraced Christianity under Theodosius in A.D. 381, while Augustine, one of the founders and a vital link in the Catholic tradition, was baptized a Christian in 387. He grew up a pagan in Carthage but had an excellent education before turning to Christianity. His major works are the *Confessions* and *The City of God,* but he wrote voluminously and influenced future generations more than his own. In fact, historians generally agree that his ideas have shaped the theology, morals, politics, and philosophy of the West in no small measure (Greer 1972, 105). We can appreciate St. Augustine because he spoke not only for his own time but for what became Christian theology until the sixteenth century.

St. Augustine's ideas represent a continuation of the philosophy of the Satiable Self that Aristotle and Seneca articulated, and they reinforce the Culture of Security that grounded both the classical Roman period and the Middle Ages. Augustine struggled with his conversion to Christianity. It wasn't a detached or philosophical conclusion arrived at through intellectual debate with himself. It was through emotional trauma that he was led to God. But this had a major influence on his theological writings over the remainder of his life. It turned him into a philosopher of the Satiable Self. "From his personal experiences Augustine concluded that bodily appetites (as well as false philosophies) distract men from the contemplation of God. He denounced as sinful, therefore, even the simplest of physical pleasures" (Greer 1972, 105). Augustine gave up his wife and child, practiced self-denial, and thought that all Christians—if they were to be saved—must plead to God for help in denying the physical world and its temptations. He was a forerunner of Christian asceticism.

Mention of asceticism is important because it suggests an attitude of satiability in Augustinian thought: there is more to life than having more, being more, and getting more. What life is about, says Augustine, is not Be All You Can Be, nor is it self-actualization of unlimited potential. Life is about faith. Life is about salvation through total embrace of Jesus as the Savior. Asceticism and the Satiable Self correlate. It would be contradictory to embrace both asceticism and insatiability. Asceticism in Augustine parallels the minimalism of both Aristotle and Seneca. All three thinkers agree that the pursuit of "more is better" leads an individual down the wrong path. For Augustine, the ultimate goal is salvation through faith, while for Plato, Aristotle, and Seneca, it is wisdom through virtue. Yet Augustine wanted to reconcile the Greek idea of reason with the Christian value of faith (Markus 1967; Gilson 1960). He started with Heraclitus' command: "Know Thyself." He put faith first but saw it as a particular use of reason: "Believe in order that you may understand; unless you shall believe, you shall not understand" (Markus 1967, 199). The point is that Augustine's views follow the early classical traditions, and in taking from his Greek predecessors, he also adopted their notion that "what is good is what is satiable."

All of these classical thinkers put something based upon satiability first in life. Faith is an ultimate act that is based upon our freedom of choice. You simply do it, or you don't. It is satiable and finite. The good life (*eudaimonia*), happiness, virtue, and wisdom are likewise for Plato, Aristotle, and Seneca: they are choices made by the individual that are satiable. None of these ultimate goals, whether we talk about faith, the good life, virtue, or wisdom, are life processes that we pursue and never reach. They don't have the character of an endless quest that is expressed through continual self-development and insatiable improvement.

If we extended today's notion of Be All You Can Be to our ancient forebears, we'd say that faith, virtue, wisdom, and happiness are objects for our infinite potential always to be more. They are insatiable quests, we might argue. We therefore aim for them, but by so doing, we also accept the fact that we will never ultimately hit the target. The target of wisdom, virtue, and faith expands their parameters and limits as we expand our being toward them. They will always elude us, because, as goals, they are projections of our own insatiability. They are not stationary targets or fixed goals because they are expressions of our limitless potential always to be more. Thus, unlike Plato, Aristotle, Seneca, and Augustine, we define our goals as insatiable in tandem with our striving to achieve them.

The goal and our effort to actualize it are, for us today a dualism that moves together as one unit. They are tethered. It is like casting a fishing line with both a hook and a bobber on it. If the purpose in casting the line is to make the bobber catch up with the hook, it's not going to happen. No matter how hard one casts the line, the bobber will never slide down the line to the hook. The hook will always elude and stay ahead of the bobber. Perceiving ourselves as the insatiable improvers, always able to be more tomorrow than we are today, is what we are doing when we cast the fishing line. We have gotten better and better at casting and getting the line farther and farther into the lake, but we'll never get the bobber to catch up to the hook. So we would look at the ancients and say that, from our point of view, not only can we always be more wise and virtuous tomorrow, but our notion of wisdom and virtue can expand and become more, along with our efforts to actualize them.

For the early philosophers of the Satiable Self, this was not the case. They saw all of their goals including wisdom, virtue, and faith, as doable and realizable. Unlike our contemporary view, they didn't maintain that these ultimate human ends were insatiable and never fully achievable. They weren't easy, but they could be done.

Augustine was clearly, like the Roman and Greek philosophers whom we've examined, an advocate for the contemplative life. He, too, observed insatiability of the human appetite in the Roman Empire. The Goths sacked Rome in 410, and Augustine suggested that it was an "earthly city," destined to fall from decadence, dereliction, and depravity. Only the "City of God" was eternal, according to Augustine. Consequently, his views helped to foster Christian monasticism (Greer 1972, 107).

The monastic and ascetic tendencies in early Christianity stem from the awareness that "pleasures of the flesh" are, in fact, insatiable. Again like the Greek and Roman philosophers, early Christians like the Apostle Paul and Anthony of Alexandria (a famous Christian hermit, circa 270), maintained that to be saved, one must resist the insatiable appetites of the material world. They associated insatiability with the wrong path and satiability with the virtuous, Christian way. Of course, the monastic drift was, in part, a function of what was happening to the official church. When Theodosius proclaimed Christianity to be the religion of the empire, the church took a higher profile and became more worldly and secular. Many Christian followers were concerned with the Church's worldly appearance and, since they wanted to follow in Christ's footsteps, they chose the monastic life of withdrawal from the world rather than martyrdom. Even Augustine founded a monastery in North Africa (Greer 1972, 110–111).

With the collapse of the Roman Empire after 400, there was political change, but there was little change in the essential culture that functioned to maintain human life and social reproduction. The Culture of Security, that is, the embedded character of both the pre-Neolithic and early Western civilizations, did not disintegrate but held together. Economic activity, as it was for all pre-Roman human existence, continued to be subordinated to political and religious norms, customs, and traditions. The fall of Rome did not create the fall of the Culture of Security. Economic activity was not the driving force behind the Roman Empire, and it was not the driving force after it. As with our hunter-gatherer ancestors, life during Pax Romana (27 B.C.–A.D. 180) and the late imperial period up to Theodosius (A.D. 400) was about provisioning and security, not about the insatiable quest for more is better.

The privileged classes and political leaders understood that more can be had, that one can be more tomorrow than today, and that getting more is possible and often desirable, but they did not view their role in the world as leaders of economic improvement. They viewed their expansionist designs as religious and political rather than economic. Economic growth occurred, and technological innovations happened, but these were not the driving forces. The ruling classes, unlike the subsequent capitalist class 1,000 years later, did not see themselves as an economic vanguard or the bearers of economic prosperity for all common folks in the domain. Their purpose, as they defined it, was not to expand the level of economic activity. It was to extend Christianity, Islam, or the cultural hegemony of Rome. The leaders of these worlds knew that they could have more and be more as a result of all of this, but they tended to view their privileges and higher standard of living as a necessary means to enhance their guiding role, rather than ends in themselves.

Even Aristotle distinguished between "use value" and "exchange value." He knew that the division of labor, trade, markets, and prices were significant features of the commercial landscape evolving around him. But he cautioned that as long as people traded in order to gain the "use" of different commodities, then all was well. But he didn't trust the merchant class, as he also was aware that they could, and sometimes did, intend to "profit" from the exchanges, that is, try to pursue "exchange value" rather than settle for "use value." As Polanyi argues, an economy that functions with trade for use value is an embedded economy (Polanyi [1944] 1957). As Karl Marx clarified, an economy like capitalism is all about profiting from commercial exchanges, that is, making exchange value the central function of economic activity. Once this happens, the economy is not only "driven" but "disembedded" as well.

But in the Culture of Security that prevailed during the ancient era and then into the Middle Ages, use value dominated over exchange value, and the focus was on "distributive ethics." This meant that if one group gained it must have come at the expense of another group. To Aristotle and the Romans, this was obvious. That is, if the economic status of Rome increased, it was because the Romans were able to redistribute wealth from subordinate and governed classes elsewhere in the empire. Unlike our perspective today, where we say that with economic growth all classes can improve without redistribution, the ancients focused on redistribution: more for one meant less for another. In part, the reason for their distributive ethics was that they were not commercial societies. Economics did not drive them. They were not cultures driven by insatiable improvement, as economic activity was a subordinate dimension to life. There was no academic discipline of economics. In general, the "embedded" character of economic activity shifted the focus to religion and politics and away from economics and the material standard of living. Economic activity was not based upon the pursuit of individual gain and not driven by individual desires for more of everything that life has to offer. Economics was about subsistence, meeting material needs that were not considered to be insatiable, and sufficiency of means.

The Culture of Security that grounded both ancient and medieval life suggests that the underlying meaning of economic activity is "to take care of one another." Economic activity, in other words, is for provisioning the material means that are a necessary condition for other pursuits (at least for the privileged classes). "Taking care of each other" does not mean doing it in an equal or democratic fashion, but it does mean that the fundamental basis and meaning for doing economic activity are to assure security at one's assigned station in life. The roots of this notion lie in the million years of tribal life that preceded settled civilization. So for Aristotle, for the Roman Empire that followed him, and for the Middle Ages, economic activity is absolutely essential for both social and individual security, but it is not the purpose of life itself. This is the meaning of the Culture of Security that continued to prevail after the fall of Rome and for the next 1,000 years. Their economies were not viewed as the essential means for "getting ahead," but they were essential means for material security.

FEUDAL IDEOLOGY AND THE CULTURE OF SECURITY

Three cultural regions emerged after A.D. 400. In the north were the Franks; in the east was the Byzantine Empire (Constantinople was called Byzantium); and Africa and the Middle East were the Islamic Empire. But for what became Southern and Western Europe, it was the Christian Church that provided the stability and continuity to bridge the period between the fall of the Roman Empire and the Middle Ages (Greer 1972, 117–118). As a result, the asceticism of Christianity prevailed and so did the ideal of the Satiable Self.

This marked the beginning of the Middle Ages. In what is known as Western Christendom, the Germanic tribes dominated the cultural scene—the Franks and the Anglo-Saxons. By 814 Charles the Great, or Charlemagne, as he was later known, consolidated the Carolingian dynasty that included France, Germany, and the North. By the eleventh century there were three major regions of European feudalism: the Holy Roman Empire, the Kingdom of France, and the Kingdom of England (Greer 1972, 144–145).

Feudal ideology was not only anticapitalist but clearly focused on security rather than growth. It was not a period that any historian has considered to be "driven" by insatiability. It had the ascetic quality that served to limit and restrain the pursuit of self-development and insatiable improvement. Feudal ideology was about security and protection rather than "more." As K. Hunt states, in the feudal hierarchy, "the serf, or peasant, was protected by the lord of the manor, who, in turn, owed allegiance to and was protected by a higher overlord. The strong protected the weak. Custom and tradition are the keys to understanding medieval relationships. The entire medieval organization was based on a system of mutual obligations and services up and down the hierarchy" (Hunt 1990, 3). Moreover, the church was the primary vehicle for spreading the ideology of paternalism and security. "This was also an age during which the religious teaching of the church has a very strong and pervasive influence throughout western Europe" (4). It was the biggest landowner, as well. The manors were basically self-sufficient agricultural units based upon obligations and reciprocal relations in which lords provided protection in exchange for a labor-service obligation by the serf.

Hunt labels the ideology of feudal Europe the "Christian paternalist ethic," as this emphasizes both the ascetic and paternalist character of the period. The rich had a moral obligation to care for the poor. But the point here is that this reflects the Culture of Security that continued after the Roman Empire. According to Hunt, "the Christian paternalist ethic, with its parental obligations of the wealthy toward the poor, was developed more specifically and elaborately by most of the Christian fathers. The writings of Clement of Alexandria are a reasonably good reflection of the traditional attitudes of the early church. He emphasized the dangers of greed, love of material things, and acquisition of wealth. Those who had wealth were under a special obligation to treat it as a gift from God and to use it wisely in the promotion of the general well-being of others" (Hunt 1990, 7). The rich were not expected to make themselves poor or be poor in solidarity with their brethren, but they were expected to care for the poor without sacrificing their assigned station in life.

This ideology suggested not only that security was more important than personal freedom but that it likewise suppressed the logic of "more is better" and Be All You Can Be. The purpose of life in feudal Europe was not to get ahead but to be saved—salvation through faith. "In a similar vein, Ambrose wrote that 'riches themselves are not blamable' as long as they are used righteously. In order to use wealth righteously, 'we ought to be of mutual help one to the other, and to vie with each other in doing duties, to lay all advantages before all, and to bring help one to the other.' Greed, avarice, materialistic self-seeking, were sharply condemned. The acquisitive, individualistic person was considered the very antithesis of the good man, who concerned himself with the wellbeing of all his brothers" (Hunt 1990, 7; see Gray 1963). So protection, obligation, taking care of each other, acceptance of assigned station in life, faith, and salvation constituted the feudal way in Christian Europe after A.D. 400. It was a minimalist way that favored acceptance of God's ordained order rather than the exercise of the freedom to "get ahead." This was not a world driven by growth, "more is better," or Be All You Can Be. It was simply not a driven world.

This is the historical backdrop for looking at St. Thomas Aquinas (1225–1274). His, like those before him, is a philosophy of the Satiable Self. Aquinas' major work is *Summa Theologica*, and in this and much of his other voluminous writings he tried to reconcile the reason of the classical Greek thinkers with the faith of his Christian predecessors. As Etienne Gilson notes, "For St. Thomas, as for all the Christian doctors—one might add, for the Arabic and Jewish doctors as well—another problem takes precedence over that of human knowledge: namely, the problem of the relations between Reason and Faith. Whereas the philosopher as such professed to draw truth from the spring of Reason alone, the philosophical theologian draws truth from two different sources: from Reason, and since he is a theologian—from Faith in the truth revealed by God, and its interpreter, the Church" (Gilson 1986, 37). Aquinas accepted the role of reason and logic in the world of ideas as long it was grounded in faith and as long as it was used to bolster faith (Greer 1972, 182; Gilson 1986). While Aquinas was canonized in 1323, his ideas have left their mark on Christian theology. He is considered to be one of the most important theologians in this tradition along with Paul and Augustine (Davies 1992, vii).

Aquinas had a strong Aristotelian bent, even though he situated this in a Christian context. He believed that humans have a will, free choice, and desires. He felt that people seek that which fulfills them or perfects them. This is the desire to be happy, yet the only way to be happy is to come to God. Accepting God is the means to happiness, completion, and fulfillment. Is this an insatiable quest for ever more "closeness to God"? Aquinas says no. But his concept of happiness is not what or how many consider it today. By happiness he meant spiritual fulfillment and contentment, rather than the gratification that we moderns might derive from immediate gratification. "Happiness, for him, is not a matter of 'whatever turns you on'" (Davies 1992, 228). Happiness results, says Aquinas, from understanding that life does have a goal, and the goal is God, and it is a goal that is not insatiable but doable.

How so? Aquinas says that there are ultimate ends and that even though there are material pleasures, these, too, have some ultimate goal. They are completely self-sufficient ends in themselves. These are not "endless ends," so, therefore, the life devoted to God is not about an insatiable quest but simply understanding that everything and every activity serve the one ultimate end of God's will. One must follow this path, which, in fact, does have an end (Davies 1992, 228). You either do it, or you don't. Likewise, Aquinas' view about the need for material goods is much like that of his classical predecessors: material wealth can be an insatiable sinkhole, so don't follow it. Goods are merely a means to an end, not an end in themselves (Davies 1992, 228). As with Aristotle and Seneca, the point in life is *not* to Be All You Can Be but simply to choose virtue and wisdom. For Aquinas and Augustine, the point is to choose God. It's satiable. You merely make the choice—a very difficult choice sometimes but one that can be completed. It's not a case of trying to actualize ever more potential, as we might think from our perspective today. Aquinas is stating that human virtue means behaving in accord with our nature, and, fortunately, we can use our reasoning capacities to know our nature. So "our primary moral imperative, you might say, is to recognize what we are and to act accordingly" (Davies 1992, 231). Just go do the right thing, and all will be well. For Augustine and Aquinas, the right thing is God, while for Plato, Aristotle, and Seneca, the right thing is virtue and wisdom. Yet all of these thinkers lay claim to happiness as a by-product of choosing the good life. The self is satiable.

Moreover, like the self of Aristotle, Aquinas' self needs to have virtues that serve reason and faith, and these virtues are cultivated through good habits. Davies notes that virtues, for Aquinas, are dispositions that help humans or make it easier for us to do the right thing. Humans have inherent abilities to behave rightly, but these abilities must be conditioned by the discipline of habituation (Davies 1992, 239). "'Virtue,' says Aquinas, 'is a *habitus* which is always for good.' It is a *habitus* by which a person acts well" (239).

In *Summa Theologica,* Aquinas adds, *"Virtue denotes a determinate perfection of a power*. The rational powers, proper to people, however, are not determined to one act, but in themselves are poised before many. It is through habits (*per habitus)* that they are set towards acts" (Davies 1992, 240; emphasis added). Thus, contrary to our contemporary view, Aquinas follows the ancients in assuming that although there is potential to be more, it is a satiable quest. His statement that virtue implies a determinate perfection of a power, coupled with his Aristotelian concept of powers as habits, suggests the notion of satiability. "You, too, can be virtuous." It is possible and determinate rather than unlimited and insatiable. Simply go out and use good habits and good judgments, and everything will be fine. This is what it means to be a Christian for Aquinas. Still, we have to remember that faith is the key value. Unlike Judaism, the feudal

Christian theologians placed more emphasis on faith and belief in God than on the power of "good works."

But the point is that people, for Aquinas and the ancients, had within them the ability to be good, decent, God-fearing folks. They did not see this type of self-realization, self-actualization, or self- development as an insatiable project to continually improve with no end in sight. It has to be emphasized that there is a huge difference between a form of self-realization that is unlimited and one that is determinate and satiable. Both forms imply that there is a gap between what one is and what one can become. From Aristotle to Aquinas there is a recognition that "people can be more tomorrow than they are today." But from the ancient through the feudal eras, they saw the gap as closable and finite. They didn't view self-realization or "becoming more" as insatiable. They saw great value in closing the gap, but they didn't view the "process" of closing the gap, becoming more virtuous, wise, or God-fearing as what it's all about. It was "being closer to God" that Aquinas valued. Unlike ourselves, he did not focus on the process of becoming itself.

If one views self-realization as having infinite potentiality, then the gap will never be closed between what one is and what one can become, because you can always become more. By so doing, it forces us today to emphasize the process of "becoming more" itself, rather than the ends to which this process is put. If there is no end to self-realization, then the focus shifts to this process as a means, and consequently the means becomes the end. For we moderns of the twenty-first century, it is not so much what you become but the fact that you demonstrate to your peers that you are always trying to become more. The process itself of becoming more counts, rather than what you become. Why? Because for us, you can never become too much; you can never overdo something that is inherently insatiable.

We have made an ultimate end out of Be All You Can Be, because as a means to an end that can never be reached, it's the means that has to be valued in and of itself. Thus, for us, it is not *what* one becomes that matters so much as that one continually strives *to become more*. It is the act of striving to be more, given the insatiability of it, that counts. This was not the case for Aquinas and his predecessors. They were philosophers of the Satiable Self. If the end for which one struggles is doable and satiable, then it is "fixed." This being the case for Aquinas, the focus is on the end itself, and what matters is *what one becomes*. The end is viewable, and one can get there. But for us, the means become the end, as the end is always beyond our reach.

Aquinas lived on the cusp of a new era. Essentially, between 1100 and 1500 there were four centuries of transition from the feudal Christian world in Western Europe to the capitalist era that we experience today. The transition was immensely fast compared to the Neolithic Revolution 8,000 years earlier. But the changes were of equivalent magnitude. Here's what happened:

- Between the time of *Homo habilis* a million and a half years ago and Aquinas' time in the eleventh century, the Culture of Security prevailed everywhere in the world, regardless of whether or not humans were in (1) hunter-gatherer communities, (2) slave systems, or (3) feudal systems. This is the one commonality.

- For the million or so years (1 million B.P.–30,000 B.P.) that it took for *Homo sapiens sapiens* (today's humans) to evolve from *Homo habilis*, people were hunter-gatherers and walked over most of the earth. There was a Satiable Self, but there was very little change in lifestyle and not much awareness of "more is better" or that people could or should "be more" or "have more."

- Then with the Neolithic Revolution around 10,000–8000 B.C., humans (*Homo sapiens sapiens*) settled down, stayed in one place, and became farmers.

- The Neolithic Revolution brought about (1) economic classes in which a dominant class began to live off the labor of a subordinate class; that is, a Marxist class structure emerged as a result of the agricultural surplus and (2) an awareness that people can be more and can have more and that being, ontologically speaking, is unlimited and contains an insatiable quality.

- Consequently, it brought about the awareness that "self-realization" is possible and real but reserved for those in the dominant/privileged classes. Paradoxically, the notion of self-realization is viewed as a fixed, determinate goal rather than insatiable and subject to unlimited potential.

- With civilization there was more growth, economic improvement, technology, and awareness of the potential for human self-development. Yet this is a highly restricted and constrained concept because the Culture of Security restricted individualism, particularly individual freedom to be more, to be all one might be and to have more, as well. In effect, self realization and insatiable potentiality were not linked until capitalism.

With the emergence of capitalism between the thirteenth and sixteenth centuries, not only did the Culture of Security recede, but the insatiable self emerged as well, "Freedom from constraint" became the operative phrase. The Italian merchants initiated the growth of trade by the eleventh century. They were some of the earliest capitalists, in part because they made huge profits from the trade in luxuries, and, being unable to spend them all, they decided to reinvest them in both existing and novel entrepreneurial opportunities. They saw no inherent limits to this and tasted early on the lure of insatiabilty (Greer 1972, 203). They sensed quite clearly their own insatiable selves emerging from these lucrative activities.

So after the Neolithic Revolution, the privileged classes became aware of their ability to have more, be more, and understand the unlimited character of their being. They could pursue "more" but not insatiably, because their freedom to do so, like that of everyone else, was constrained by the Culture of Security. They knew that as humans they had insatiable potential, but the culture did not nurture the expression or actualization of this. For them and ultimately for everyone, it took the birth of capitalism and the *Culture of Insatiable Freedom* for the insatiable self to be born.

PART TWO

Where We Are—
The Culture of Insatiable
Freedom

Chapter 3

Capitalism and the Sixteenth Century: The Universalization of the Insatiable Self: *Everyone SHOULD Be All They Can Be*

For several reasons, the development of capitalism is significant for the emergence of the insatiable self. The rapid and observable economic growth linked to the emergence of capitalism created a shift away from distributive ethics. Capitalism not only created the obvious economic growth but meant that the poor could have more without their gain coming at the expense of the rich. It also meant that *everyone could have more.*

Before capitalism, there was awareness that economic growth could and did take place. Yet economic growth was not what feudalism or slave systems were about. Precapitalist systems were not growth-driven. The Culture of Security prevented these systems from being driven by economic growth. So it was believed that if one group was to have more, then it was generally understood that another would have less—thus, the focus on distributive ethics. This also meant empire building, as with the Romans, among others. But with rapid economic growth in tandem with capitalism, equal rights to Be All You Can Be, to realize one's potential became possible. The collapse of the old Culture of Security and its replacement by the Insatiable Freedom Culture brought this about. Growth, as a legitimate possibility for all peoples and societies, suggested that now the right to be more, to Be All You Can Be could be extended to everyone. We can examine this from the perspective of the economic surplus, as well. Loosely defined and in the traditional Marxist sense, the economic surplus is that amount of production that exceeds the necessities of life (see Stanfield 1973). So in the pre-Neolithic period of hunters and gatherers there was no observable economic surplus. Yet we have to be careful, because as economic anthropologists like Marshall Sahlins suggest, for our ancestors their economic surplus took the form of leisure. They could have produced more than they needed but didn't. Rather than having surplus output, they had leisure. Still, there was no measurable surplus. Then with the Neolithic Revolution an observable economic surplus was produced. But from that point 10,000 years ago until the sixteenth century, the economic surplus accrued to the privileged classes. It was small by comparison to today's economy, and there was enough of a surplus to provide for a more comfortable lifestyle for the rich as well as the production of art and cultural activities for that class. It meant that some (the privileged classes) could be more and have more, as well.

But the Culture of Security inhibited both the production of economic surplus and its distribution to the common folk. Commoners had little or no access to either the surplus itself or its expanded production. These class societies before capitalism had both a limited surplus and limited access to its production and consumption. They were not driven by the desire to expand the economic surplus. They were not "surplus-driven" economies and didn't conceive of production as the means to increase the surplus. However, with the birth of capitalism, the economy changed its focus. Not only did the surplus expand under capitalism in unimaginable ways, but production and appropriation were more accessible to all participants in the economy—capitalists and workers alike.

Capitalism is not only growth-driven but surplus-driven. The economic surplus grows intentionally because all of the economic players are driven by insatiability, and access to it is unequal but greater than in the precapitalist economies. There is more surplus and more access to it by more folks than in the earlier societies, because the Culture of Security no longer constrains anyone. Everyone in capitalism is free to get ahead, get a piece of the growing economic pie, and become a winner. But not all people are equally free to do this. Those with money, inheritance, better educations, and all of the advantages that we recognize today have greater access than those on the bottom rung of the economic ladder.

As the time-line chart in Figure 3.1 indicates, the Culture of Security constrained both economic growth and the birth of the insatiable self. During the period between the Agricultural Revolution and the emergence of capitalism, those of the privileged classes had at least a vague understanding that they could both be more and have more. There was an economic surplus, but it was small, and the purpose of their economies was not to make it bigger. The dominant classes had "growth-awareness," as they knew that "more" was possible. They saw it and experienced it. But without a growth-driven economy, the notion that "more is better" was suppressed. They thought in terms of satiability, not in terms of the actualization of insatiable potential. Without the knowledge that there could be enough produced for all to "have more" or enough produced for all to "be more," the idea that all humans could and should "be all they can be" couldn't be universalized. It took capitalism for this to happen. It took an economy driven by "more is better," insatiability, and surplus expansion.

Figure 3.1
The Culture Time Line

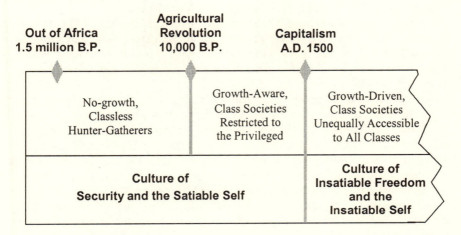

Once capitalism arrives, then each individual is free to get ahead, and to the extent that he or she tries, growth is built into the system. It becomes growth-driven and surplus-driven, as Figure 3.1 states. Capitalism, as Marx knew, is a still a class society, but all are free to climb upward in their class standing. The economic pie and its surplus are open for all common folks who want to work hard enough for upward social mobility. Unlike precapitalist societies in the Culture of Security, ordinary people are no longer cautioned to accept their assigned station in life. All folks are now able to "be all they can be." The "goods life" is open to all, but clearly not on an equal basis. Polanyi calls this transition to capitalism *The Great Transformation* (Polanyi [1944] 1957).

THE POLANYI THESIS

The *great transformation* was a 400-year process that began around the twelfth century with the innovation of the three-field system of crop rotation in Europe. With more food, population grew and doubled in Europe between 1100 and 1300 (Hunt 1990, 12). We can't overstate the magnitude of these population changes and the economic growth that was both cause and effect in this process. For the first 2 million years of human existence population stayed under 10 million. Thus, at the beginning of the Agricultural Revolution there were only 10 million people worldwide. By 5000 B.C. there were 50 million. By 1400 B.C. there were 100 million people, and then by A.D. 1800 there were a billion. But, as Hunt states, the sixteenth century was a watershed in economic history (18). Even though the Black Plague and the Hundred Years' War between France and England reduced Europe's population dramatically, after A.D. 1450 growth of both population and material things surged. "The population of western Europe, which had been relatively stagnant for a century and a half, increased by nearly one-third in the sixteenth century and stood at about 70 million in 1600" (18).

With the gold discoveries in Africa and the Western Hemisphere and the enclosure movements in Europe, merchants with money to spend and landless peasants with labor to sell hooked up, and capitalism began.

The great transformation brought about three major changes: (1) economic growth, (2) a new culture that replaced security with freedom—the Culture of Insatiable Freedom, and (3) a new notion of what it means to be a human being—the insatiable self. All three are interdependent, mutually reinforcing, and codetermining. This entire process is what Polanyi has also called the "disembedding of economy from society." This makes capitalism the first disembedded economy in human history (Polanyi [1944] 1957).

What are the implications? Polanyi's thesis is critical for understanding the shift from the Culture of Security to that of Insatiable Freedom. Precapitalist societies were embedded because economic activity within them was subordinated to social norms, customs, and traditions. Economic activity was not about getting rich or getting ahead. The ability of the individual to pursue his or her economic self-interest was largely suppressed and constrained. The individual was not free in today's sense to buy and sell and pursue economic greed. Embeddedness implies that the individual is "embedded," too. There is little economic freedom for the individual. One's motive to go out and produce was not that of "getting ahead" at all.

Individual motives to work were based upon obligation and command. One went into the fields or into the shop because that's what was expected of anyone as a member of the tribe, village, or society. So although this culture lacked the individual freedom to pursue gain, its benefit was security. Even though the tribe or village faced economic uncertainty or the perils of nature, the individual was, by virtue of being a member of the community, taken care of. The individual's motive to produce was not "fear of starvation."

The collective motive for these societies and tribes was understood to be that we "work to live," and without doing so, we suffer insecurity or hardship. But the individual was not motivated by "insecurity" as we are today, since we realize that if we don't get out there and hustle, we will suffer the consequences. Thus, "embeddedness" implies security, whether it takes the form of the feudal lords' obligation to care for the common serfs on their land or a tribe's collective obligation to care for its members. "Disembeddedness" implies that "you're on your own, pal"; that is, it implies freedom. But the real wealth of precapitalist societies, particularly the early hunters and gatherers, was their security. As Daniel Quinn states in *My Ishmael*, "The foremost wealth of tribal peoples is cradle-to-grave security for each and every member." As for us today in the Culture of Insatiable Freedom, he says: "There are hundreds of millions of you, however, who live in stark terror of the future because they see no security in it for themselves anywhere" (Quinn 1997, 173).

No one in the embedded economies of security was driven by improvement. The economic activity that defined these embedded cultures was constrained because the individual was constrained. People didn't think in terms of economically improving their status through trade or markets, and if they did, they were generally admonished for doing so by the moral establishment, that is, by folks like Aristotle or, later, the Vatican and church fathers.

An example of the embedded character of precapitalist Europe is the "just price" and the usury laws. The embedded economies of the precapitalist world had economic mechanisms that we often associate with capitalism: trade, markets, prices, exchange, and so on. But these mechanisms were also embedded. The "just price" that was discussed by Aristotle and then the church fathers in feudal Europe was a price for a good that didn't alter the economic status of either party. The goods/money were exchanged for the use value that each could gain, but the price had to be one that kept both parties at the same standard of living. It was a "just" price then. Today with capitalism, there is no just price. Prices today are based upon supply and demand and what the market will bear, not a particular concept of fairness that keeps people from "getting ahead."

The whole purpose today in our disembedded economy is to "get ahead." If one can do this in the course of buying and selling and within legal parameters, then so be it. We say that it's not a matter of "justice" at all. The feudal concept of usury was similar to that of the just price. Usury is interest charged for lending money. The general view held by the church was that charging people interest for money that they might need was immoral. It was usurious, as the lender, who obviously didn't need the money, would be getting something for nothing at another's expense. Of course, this was never strictly enforced. Even Aquinas said that lending with an interest charge could be considered acceptable if the borrower was going to use the money for his or her own benefit. But the just price and usury laws give us an indication of the "embedded" character of precapitalist society. These economic activities were embedded by the Culture of Security and suggest the extent to which the Satiable Self was the cultural and moral norm.

With the emergence of capitalism in the sixteenth century economic activity was disembedded from the Culture of Security, and not only did this happen, but the old culture was replaced by a new one based on freedom, and buying and selling in markets and motivated by the individual's desire both to avoid insecurity and to get ahead.

What exactly is the disembedding process? It's about how capitalism emerged, and capitalism is a "market economy," where the most basic needs are met by exchanging things in markets. Labor has to be exchanged in labor markets so that propertyless people can get the income that they need to buy their necessities. But labor markets had to be created. The creation of labor markets in Europe took several hundred years, and the enclosure movements, peasants' desire to flee the manor and obtain greater freedom in towns, and the end of poor laws all played a part. Also, in a market economy, those who own means of production, the capitalists, have to be able to buy labor and also have to be able to find buyers for their products. In the new market economy everybody is dependent upon finding buyers for something that they have to sell. Otherwise, they suffer the consequences of economic hardship. Making the exchanges is imperative. This is not planned out in advance, nor is it controlled by government. It's up to each individual player, whether worker or business, to find a buyer(s).

This fact alone makes capitalism totally inconsistent with the Culture of Security. Insecurity is the fundamental premise of this system. How can it be otherwise? The laws of supply and demand rule, and so does competition. You can never be sure what is going to happen, because there is no guarantee that you will find the buyers whom you need at a price that will sustain you. It doesn't matter whether it is workers or firms, finding the buyers and making the necessary exchanges are essential, and there's no way to know in advance. That's why we can say that the market economy is grounded on insecurity. "You are at the mercy of the market" is a phrase that we are all too familiar with today! Of course, we also say, "Trust in the magic of the market." But "trust" simply means that, given our initial insecurity, we have to place our faith in the prospect that what we have to offer will find the needed demand.

Karl Polanyi, even more so than Marx, was no doubt one of the first to really appreciate the dramatic impact that the disembedding of economic activity had on people's lives. What he means by "self-regulating" markets is that with capitalism's birth it was presumed by early defenders of the market economy (the classical economists, beginning with Adam Smith) that markets would be free of both government intervention and monopolistic influences so that only market-driven competition would determine outputs and prices. Therefore, a system of self-regulating markets would be the actualization of the textbook case of "Pure Competition." Then Polanyi states that a market economy, as self-regulating, means "an economy directed by market prices and nothing but market prices" (Polanyi [1944] 1957, 43). He maintains that although all societies must have some kind of economy for meeting human needs, the market-based and competition-driven system of capitalism is totally unique in human history. Why? Because, in its pure or extreme form, nothing but individual competition controls it (43). No government controls it; no individual business or capitalist controls it; no group of consumers or workers controls it. Nobody actually controls the self-regulating market system. Everyone must fend for himself or herself. Clearly, markets did exist before capitalism, but they were not the priority means for meeting basic material needs. They were only "incidental," says Polanyi and generally were not driven by competition (43). Precapitalist societies were mostly self-sufficient agricultural economies in which markets were ritualistic, exchanged surpluses and had their prices and outputs governed directly by people, not competition. The reason, we should add, that markets were no more than incidental before capitalism is that they were embedded in the Culture of Security and not part of a growth or profit-driven logic of insatiability.

Polanyi also argues that the real beginning of the "self-regulating" system was not until the nineteenth century, and this is because at that time all of the previous feudal paternalistic programs, like the English Speenhamland Act, were finally repealed. With this move, there were no longer any legal obstructions to the creation of competitive labor markets. In Marx's terms, there was by the nineteenth century a mobile labor force with nothing to sell but its labor. The very act of creating a propertyless and mobile labor force, in part, defines *the market economy as based upon insecurity* and the freedom to sell. Again, because of this fact alone, capitalism cannot be viewed as the next progression within the old Culture of Security. Naturally, for those with property and money there is much less insecurity, and their motive for participating in the production process is the lure of getting rich. The nineteenth century was different, says Polanyi, "for it chose to base itself on a motive only rarely acknowledged as valid in the history of human societies, namely, 'gain'" (Polanyi [1944] 1957, 42).

The emergence of capitalism as a self-regulating economy made insecurity and fear of economic hardship the motive to supply labor for the working class, while for the business class, their motive to supply capital was economic gain. But both classes are driven by the insecurity of having to sell something in a market in order to live. All social classes face the "vagaries" of the market, in other words. Both classes are subject to the insecurity of having to compete and having to rely on themselves and their individual initiatives. Supply and demand motored by impersonal competition became the "blind market forces."

In the self-regulating, disembedded economy, no one controls the process— no firm, no individual, no government. Control is lodged in the competitive struggle itself. Control is exercised by everyone in general and no one in particular. This is what is meant by stating that capitalism is grounded in a fundamental insecurity and therefore driven by personal freedom. As Polanyi states, self-regulation suggests that everything produced is headed for the market to be sold. This being the case, it means that our entire income, whether we are owner or worker, is dependent upon selling something in the market. Our security is totally at the mercy of the market, in other words (Polanyi [1944] 1957, 69). Again, in today's jargon we'd say, "You are on your own, pal." Yet this is what motivates both rich and poor. So, "no one is going to take care of you," as "it is up to you to sink or swim" in the wake of the market-driven competitive process. The point is that this is an economy that is driven by individual freedom. You may face insecurity unlike that of any previous economy, but, on the other hand, you have the individual freedom to pursue your economic self-interest. As Nobel laureate Milton Friedman says, you are "free to choose" in capitalism (Friedman and Friedman 1981). Yet leftists have added that you are likewise "free to lose."

The pursuit of security motivates individuals in capitalism, but this pursuit is carried out on the basis of individual freedom. This was not the case in earlier societies. Polanyi suggests that people would normally not choose to create such an economy, and therefore he tries to explain why and how it happened. To him it is unnatural and certainly not the spontaneous or organic outcome of the mercantilist world that preceded it. He says that "the 'freeing' of trade performed by mercantilism merely extended the scope of regulation," as the economic system was still subordinate to political institutions—monarchs and customs continued to rule over both politics and commercial life (Polanyi [1944] 1957, 67).

The disembedding of economic activity was accomplished by freeing up the individual. It not only created the Culture of Insatiable Freedom but created "the Economy" as a separate sphere of activity divorced from the political sphere and other social spheres like that of the family and religion. In the market economy, economic activity takes on a life of its own and not only becomes separated from the rest of society but also tends to dominate all of the other spheres, which then find themselves subordinated to its logic of "more is better" and the insatiable pursuit of self-actualization. The economy becomes the driving force behind all else. Clearly, all spheres are codetermining. It's not a case of economic determinism. But our economy today is not only a separate sphere of activity based upon insatiable improvement and self-interest; its logic also tends to subordinate all other spheres to itself. Its influence is disproportionately strong compared to that of the other spheres. That's why we say that capitalism secularizes life and creates a materialist culture. With the disembedding of economic activity, religion's hold on the Satiable Self is loosened. Through the disembedding process starting in the sixteenth century, the individual is freed from the constraints of religion, customs, mercantilist regulation, and traditions. This unleashed the self to Be All You Can Be. Additionally, it created the awareness that "being more" is insatiable.

Figure 3.2 illustrates the disembedding process, the embedded economy of precapitalist times. It shows that there is not a separate sphere that we can identify as "the economy." The dashed lines indicate that there is economic activity, but it is subordinated to, and immersed within, the broader circle of society itself. This also implies that although individual economic freedom doesn't exist, security does. By embedding economic activity, it therefore embedded the individual's power to pursue insatiable self-development. The Satiable Self and security were preserved at the expense of freedom. The collective motive to work is fear of hunger and hardship. This applies to the group, village, or tribe as a whole. This motive is for everyone in general but no one in particular. But the individual motive to work is different. Fear of hunger is not what motivates each person considered individually.

Figure 3.2
The Embedded Economy

Figure 3.3
The Disembedding of Economy

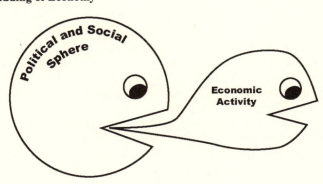

The individual motive to work is obligation and command. One did what was expected by virtue of the group's norms and customs. So for the collective, insecurity existed, but for the individual, insecurity is not the motive to produce. Today we tend to extrapolate from our own situation and conclude that our ancestors were motivated in the same way that we are. But in the precapitalist world, each person admitted to the collective was taken care of; fear of hunger was applicable only to the collective, not to the individual members.

The disembedding of economic activity is illustrated in Figure 3.3. Between the eleventh and sixteenth centuries economic activity was separated from society as a result of the legitimation of individual economic self-interest. The allowance for the pursuit of one's economic freedom caused the economic sphere. In this process the individual's ability to "get ahead" drives the creation of the economy. Economic freedom and the individual motives to get rich and pursue insatiable potential are released from the social and political spheres.

Finally, there's the disembedded economy of capitalism (Figure 3.4).

Figure 3.4
The Disembedded Economy of Capitalism

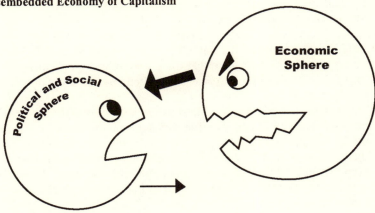

Here the economy is both separate from the social and political sphere and a larger circle. Economic activity is no longer subordinated to social norms, customs, traditions, and politics. The economy circle is larger because it not only takes on a life of its own—what we mean by the statement that capitalism is the first truly economic society—but tends to dominate all the rest of society. Yet if we notice the arrows that are between the circles, the arrow from the economy to the social sphere is the larger of the two. Why? Because although these spheres are co-determining and influence each other, in the disembedded market economy, the economy is disproportionately influential. The arrow from the society to the economy suggests that the political and social spheres also have a shaping and molding effect on the economy. In common political jargon, the capitalist state can shape the behavior of corporations in the private economic sector, while, simultaneously, the corporate world of the economy tends to dominate, as it is not the state that determines production, consumption, incomes, and basic material security.

Our needs in the disembedded market economy are not met by the state or by state-directed controls over the private sector. For example, the embedded economy of precapitalism had trade, markets, and prices, but these mechanisms were subordinated to social norms and customs. To the extent that there were prices, as we stated earlier, most pricing was subject to the moral norm of the "just price." These were "price-determined" markets, as competition and supply–demand did not determine the price. The price was established externally to the market. If the state set prices, as it did in the Soviet economy, then we would also call these markets "price-determined," and this would make the economy "embedded" as in Figure 3.2. So, the Soviet economy was an embedded economy! But in the disembedded economy, the separate sphere of the economy has "self-regulating" markets in which prices result from market forces themselves. These are "price-determining" markets, and as classical economic theory maintains, prices are signals that call forth more or less supply and demand and presumably "clear" the market as equilibrium is established. The state plays a minimal role in how much gets produced and who gets what, because it lets the impersonal forces of market competition rule.

Our material needs and the security that derives from them are linked directly to the market. Then and only then can we say that the market is influenced by the policies of the state. Regardless of the actual role of the state in capitalist society, we recognize that the economy in capitalism is a separate and powerful entity driven by everyone's need and desire to obtain security, as well as to "get ahead."

With respect to work motives, the situation is entirely different from that in the embedded economy. With the disembedded economy the collective motive to work is "continuous improvement" or "insatiable improvement." Yet the individual motive is insecurity and fear of economic hardship for those with the least property and the lure of wealth for those with the most. Insecurity is a collective motive in the embedded economy but an individual motive in the disembedded economy.

If we accept Polanyi's thesis, capitalism becomes the first truly "economic" or "commercial" society. Its logic tends to shape and mold the other spheres disproportionately. *Capitalism is a wealth-producing juggernaut.* The purpose of the market economy is to produce wealth on an unlimited scale, and, driven by competition in conjunction with the individual's insatiable freedom to improve everything good, it does so. But it should also be clear that its purpose is not to take care of people or to provide security. Security is not integral to this system's purpose and becomes a hoped-for outcome of one's successful exercise of individual self-interest. In capitalism we obtain security by exercising our freedom to get ahead. Security has to be achieved, has to be accomplished, and has to be pursued. It is not a feature of the system, even though freedom is.

This sacrifice of security and capitalism's way of linking it to the successful use of freedom is basic. In other words, each person's material security is dependent upon using his or her freedom to win at the compete-or-die logic of the market game. In the early nineteenth century the British Poor Laws functioned to suppress the supply–demand, competitive labor market, and Polanyi says that capitalists wanted an end to the Poor Laws since they "prevented the rise of an industrial working class which *depended for its income on achievement*" (Polanyi [1944] 1957, 137; emphasis added). Since achieving security becomes a goal that one must accomplish, and because this is the common reality of the self-regulating economy, it creates an almost intuitive, knee-jerk reaction to disembedding.

Polanyi adds that to let the market system and its compete-or-die logic determine our lives would actually "result in the demolition of society" (Polanyi [1944] 1957, 73). He is saying this: a truly self-regulating market system is scary. There's no assurance of any security. No one is obligated to provide anything to anyone else. To turn the material reproduction of an entire society over to the impersonal forces of the competitive market is not likely to happen, according to Polanyi, because people, both businesses and workers, will intuitively react by seeking protection from the "vagaries of the market"—its uncertainties and unpredictabilities. Polanyi maintains that "actually, the worker has no security in his job under a system of private enterprise," and in this respect, he concludes, the worker's status is even lower than in precapitalist economies (231). We can be laid off at will. It might be explained to us as necessary, as cyclical in nature, due to downsizing, rightsizing, cheaper labor elsewhere, or deindustrialization. But the explanation doesn't remove the essential insecurity that accompanies the disembedded economy.

Arming people with their freedom to pursue economic self-interest is not enough to calm their anxieties about their fate. There's an analogy for this. For example, assume that there is a deep swimming pool surrounded by a large crowd of people who can't swim. Then someone says to the crowd, "If you all hold hands and jump together into the pool, you'll displace enough water to lower the level and allow everyone to live and not drown. Your heads will be above the waterline. Trust me!" Obviously, if only part of the crowd jumps, then the plan won't work. They all have to do this together and trust each other to jump simultaneously. This is something like the Prisoner's Paradox. There's a strong likelihood that the fear of drowning will prevail. People won't jump. For Polanyi, the self-regulating market economy is similar. To make it work, everyone has to trust in the impersonal forces of competition and his or her own initiative in order to obtain security.

Polanyi says that fear won out in the disembedding process, and, although the economic activity did become disembedded, and an economic sphere was created, people also ran for protection at the same time. They sought protection from market forces. In the analogy this is like everyone's pulling back when the count gets to three in order to grab a life jacket. Some people jump and drown, while others frantically scour the poolside for the few life jackets that they see. "Society protected itself against the perils inherent in a self-regulating market economy—this was the one comprehensive feature in the history of the age" (Polanyi [1944] 1957, 76).

A countermovement accompanied the disembedding process, in other words. This, for Polanyi, is called the "protective response." Fear of the consequences from subordinating our lives to forces that none of us control led people to seek protection. They did this by organizing unions, by going to their governments to lobby for protective legislation, and by trying to establish monopoly power. Both workers and capitalists sought protection. This is no different from saying that no one likes competition. Businesses don't, and neither do workers. Workers form unions, and capitalists form trusts. They both go to the state and ask for protection, subsidies, and various forms of the social safety net. Of the protective response, Polanyi says it is "the principle of social protection aiming at the conservation of man and nature" (Polanyi [1944] 1957, 132). It was motivated by all those who experienced the insecurity that comes from disembedding and used "protective legislation, restrictive associations, and other instruments of intervention" (Polanyi [1944] 1957, 132).

The modern welfare state is the historical result. This countermovement of the protective response is a "reembedding" movement that occurred simultaneously with the disembedding movement. The whole process of the creation of the market economy was, therefore, a "double movement." As Polanyi says, "the dynamics of modern society was governed by a *double* movement: the market expanded continuously but this movement was met by a counter-movement" that tried to block the drift toward self-regulation (Polanyi [1944] 1957, 130). This ultimately explains much of the last 300 years of capitalist development. The tension between the forces of self-regulating markets and those of the protective response are actually a manifestation of a deeper and richer tension between freedom and security. Do we want a society where we use freedom to obtain security, or do we want one that uses the assurance of security as the basis for the enjoyment of freedom? To the extent that the protective response represents a genuine and intuitive, gut-level reaction to insecurity, it suggests that most folks have a real need for security.

Capitalism emerged but not, strictly speaking, as a purely "self-regulating" market economy. Had there been no protective response, then we would have a truly "self-regulating" market system. But the protective response prevented that from happening as legislation, unionization, and government subsidies intervened in the market process to dampen the effects of self-regulation. The disembedding and its countermovement were enough to undermine the Culture of Security but not enough to totalize life under the regime of vicious, dog-eat-dog competition. Most would figure that the social safety net and welfare state are products of the twentieth century, yet they really were born along with the capitalism and labor markets in the nineteenth. As the Hungarian social theorist Mihaly Vajda argues: "The situation in England during and after the industrial revolution, which revealed the prevailing laws of the self-regulating market and, at the same time, their catastrophic consequences, was a brief, transitional period in the history of capitalism. The liberal theory thus appears as one of the least realizable (negative) utopias in the history of humanity. If Polanyi's theses are on target, and surely they are, then the historical tendency of capitalist society does not and cannot correspond to that which Marx predicted" (Vajda 1981, 47).

Vajda's point is that Marx based his self-destructive predictions about capitalism on the idea that capitalism was a purely "self-regulating" market. But it was not and never has been. Why? Because ordinary people intuitively resist such a system and did so from the very beginning. Why? Because it is too scary; no security at all is built into the structure of such a system. Security is completely determined by the effectiveness of each and every person's ambition in the compete-or-die game. Such a world is a negative utopia. It is utopian because people always resist a world like this, and it's negative because it would be a bad world as well. What this means is that the likelihood of a crowd of nonswimmers jumping into a deep pool all at the same time is not great. From the Industrial Revolution until today, we have documented the extent to which the state has intervened on behalf of all sorts of victims of the competitive market. There was never enough protective legislation to totally reembed the economic sphere, but it has provisioned a measure of material security to buffer both business and workers from the effects of self-regulation. Therefore, capitalism has been known as the "mixed economy." In fact, in Figure 3.4 illustrating the disembedded economy, the arrow that runs from the social/political sphere to that of the economy represents the protective response. Its moderating effect has helped to stabilize the market economy and provide substantial legitimation for it. But it has not reembedded it, and therefore we can conclude that the system today is still driven by the insecurity of its actors and their willingness to struggle for their security by using personal economic freedom.

An important qualification needs to be made, however, with respect to the term "embedded." Isn't it true that all economic activity—and any "economy" that we consider—is "embedded" at some level within the culture of the given society? Yes. Even capitalism as an economic system is "embedded" in the Culture of Insatiable Freedom, consumerism, and "more is better." In a pure sense there is no such thing as a "disembedded" economy that lies outside a society's cultural parameters. But what Polanyi is arguing with respect to capitalism's "disembeddedness" is different. The extent of "disembeddedness" is measured by the degree of constraints on individual economic freedom. Clearly, our individual freedom is shaped and influenced by the culture in which it operates. Our pursuit of economic freedom is embedded in the culture itself. But the ability to actualize this freedom in economic activity is what Polanyi is getting at. By disembedding economic activity from the social and political spheres of life, it releases the individual from prior constraints but does not release the individual from the culture itself. In precapitalist life, the social and political institutions that embedded economic activity functioned to constrain the self and its freedom. That's why there was the Satiable Self.

We can clarify "embeddedness" by modifying the previous diagrams to look like Figure 3.5. Figure 3.5 also illustrates something else: when economic activity became disembedded from the social and political spheres, it also changed the culture from that of Security to our present Culture of Insatiable Freedom. The disembedding process did two things. It created a separate economic sphere, and it created a cultural transformation. No wonder Polanyi calls the emergence of capitalism the great transformation.

FROM THE CULTURE OF SECURITY TO
THAT OF INSATIABLE FREEDOM

The cultural transformation from security to freedom set the stage for the birth of the insatiable self. It begins with the awareness that the new Culture of Insatiable Freedom is simultaneously a culture driven by insecurity. John Kenneth Galbraith, the twentieth century's Goliath of social economics, in his classic critique of consumer culture, *The Affluent Society*, devoted an entire chapter to the issue of insecurity in capitalism (Galbraith 1958). He says:

Figure 3.5
Culture in Precapitalism and Capitalism

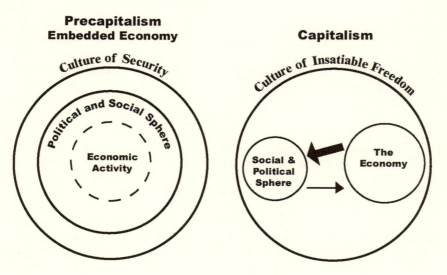

In the model of the competitive society such insecurity was inherent. The individual producer or worker might, at any time, suffer a sudden decline in his fortunes. This could be the result of laziness or incompetence which would lose him his customers or his job. But the best of men might suffer from a sudden change in consumer tastes or as the result, not of their own inadequacy but of that of their employer. These unpredictable changes in fortune were both inevitable and useful. They were inevitable, for they were part of the capacity of the system to accommodate itself to change. The insecurity was useful, for it drove men—businessmen, workers, the self-employed—to render their best and most efficient service, for severe punishment was visited impersonally on those who did not. (Galbraith 1958, 98)

Marx would have agreed, as well. From Marx's point of view, simply by virtue of wage workers being dependent upon the profits-first logic of capitalist production, they are fundamentally in a position of insecurity. But Polanyi's point is even more basic, for he would argue that the market system itself constitutes the basis for insecurity. Everybody, as Galbraith suggests, from poorly paid wage workers to wealthy capitalists, exists within a climate of insecurity. Everybody is dependent upon the sale of either labor or goods to obtain his or her material security, and there's no assurance that the sale or exchanges in markets will take place as needed. Of course, our modern form of "structural" or institutionalized insecurity exists within a competitive environment: we must compete with others in our effort to overcome it. C. Wright Mills stated in *White Collar* (1951), "Life in a society of masses implants insecurity and furthers impotence; it makes men uneasy and vaguely anxious; it isolates the individual from the solid group; it destroys firm group standards. Acting without goals, man in the mass just feels pointless" (Novack 1966, 7–8). Although Mills was right on with his view about insecurity and anxiety, the cultural observation that most of us would make suggests that insecurity drives people to potency rather than impotency. Competition does destroy our group bonds, but the market mechanism also coerces most people into getting goals in an effort to avoid being left behind. *If* we fail to be sufficiently "goal-oriented" and "self-directed," *then* we may begin to feel pointless in the existential sense and in Mills' sense.

Galbraith repeats Polanyi's point that although all people claim to like the insecurity that forces us to perform, they don't like it applied to themselves. As he states, "This insecurity, valuable though it seemed in principle, was cherished almost exclusively either in the second person or in the abstract. Its need was thought urgent for inspiring the efforts of other persons or people in general. It seldom seemed vital for the individual himself." In addition, "In the conventional wisdom of conservatives, the modern search for security is regularly billed as the greatest single threat to economic progress" (Galbraith 1958, 99). What Galbraith is saying is that (1) people may abstractly support the notion that insecurity works to motivate achievement, but they act to eliminate it as a motive for themselves and that (2) without insecurity as a whip, we would stagnate both individually and collectively.

Evidence of the extent to which "the conventional wisdom" has been acculturated exists everywhere. For instance, I asked students in my macroeconomics courses to write a short essay about insatiability. They were to create their own question about the topic and then write about it. One group came up with this: "Is the risk of having a high level of poverty worth our freedom to obtain wealth?" A student wrote: "Is it not undeniably true that everyone in this great country has the potential to make it big? Yes! Knowing that I have the opportunity to make millions is worth the risk of poverty. This economy flourishes because of the wealthy. If there were no reward for working so hard then people would not strive to be the best they can be." His comment is hardly uncommon. Another student wrote, "If everyone earned the same amount of income there would no longer be the push or drive to work hard and to get ahead of others financially. I am a firm believer in the idea that without competition there is no incentive to achieve." The point is that in the popular consciousness of our Culture of Insatiable Freedom, we have accepted the idea that insecurity drives us to use our freedom to insatiably Be All You Can Be.

Insecurity is basic to the market economy, affects all players, both capitalists and workers—although not equally—and allows for the pervasive cultural assimilation of the imperative of Be All You Can Be. Because virtually everybody faces the condition of having to "achieve" security, it is logical that everybody would quickly realize that the solution is to exercise one's freedom to "be more," and by "being more," one can "have more" and obtain a measure of security.

So although the disembedded economy of capitalism uses the whip of insecurity to coerce our performance, it grants us the carrot of personal economic freedom to "get ahead," and if we do, we receive the reward of the "goods life." The bottom line is that with capitalism, not only can you "be more," but you can "have more." More importantly, the system, driven as it is by insecurity, says that you *should* "be more" and *must* "be more." But how much of "being more" is enough? There's never enough, because "you can always be more tomorrow than you are today." "Being more" is inherently insatiable, as we have realized over the last 10,000 years. Humans exist with unlimited being, that is, as the insatiable potentiality to actualize ever more abilities, skills, talents, and capacities.

THE IMPERATIVE OF INSATIABLE SELF-DEVELOPMENT

The Enlightenment in the eighteenth century was influential in popularizing the notion that humans have as their essence the unlimited potentiality always to be more. But the Enlightenment, which technically is the period between Newton's *Principia* in 1687 and the French Revolution in 1789, was also an expression of the cultural changes that accompanied the birth of the market economy, modern science, and modernist philosophy (British empiricism and continental rationalism). With the sixteenth century we witness tremendous economic growth, global exploration and expansion, and the secularization of life. Newton's message was a synthesis of the scientific precedents set by Copernicus (1543), Kepler and Galileo (1609), and Bacon and Descartes (1637). Newton saw no conflict between physics and astronomy, as it was Newton who linked Galileo to Kepler. By doing so, he was the first to establish proofs for universal and eternal laws (Greer 1972, 325). The upshot of this was the popular acceptance of the view that "through science and technology he [man] could *improve his well-being* and press nature into his service" (330; emphasis added). With scientific knowledge, in other words, humans were presumed to be capable of unlimited and insatiable improvement of everything good in themselves, their living standards, and the world around them.

The Enlightenment philosophers, or *philosophes*, included Voltaire, Diderot, Condorcet, Holbach, and Beccaria. In general, they argued that humans have tremendous reasoning capacities, and they placed great emphasis and faith on the rational powers of people. They were inspired by the achievements of the emerging scientific method. "By the early eighteenth century, the achievements in mathematics, astronomy, and physics which culminated in Newton's *Principia* (1687) had penetrated widely if not deeply into the public mind of the West" (Brinton 1967, 525).

The *philosophes* were the forerunners of our notion of modernism. They believed that by tapping the unlimited powers of rationality and through the use of science, humans might come to understand and know themselves and their world. These philosophers of the Enlightenment concluded that nature was easier to know and understand than God. Nature was shown to be more predictable than God. A new kind of faith was being embraced (Greer 1972, 331).

Ultimately, their thought suggests that there are eternal truths, objective knowledge, and universal concepts. The Enlightenment ideas argued that humans not only can understand their world but, through science, can control it, use it, and reign over it. Also the notion that there are universal and eternal truths that humans can comprehend suggested that humans can come together and through this shared commonality create a reasonable and harmonious system of life—the perfect world is possible, in other words. Thus, through reason and science we can control ourselves and the world—liberty, equality, and fraternity are real possibilities. They were optimists and believed in reason, nature, and progress. Their thought contributed in no small way to our conventional wisdom that humans are essentially about insatiable improvement. That's what it means to be "enlightened," they might say.

Their notion of progress was a radical and novel idea then. Yet "Americans especially are so accustomed to accepting the notion of Progress as something self-evident that they find it hard to realize how new this doctrine really is" (Brinton 1967, 521). In the Judeo-Christian tradition, as we have pointed out, there was no comparable concept. In fact, from Antiquity to the Renaissance, the conventional wisdom held that humans had fallen from the perfect state and could, at best, hope and struggle for salvation. For example, in Augustine's *City of God*, he stated that an improved human condition, "though seen to be ahead as well as behind, is not one attained by the steady improvement of man's lot on this earth in the *civitas terrena*, but by a promise of a Second Coming of Christ" (521). On the other hand, Turgot gave a speech at the Sorbonne in 1750 that was titled "On the Successive Advances of the Human Mind." Subsequently, his disciple and friend Condorcet wrote *Sketch for a Historical Picture of the Human Mind*, which, in effect, was an "extraordinarily optimistic utopia of indefinite progress toward what has been called a doctrine of 'natural salvation'—the attainment by everyone of immortality in this flesh on earth" (521). Condorcet's euphoric optimism and faith in insatiable progress were ridiculed at the time, yet, ironically, today such a view is accepted as common sense.

The point is that with the developments in philosophy starting on the European continent with Descartes (1596–1650), then Spinoza (1632–1677) and Leibniz (1646–1716), and in Britain with Hobbes (1588–1679) and Locke (1632–1704), there were clusters of ideas about progress, human potentiality, natural rights, and democracy, all of which served a common purpose: to give birth to a new idea about unlimited individual and social improvement. The Enlightenment is simply an expression of this radical new belief.

The basis for all of these changes is no doubt the material growth that capitalism was making possible. It was observable growth, and the fact that it was a by-product of the new right to pursue economic self-interest was observable as well. Everyone was free—though unequally free—to go about getting ahead. Insecurity, freedom, and the competitive market became facts of life. Economic growth, likewise, became a fact of life. For the first time in human history there was such an abundance of material wealth that all humans could have more of everything. With the new science, armed more importantly with the scientific method, there was no reason that more of everything good in life could not be obtained by everyone willing to work for it.

Yet the notion of equal rights to be more and to pursue one's self-actualization made little sense in precapitalist societies. The distribution of the material means to "be more" was constrained. With the economic-growth awareness that accompanied capitalism, the means to be more was essentially unlimited. This also created the foundation for the extension of democracy. Democracy and the movements that demanded it argued for the equal right and opportunity for each and every individual to be all that he or she could be. In other words, the physical means for each to *have more* led to the opportunity for each to be able to *be more*. But capitalism also meant that the Culture of Security was to yield to the new Culture of Insatiable Freedom. People were free to try to have more. This notion is integral to classical liberalism, of course.

PRODUCTIVISM AND CONSUMERISM

With the birth of capitalism there is the shift from the Culture of Security to the Culture of Insatiable Freedom. We say "insatiable freedom" because the idea that humans have unlimited potential always to be more makes no sense unless it is understood that they have the existential freedom, that is, the power, to make choices and act on them, to at least try to actualize this potentiality. Our freedom is insatiable because it is simply the power to pursue being more, and since one can always be more tomorrow than what one is today, that freedom is insatiable. By calling it existential freedom, we mean that all humans have this capacity regardless of their objective class/race/gender/ethnic position. Obviously, there's a huge difference in objective freedom between an oppressed, Third World female doing sweatshop labor and Bill Gates. Yet both have a type of existential freedom to "be more." What capitalism did was remove a variety of objective cultural barriers to the individual's pursuit of self-development and self-/social improvement.

The difference between capitalism and Antiquity is simply that the economic growth that occurred with the market economy made it possible to generalize being more and having more to virtually everyone from wage worker to capitalist. Economic growth made it apparent that all folks could have more and be more rather than this being restricted to the dominant classes, as had been the case previously. Having more and being more were no longer the exclusive prerogative of the privileged. Additionally, the removal of security and the imposition of insecurity-cum-freedom meant that in the new Culture of Insatiable Freedom everyone would begin to gravitate toward the complete embrace of being and having more.

Everyone's ticket to material security, regardless of rich or poor, capitalist or worker, became linked to, and dependent upon, the pursuit of "being more." Capitalism created a culture in which virtually everyone has to try to "be more" just to survive. This was not the case in the old Culture of Security, where there was no reason for anyone to have to be more. "Being more" did not drive the economy in the old culture, but it does in capitalism. If the old culture's form of security was taken away by the market, it is only logical that those who have to hustle to live are going to demand equal rights and democratic participation. If you have no other way to get security except to work for it, then you'll want to have access to the social mechanisms that will allow you to "be more." This is simply because being more is the only way to get anywhere in a competitive process. The desire and demand for equal rights, equal opportunity, and a democratic say in the political process are logical consequences of what it means when people are told, "You're on your own, pal."

So the disembedding of the economy from society and the insecurity-cum-freedom incentive system gave everyone the green light to try to get ahead. Because "you're on your own, pal" became the operative incentive, there is an element of coercion and compulsion to "being more" and "having more." If you don't hustle, you lose. The new system of capitalism requires that people take steps to do something with their lives, because, failing this, they don't get the good jobs or the decent standard of living or sell their products and make their profits. They get left behind in the compete-or-die world.

Yet capitalism did something else to reinforce this: it separated the activities of production and consumption and relegated each to a different sphere. We can examine the implications of this in Figure 3.6.

In the Culture of Security there are no separate spheres of consumption and production. Producing and consuming are not divorced from one another, because these are essentially self-sufficient agricultural economies based either on slaves or on some form of peasant or serf labor. The activities of producing goods, dividing up who gets what (distribution), and then consuming the goods

Figure 3.6
Productivism and Consumerism

Product Markets
Consumerism
Have All You Can Have

Capitalism

Factor Markets
Productivism
Be All You Can Be

were an integrated process in which the usual approach was simply that serfs, peasants, or slaves worked the fields and shops and turned over a portion of their output to their masters or lords. This is a fairly straightforward procedure.

Markets didn't act like mediators or intermediaries between the various players. But marketization creates separate spheres, makes production into something quite different from consumption, and gets folks pretty confused about who does what and who gets what. Of course, this is a point made by Marx and the early socialists as they became aware of how exploitation of labor occurs in the production sphere of the process. Their concern was with the fact that by creating separate markets for labor, on the one hand, and consumer goods, on the other, workers' ability to experience the exploitation was obscured by the market process itself.

Marx talked about how production and consumption codetermine each other in the *Grundrisse* (Marx 1973), written in 1857–1858. But we need to take note of the labels used in Figure 3.6. We are talking not about "consumption" but "consumer*ism*"—the ideology of "have all you can have." We are not talking about "production," but "productiv*ism*"—the ideology of "be all you can be." The fact that capitalism takes production and consumption and divorces them by creating separate markets for factors of production, on the one hand, and goods and services, on the other hand, also implies that two ideologies operate: consumerism and productivism. But they are two sides of the same coin, and you can't have one without the other. The ideologies are mutually reinforcing. Since the basic premise of this book is that the insatiable desire to have more is a result of the insatiable desire to be more, consumerism and productivism are mutually reinforcing and codetermining. Figure 3.6 illustrates this.

If we take Marx's approach to consumption and production seriously, we can apply it to Figure 3.6. First, Marx says that production is consumption and that consumption is production. Although this sounds a bit convoluted, his point is that people don't produce without needs that are fulfilled in consumption. Likewise, when they consume, they are using up the products, thus setting the stage for a new round of production. He says that "production creates the objects which correspond to the given needs; in consumption, the product becomes a direct object and servant of individual needs. Thus production appears as the point of departure, consumption as the conclusion" (Marx 1973, 89). He adds that consumption and production form a "regular syllogism."

But Marx is getting at something else. Yes, any of us would agree that production can't exist without consumption and that consumption can't exist without production. You can't have one without the other. This much is obvious. Marx states that a "mediating movement" occurs between consumption and production in which without production, "consumption would lack an object." But consumption "alone creates for the products the subject for whom they are products" (Marx 1973, 91). Marx is making another important point: production is the primary activity, the dominant activity, while consumption is more passive.

Why does Marx say that production dominates over consumption? While the two are codetermining, Marx wants to argue that production has disproportionate influence. He says that consumption "*ideally posits* the object of production as an internal image, as a need, as drive and as purpose. No production without a need. But consumption reproduces the need" (Marx 1973, 92). His point is that needs can be filled in a variety of ways and that just because there is a need to be satisfied, this need in itself does not determine the specific form or product that will be used to satisfy it. He says, "Hunger is hunger, but the hunger gratified by cooked meat eaten with a knife and fork is a different hunger from that which bolts down raw meat with the aid of hand, nail, and tooth. Production thus produces not only the object but also the manner of consumption. Production thus not only creates an object for the subject, but also a subject for the object" (92). So if technology exists for the production of knives and forks, and these are produced, then consumption of food will be done using these instruments. People will therefore develop table manners and proper and polite behavior for eating. Thus, for Marx, the specific way in which hunger is satisfied is largely determined by the state of the productive process. In other words, the way in which we fulfill our needs originates in the productive process itself. It shapes our need fulfillment and influences how we are as consumers, what we look like, and how we behave!

Now if we apply this reasoning to Figure 3.6, by extrapolation we can make some rough conclusions about the relationship between consumerism and productivism. Consumerism refers to that ideological pillar of capitalism that the "goods life is the good life." Consumerism implies that we should find happiness through buying, that we should "shop till we drop." As we recognize, there are many ways to fulfill a vague and amorphous need, like the need to belong, to give and receive love, to have a feeling of self-worth, and so on. But capitalism tends to bias our need fulfillment by emphasizing the satisfaction of needs through the purchase of commodities in markets. A vast literature documents this fact (see Leiss 1976; Preteceille and Terrail 1985; Ewen 1976; Ewen and Ewen 1982; Wachtel 1989). But the critical issue is that consumerism is about "having all you can have." It identifies a set of beliefs and values that says to us, "You can have it all, and there's no inherent end to having more of everything in life." As consumers, the more money that we can get our hands on and the more goods that we can buy, the happier we are supposed to be, and businesses are happy to supply our needs for ever more products. That's consumerism.

What about productivism? This, too, is an ideological pillar, and it is about ambition, goal orientation, achievement, and, ultimately, Be All You Can Be. It speaks to our conventional wisdom that the purpose of life is to be more, get more, achieve more, actualize more, and develop yourself to the fullest. Because we can always be more tomorrow than we are today, actualizing ourselves to the "fullest" is insatiable, just as having all we can have is likewise insatiable. But productivism also applies to businesses and corporations as well. *Productivism is fundamentally about maximization of performance, and it applies to all economic actors, individuals, sole proprietorships, and corporations.* Moreover, productivism is a cultural norm that applies to all activities, both economic and otherwise. The corporation, as an economic and political entity, must embrace Be All You Can Be if it is to be a winner in the competitive struggle. It must have goals, be self-directed, be ambitious, and seek to actualize its potential. Like individual people, it can always be more tomorrow than it is today. The corporation defines itself in these kinds of human terms. It measures itself on the basis of accomplishments and achievements and wants to Be All You Can Be.

Productivism is another way of talking about the Culture of Insatiable Freedom. The freedom that is insatiable is the freedom always to be more, always to pursue "getting ahead." Productivism is usually associated with economic activity, but it is a label that we can use to accurately describe our entire way of life. By stating that humans now define themselves as the life form that can always be more, we have therefore defined our essence as "insatiable improvers" and, thus, "productivists." So although in the consumerism-productivism diagram we are examining the logic of the market economy, productivism is a defining feature of our culture. Humans are productivists—at least that is how we now define ourselves. We are the insatiable achievers, the performance people. Life gets reduced to being about performance, that is, about productivism.

The arrows in Figure 3.6 suggest that the ideological pillars of consumerism and productivism are codetermining and mutually reinforcing. For example, the primary means for having all we can have is to get a good job, and to do this requires Be All You Can Be (like the left-hand arrow from consumerism to productivism). So if the corporation goes into the competitive market, it, too, must Be All You Can Be if it wants to have more. Its payoff for maximal performance and productivism is that it can have all it can have—maximal profits, market share, asset values, and such. On the other hand, for individual economic players, when we go about acquiring more job skills and struggling for upward career mobility, one of the primary payoffs for our human capital investment is that we get better-paying jobs and are rewarded by having all we can have—more income, more wealth, and the rewards of the goods life. Thus, "insatiably being more" enables us to "insatiably have more." There is effective compensation for our effort (the arrow from productivism to consumerism on the right-hand side). Being more *enables* us to have more (the upward arrow), and having more *requires* us to be more (the downward arrow). Capitalism separates Have All You Can Have from Be All You Can Be by distinguishing between consumerism and productivism. It does so by divorcing the sphere of consumption from the sphere of production.

If Marx's logic is accepted, we have to acknowledge not only that the two "isms" are codetermining but that Be All You Can Be can take many forms. In capitalism Be All You Can Be *tends* to be channeled into economic activities rather than other spheres, and this reinforces the consumerist mentality of Have All You Can Have. Since production dominates consumption, productivism dominates consumerism.

How so? First, it must be noted that with separate spheres of consumerism and productivism, these two types of consciousness (which is effectively what they are) can be pursued independently. For example, an ambitious individual may be a productivist when it comes to acquiring job skills and accomplishing career-related goals, as he or she has internalized this cultural norm. In other words, "You are what you accomplish in your career." Yet this same person may not be into consumerism and may actually practice "voluntary simplicity" (see Elgin 1993; Dominguez and Robin 1992). On the other hand, there are those who are voracious consumers, living the goods life, but because they have inherited substantial wealth, they don't have to be productivists.

Consequently, you can have all you can have without having to Be All You Can Be, and vice versa. Yet most of us are wrapped up in the circular causality of both types of consciousness. Is productivism the dominant "moment," as Marx might have argued? There's a strong case for this, because of one factor: *the structural and fundamental insecurity that motors the market system does not in itself drive us to have all we can have. However, it does necessitate that we Be All We Can Be.* The initial condition of being faced with "you're on your own, pal" makes us want to be more in order to have anything at all. Faced with the prospects of economic hardship, we are driven to action in the labor market. Subsequently, we can then look forward to the goods life. The economic insecurity of capitalism directs our consciousness to being more *in the economy*.

This serves to legitimate the consumerist consciousness. So the point is that our ability to insatiably be more can be focused on any number of objects (being more spiritual, being more virtuous, being a better lover, etc.). But because of the economic form of insecurity that confronts everyone, that insatiable ability to be more takes a specific economic expression. It is channeled toward an economic productivism that then establishes consumerism and the goods life as a legitimate payoff.

How is it that this particular economic manifestation of Be All You Can Be—what we call productivism—ultimately transcends the economic sphere and becomes a cultural norm? If we argued from an economic determinist perspective, we'd have to say that, because the economy is so basic to all life, what happens there carries over to, or determines, what happens everywhere. In other words, because we are driven to actualize our insatiable potential in the economy due to the fundamental insecurity that we all face (except those with inherited wealth), we universalize this to our whole life. Thus, if *economically* we must develop ourselves, *we must,* therefore, *be the "insatiable self-developers."*

Consequently, economic determinism is one way to explain how we have evolved to the point of defining ourselves as the "insatiable improvers." If improving is what we do to survive in the competitive market system, then we become improvers in all ways, in all spheres, and ontologically as well: to Be is to Be All You Can Be.

A less deterministic explanation is that with the material growth that accompanied the birth of capitalism, the means for "being more" and the awareness that humans have unlimited potential to improve themselves became more obvious and visible. Added to that, the economy acted as a catalyst to bring out the improvement capabilities in people. With capitalism and economic growth, people became more conscious of their capabilities and experienced the reality of the freedom to act, to get ahead, to be more, and to have more. All of these forces operated together in a codetermining fashion. It's also important to talk about the "experience" of capitalism and the extent to which this phenomenological or existential experience that precedes reflective thought contributes to the creation of the Insatiable Freedom Culture.

What is the fundamental experience of capitalism, if there is one? Marx argued that it is exploitation, and maybe during the Industrial Revolution this was true. Marx maintained that workers, with no recourse for a livelihood except to sell their labor to capitalists, would find themselves in factories, working under conditions that they didn't direct, subject to the authority of bosses, and thus their most essential experience of life in capitalist society would be that of exploitation. Of course, he anticipated that workers suffering this experience would not only be aware of it but then band together and demand social change. Yet, as we know, this hasn't been the case in very many places over the last 200 years.

Why workers haven't done what Marx expected is the subject of a vast literature, a very rich literature indeed, the legacy of which is neo-Marxism, critical theory (like the Frankfurt school), existential Marxism, humanistic Marxism, and now post-Marxism (see McLellan 1979; Agger 1979; the journals

Telos and *Rethinking Marxism*). In general, these views all have one conclusion: Marx suffered from excessive economic determinism. Marx figured that by virtue of a person's being a wage worker, this condition would not only be the basic feature of his or her life but would be how people defined themselves. In other words, "to be" in capitalism is to be a wage worker (unless you own enough capital to avoid it). Thus, for Marx, people are fundamentally "toolmaking" creatures for whom "labor" is so basic to what it means to be a person that, as wage workers, they would "experience" this as "alienated labor."

If Marx asks the question, "What is the defining feature of life?", his response is, Labor. Then, if he asks, "What is the defining feature of capitalist life?", his reply is, Alienated labor. Marx saw the economy as so important that he felt that people, when asked, "Who are you?", would respond by saying, Workers. And consequently when forced to work under the alienating conditions of the factory-machine process, they would experience this alienation, resist, and ultimately rebel. But do people always define themselves as workers in capitalist society simply because they sell their labor? It seems historically that they do not.

When people are asked how they define themselves, they give a multitude of answers other than "workers." They may say that fundamentally they are women, husbands, Christians, African Americans, and so on. They may even say that they are fundamentally "consumers"! So simply by virtue of being a wage worker, this hasn't meant that people define themselves as such. The economy of wage labor, as alienating as it has been, hasn't been *the* overriding and determining factor in how folks define themselves (see Laclau and Mouffe 1985). They have experienced capitalism as many things other than as wage labor. So they have defined themselves in a multitude of ways. Ultimately, freedom and the individualized freedom to pursue economic gain are far more experiential in capitalism than is exploitation. Freedom is not only what classical liberal defenders and ideologues say the system is about but also a fundamental way in which most people experience the system. Contrary to what Marx thought, ordinary folks in the market economy tend to define themselves in many other ways besides economically. But *Marx was a "productivist."* He tended to view people as essentially achievers, doers, realizers, and actualizers. He saw the economy and the abstract power to labor as fundamental to how people define themselves and what life is about. "To be" is to work and produce things. *For Marx, "to be" is to "produce,"* in other words, and "to produce" under conditions dictated by the needs of profit and business is to threaten a basic instinct in us. Thus, Marx thought that the alienating conditions of capitalism would be readily apparent to all workers. They would tap a very sensitive nerve and spur a socialist revolution, he hoped. But they haven't...yet!

Polanyi's approach offers a slightly different view. If Polanyi is correct, the most fundamental experience of capitalism is insecurity, not exploitation. The immediate effect of the disembedding of economy from society, as we have analyzed, is the feeling and experience of "you're on your own, pal." There is a much stronger case for insecurity's being the primordial experience rather than exploitation. The "protective response" of people mentioned previously was that of seeking protection from the vagaries of impersonal market forces. With the disembedding of the economy, everyone, both workers and capitalists, felt the effect of market forces beyond anyone's immediate control. They sought protection from the compete-or-die market and consequently went to the government for help. Workers, experiencing this insecurity, also tried to form unions. They knew that there was power in numbers and that to be unified as a single seller of labor (the union as monopsonist) gave them leverage. The "protective response" was an immediate, intuitive, and knee-jerk reaction to market-induced insecurity.

But this is not all. Along with the insecurity, there is an immediate experience of the market system as freedom. Of course, this is not a case of equal freedom for and among all players, and we have to qualify this kind of experiential freedom. Because the fundamental insecurity experience and the fact that "you're on your own, pal" also imply a form of compulsion, the freedom experience is complicated. Many Marxists and left-wing theorists have, over the past two centuries, argued that the condition of wage -labor is coercive. One's situation in the market system is dependent upon many variables, including the ownership of property. Without owning sufficient means of production, one is "forced" into the factory as a wage worker, as this is the only way to survive. An example frequently used by historians is the enclosure movements. When the European aristocracy enclosed the common lands in order to graze sheep for the burgeoning textile industry (1300–1600), the peasants were "forced" off the common lands and were "compelled" to migrate into the new industrial towns in search of buyers for the only thing that they had left to sell: their labor power.

Thus, marketization creates insecurity, and insecurity compels workers to sell their labor to the highest bidder. So there is compulsion, but there is simultaneously freedom to search for bidders, freedom to buy whatever one can afford, and freedom to pursue any form of alternative possible. Another way to state this is that in precapitalist times, the slave was tied to the master, and the serf was tied to the lord, and in capitalism the wage worker is tied to nothing. This is a standard conclusion by both Marx and his followers. It's also a standard conclusion drawn by those on the opposite side of the political spectrum: the classical liberals, that is, today's conservatives. But instead of Marx's adversaries' emphasizing the idea that the worker is tied to "nothing," they say that the worker is "free" for the first time in history.

The worker, unlike the slave or serf, is free to go wherever he or she wants, to seek out opportunities, to save and obtain capital, and ultimately to Be All You Can Be. Naturally, some face far more obstacles to their freedom to "get ahead," but each is free to come and go, make changes, and search for the good life. Each person's freedom is limited and constrained by his or her immediate economic situation in society and current income and class standing. Thus, one's freedom is "conditioned" and "conditional," based upon circumstance usually beyond one's control. Clearly, there are victims of oppression and social injustice whose freedom is limited by these circumstances. But this notwithstanding, one has the power to act, to change one's circumstances, and to actualize potential. It's just harder for so many, other than the privileged. But the logic of the economic system (in a political democracy) says to everyone, "You're all free to try, and you should, if you want to get ahead." The freedom that is an experiential part of the market economy is not a "black-or-white" or "either-or" thing. It is a spectrum or broad range from those with the most—usually the privileged classes—to those with the least—the poor, people of color, women, the underprivileged and disadvantaged of the system.

But even those at the lowest end of the capitalist freedom continuum have a measure of this type of freedom, and they experience it more directly as a result of the fundamental insecurity of which it is a part. Some dispute the experience of freedom in capitalism, stating that it is merely an existential type of freedom that is irrelevant for the poorest victims of the system. For example, even a slave has some freedom to try to overcome his or her servitude and resist the master. But this form of existential freedom is still distinguishable from that of the disadvantaged in the market system. Why? The existential freedom that one exercises as a rebellious slave is different from the freedom exercised by an oppressed victim in capitalism. The slave's situation is due to an unfree type of security. The wage worker's situation is just the opposite: an unfree type of insecurity. The slave's direct experience is security and unfreedom, while the worker's is insecurity and freedom. The freedom in capitalism we should perhaps call the freedom *to leave and search*, while the existential freedom associated with the prisoner is freedom *to resist*. One is free to go; the other is forced to stay. As Jean-Paul Sartre once stated, even the political prisoner with a gun at his or her head has a measure of freedom and choice—you can choose to save your life by submitting or value the "cause" over your life and resist. But all systems have this kind of existential freedom, and this is not what we are talking about in the case of the market economy. The freedom that even the poorest victims of the market economy retain is a basic freedom "to leave and search" that stems directly from the condition of insecurity.

In many respects, this freedom is the same freedom that Nobel laureate Milton Friedman and other classical and neo-classical liberals (like the Austrian school, Hayek, and Mises) have identified with capitalism (Friedman [1962] 1982; Friedman and Friedman 1979). In *Capitalism and Freedom*, Friedman's classic essay, he says, "As liberals, we take freedom of the individual, or perhaps the family, as our ultimate goal in judging social arrangements. Freedom as a value in this sense has to do with the interrelations among people; it has no meaning whatsoever to a Robinson Crusoe on an isolated island (without his Man Friday). Robinson Crusoe on his island is subject to 'constraint,' he has limited 'power,' and has only a limited number of alternatives, but there is no problem of freedom in the sense that is relevant to our discussion" (Friedman [1962] 1982, 12). As the freedom "to leave and search," it means that one can act to pursue "being more," and it is directly experienced because it results from the condition of insecurity in the market. So the insecurity of capitalism and the freedom "to leave and search" are a package. They go together. When "you are on your own, pal," you have to take action to deal with the situation. To the extent that this action is allowed and exercised with minimal constraints from arbitrary or authoritarian governments or paternalistic traditions, norms, and Old World customs, then freedom "to leave" one's circumstances behind and "search" for something better is real. It is this freedom that the populations of the former Soviet Union and those subjected to its economic and political model have sought since 1990.

So the bottom-line experience of capitalism, which brings about the assimilation of the imperative of Be All You Can Be, is the simultaneous experience of insecurity and freedom. This "experience," whether it is the object of reflection or not, constitutes the basis for the birth, with capitalism, of the Culture of Insatiable Freedom and the Economy of Insatiable Improvers. The *great transformation*, as Polanyi called it, was truly a cultural revolution. The Culture of Security was not a "driven" culture in the sense that capitalism has been. We experience the disembedded freedom culture of capitalism as "the need to get out there and hustle" and "get ahead or be left behind." Robert Heilbroner stated in his classic, *The Worldly Philosophers*, "The world had gotten along for centuries in the comfortable rut of tradition and command; *to abandon this security* for the dubious and perplexing workings of the market system, nothing short of a revolution was required" (Heilbroner [1953] 1972, 19; emphasis added). Very few would argue with this.

SUMMARY

The spread of the "market mentality," as Polanyi said, resulted in a competitive process in which the driving force, along with competition, is the insecurity of "you're on your own, pal." Each individual now must "struggle" for security or "earn" it, as it is no longer a right that comes from membership in society. But each has the freedom, equally so in at least a formal sense, to try to improve his or her life. All have the freedom to try to close the gap between what they are and what they could be. Each has the freedom to pursue insatiable self-realization. Each is free to Be All You Can Be. Unlimited self-development is a real possibility for all who want it.

So capitalism, the culture of freedom (and thus insecurity), the secularization of life, and economic growth have done two things. First, they made it possible for all to have more. Second, they made it essential that all should try to be more. To obtain security in the disembedded capitalist economy, one's best chance is to develop one's potential and skills. Likewise, to survive as well as prosper, businesses must seek improvement. Improvement based upon individual initiative becomes the key to success. There is no limit to this. It's insatiable.

To achieve security, one must channel one's energy and talent into Be All You Can Be. The payoff and reward are that this can lead to having all one can have. Having more is the reward for being more. Being more is the imperative pivotal to the functioning of capitalism. The insatiable self is both a product of capitalism's emergence and a cause. So there is both a material and an ontological component with the emergence of capitalism. It allows for the pursuit of being more; it coerces the pursuit of being more; and it channels this into the material realm of having more. The market economy, in other words, directly links the unlimited potential to be more to the insatiable desire to have more.

If there's stress with the imperative to be more, the compensation is the socially legitimate option of having more. Human improvement is channeled into economic improvement. The system then becomes "driven by improvement." Not only this, but "success" takes on new meaning. Improvement is measured by successes. So improvements are the end to which successes lead. Thus, capitalism is both success-driven and achievement-driven, as well as improvement-driven.

In the pre-Neolithic periods, improvements occurred accidentally and haphazardly. Because these were not improvement-driven cultures, the concept of "success" was foreign to them. Goals and successes become means to measuring improvements only when societies become improvement-driven. In today's culture the words "goal" and "success" are fundamental to our vocabulary, but these are very modern terms and make sense only in the context of an improvement-driven culture.

There's consequently a whole language discourse that coincides with our improvement-fixated culture. The Culture of Insatiable Freedom creates "goals," "successes," "ambition," "drive," "accomplishment," "achievement," "self-realization," and "self-development." This is the vocabulary of the popular "how-to" self-help books available in any bookstore. Their bookshelves offer us an infinite variety of guidance on "how to identify your goals, develop your ambition, and realize your potential"! It's unimaginable that humans prior to the last two centuries would have any idea of what this is about. Now we even hear of the "human potential movement" and the "personal growth movement"! So the idea of measuring improvements makes sense only in the present Culture of Insatiable Freedom.

Chapter 4

Marx, Mill, and Capitalism: *Driven by Improvement*

Both Karl Marx and John Stuart Mill are exemplary advocates of the insatiable self. They are nineteenth-century icons for Be All You Can Be. Their thought testifies to the elevation of Be All You Can Be as a moral imperative. As capitalism matured, so did the insatiable self. "You can be more" became "You should be more," and finally this became "You must be more." Additionally, Thorstein Veblen in his writings at the turn of the twentieth century adds a new twist to the insatiability of Be All You Can Be, as his sociological economics suggests that people try always to be more and always to have more in an endless effort to achieve social esteem and self-esteem. Veblen maintained that both the rich and poor feel self-esteem by how others judge them, so they are constantly comparing themselves with those both above and below them. There is no end to this. In Veblenian terms, we can say that the insecurity that accompanies the disembedded economy of capitalism makes all of us insecure about our self-esteem.

We need to know that others approve of us—our friends, family, the bosses, and our peers. So we have to demonstrate our worth by letting them know how much we have achieved both by having and being more. Since everyone is constantly in need of assurance about self-esteem, we are constantly trying either to keep up with, or get ahead of, everyone else. As soon as "they" get ahead, we have to do so as well. It's an insatiable treadmill of self-development for self-esteem. The point is that the cultural assimilation of Be All You Can Be is deepened and reinforced, in part, because it becomes a means to obtaining one's self-worth. To maintain and improve our self-esteem, we must "keep up with the Joneses" and not only try to have as much or more than they have but also be as much or more. The social and moral imperative of Be All You Can Be reaches its apex in Abraham Maslow's hierarchy of needs. So by 1968, when Maslow published *Toward a Psychology of Being*, the culture of freedom and insatiability had made Be All You Can Be a commonplace cliché. Consequently, it was only a matter of time before the U.S. Army popularized it as a recruiting slogan.

In the vernacular of popular psychology, self-development, the human potential movement, self-actualization, and such are the foundation for what it means to be. "You can always be more tomorrow than you are today!" "There is always more that you can be!" The fact that these are overworked clichés says something about how ingrained the insatiable self has become. Our metaphysical and ontological orientation in the world is grounded on this one core value.

JOHN STUART MILL AND THE NINETEENTH CENTURY

By the nineteenth century capitalism was in place, the Industrial Revolution was in full swing, material and economic growth was obvious to anyone, and Enlightenment ideas were generally accepted. We can measure the extent of assimilation of the imperative of Be All You Can Be and insatiable social development by examining the thought of two of the century's intellectual heavyweights: John Stuart Mill and Karl Marx. Moreover, these two icons are merely representatives of the broader development. They are not aberrations, as their thought is only the result of a gradual evolution of ideas from the Renaissance, like Rabelais and Erasmus, to the Enlightenment with Locke and Jefferson. "Central to the thinking of these men was their stress on human personality and its untrammeled development" (Greer 1972, 392). The "freedom" that these folks intended is the freedom of the new Culture of Insatiable Freedom. Also, although Marx is not considered a "liberal" in the classical sense, he was every bit as enamored with the freedom to Be All You Can Be. His only problem was that capitalism didn't foster the kind of freedom-to-be-insatiably-more in the classless and egalitarian fashion that socialism would.

First, we should mention that "education" as a personal and social value also began to change its orientation and fundamental theme. In Antiquity, if one examines the thought of the Greeks and Romans, education is considered important with respect to the assistance that it can give to the stabilization of life, the pursuit of virtue, and the pursuit of the good life. Education existed within the Culture of Security and the Satiable Self. It was not treated as the vehicle to self-actualization, the endless quest for "more is better," or insatiable self- and social improvement. By the nineteenth century, on the other hand, education's focus changes to make it *the* ticket to insatiable self-development and social improvement. The concepts of "lifelong learning" and "education as an 'end-in-itself,'" in other words, which we take for granted today, have their roots in both the Enlightenment and the birth of capitalism. As we say today,

"You can never be too educated, as there is always more you can learn." Alas, learning and education are insatiable! Mill and Marx would fully agree.

Anyone in a university teaching certification program will realize early on that the "why" of education—why have it, why do it, why support it—is about its assumed contribution to endless self-realization. Progressive education is about equipping all people with the skills and abilities to infinitely develop themselves, and, furthermore, an educated society can maximize its unlimited social improvement. In fact, in all "methods" classes, the unquestioned and, thus, given premise is that more and better education means more and better self- and social development. Thirty years ago, as education students, we read the trendy works of not only Abraham Maslow but Carl Rogers, Fritz Pearls, and Jean Piaget. It was all about one idea: Be All You Can Be. None of us getting certified ever asked, "And how much is that?" Because the answer was implicit in the question: "It's insatiable." What we understood to be the central message of educational thought and philosophy at the time was that it is integral to the human potential movement and the personal growth movement.

An early example of the shift in educational thought is the Czech philosopher John Amos Comenius (1592–1670), who in a chronological sense preceded the Enlightenment but yet anticipated it. His book the *Great Didactic* was written in 1632, when he was bishop of the Moravian Church, and in it he outlines what today is an agenda for progressive education. He believed in mass education, feeling that the world must have an informed citizenry in order to facilitate continuous improvement. In 1668 his "The Way of Light" treatise was dedicated to the Royal Society of London, saying that with its efforts "philosophy brought to perfection" would "exhibit the true and distinctive qualities of things for the *constantly progressive increase of all that makes for good to mind, body, and estate*" (Ulich 1967, 147; emphasis added). Of course, since he was highly influenced by Francis Bacon, Comenius sensed that social and self-improvement was inherently unlimited, in part, due to the advances in science that he witnessed. Following Comenius' lead, the list of philosophers of education who argued, like him, for education to serve self-realization is ubiquitous throughout the subsequent three centuries (e.g., Rousseau, Pestalozzi, Froebel, Herbart, and Emerson; see Ulich 1945, 1965). John Stuart Mill was one of these.

In the twentieth century the pragmatist philosopher and socialist John Dewey (1859–1952) was one of the most influential writers for American education. Dewey's statements on educational benefits for insatiable improvement are classic. In his 1916 book, *Democracy and Education*, he states, "When it is said that education is development, everything depends upon *how* development is conceived. Our net conclusion is that life is development, and that developing, growing, is life. Translated into its educational equivalents, that means (i) that the educational process has no end beyond itself; it is its own end; and that (ii) the educational process is one of continual reorganizing, reconstructing, transforming" (Frankena 1965, 20). Dewey anticipates Maslow's ideas, that is, that the essence of life is to grow continually as a human being. To be is to grow and self-actualize, in other words.

Dewey adds, "Since life means growth, a living creature lives as truly and positively at one stage as at another [e.g., old age as well as youth], with the same intrinsic fullness and the same absolute claims. Hence education means the enterprise of supplying the conditions which insure growth, or adequacy of life, irrespective of age" (Frankena 1965, 20). Dewey implies the concept of continuous and lifelong learning. He says that we need to realize that "life is growth" and that education must serve this. Education is not about filling a vacuum in a static sense, nor does it reduce to "casting out ignorance," which, again, implies a static notion in which the learner is a passive receptacle for the assimilation of a fixed body of knowledge. Dewey's definition is that education is a *process* that will always be a process as long as life is conceived as an endless growing experience. His "technical definition" of education: "It is that reconstruction or reorganization of experience which adds to the meaning of experience, and which increases ability to direct the course of subsequent experience" (22). How much of this is enough? No amount is enough because people can, throughout their lives, always grow more. Why? Because "experience" never ends until we die, and as long as that is the case, we can keep learning and keep growing with each new experience.

The process, the experiences, the personal growth, and education are insatiable! An example of this is Leo Ward's statement in his 1963 title *Philosophy of Education*. As a professor at Notre Dame, he reconciles education to serve God with its role to serve the secular world. He disputes Dewey's secularism but affirms his view that to learn is to grow. He says, "It is not mere rhetoric to say that the end of education is education. But education is not something subsisting in itself or existing in a vacuum. It is better to say that the end is man—the educated man or woman. That means nothing abstruse. It simply means the developed human person. These matters must be granted: educating as maturing is life-long, occurs day and night and everywhere, and is never fully completed" (Ward 1963, 130–131). Progressive education, from Comenius to Dewey, is therefore education that fosters our insatiable potential to Be All You Can Be!

We cannot talk about the cultural assimilation of Be All You Can Be in the nineteenth century without discussing J. S. Mill's (1806–1873) contribution. His thought is a perfect statement of how our Western culture defines what it means to be a human. Although most have not read anything of Mill, except possibly *On Liberty* (1859), his words sound familiar.

Mill, according to historian Thomas Greer, was the most significant representative of nineteenth-century liberalism, because he refused to accept that government, no matter how democratic it might be, had any right to stifle free expression (Greer 1972, 394). Mill's focus on free expression is clearly for the purpose of fostering insatiable self-development. Additionally, a good government was one, for Mill, that minimized irrational obstruction of this. For him, like Marx, social improvement is both the condition and consequence of the free and full development of the individual. Mill, as most know, believed that a representative, democratically elected government linked to the free market is the ideal condition for the unlimited pursuit of self-realization. In the

Encyclopedia of Philosophy, Schneewind states that Mill "was the most influential philosopher in the English-speaking world during the nineteenth century and is generally held to be one of the most profound and effective spokesmen for the liberal view of man and society" (Schneewind 1967, 314).

But we have to qualify his "liberalism." He was not a classical liberal like Adam Smith, Malthus, Ricardo, or even his father, James Mill. Mill was home-schooled by his father, brought up as a Benthamite utilitarian, but turned to Wordsworth and Coleridge and liked Comte. He was friends with Thomas Carlyle and read Dickens, as well. He didn't take to Kant or Hegel, as they were "too metaphysical for [his] essentially positivist mind" (Stromberg 1968, 82). His philosophy was utilitarianism but with an empiricist and positivist twist. With respect to his famous *Principles of Political Economy*, "his foundation was individualistic capitalism yet he was prepared to entertain exceptions to the rule wherever a sound case could be made—and the exceptions, it has been noted, grew with every edition of the *Principles*, so that Mill has been claimed as an ancestor of English socialism (Fabian)" (83). Schneewind also adds that he rethought his laissez-faire position, as he began to realize later in life that freedom without security is of little value. This is an important insight for Mill, because it suggests that, like Polanyi, Mill understood something about the trade-off between the two and that capitalism was premised on a freedom generated from fundamental insecurity. Therefore, Mill was "led to re-examine his objections to socialism. By the end of his life he had come to think that as far as economic theory was concerned, socialism was acceptable" (Schneewind 1967, 320). Yet, we have to add that as far as *political* theory was concerned, Mill continued to question the extent to which socialism could be reconciled with personal freedom of expression and individualism. He would have predicted, in other words, that the Soviet experiment a half century later would fail for lack of personal liberty.

Yet most importantly, Mill was an optimist about human progress and self-development. He favored democracy, but his concern was always that if it became too bureaucratic and impersonal, the "herd mentality" would prevail and reduce people to unthinking and uncritical automatons. He believed, like John Locke and many of the educationalists, that "people can learn." Their natures, accordingly, are not fixed, as the classical liberals often maintained with their embrace of *homo economicus*. Thus, people can learn from their mistakes, understand their world better, and further the conditions for insatiable self-development. "The goal and purpose of mankind, the only end worth striving for, was to Mill the complete development of the individual's powers to the highest possible point" (Stromberg 1968, 83). So he was not a "classical liberal," and Stromberg suggests that he, like Comte, Marx, and Spencer, was a "synthesizer of social doctrine" and a "creator of secular ideology." One of Marx and Mill's common values is not merely their commitment to the moral and social imperative of Be All You Can Be but their commitment to reshape society to bring out the best and most in the individual.

"It often seems that Mill placed more stress on individuality, or self-realization, than on general welfare, and critics frequently claim that he contradicted himself by saying that both of these constitute the sole highest good. But there is no contradiction in his views, for he held that *self-development is the best way for an individual to work for the common good"* (Schneewind 1967, 320; emphasis added). Unlimited self-development is possible for Mill because people have a measure of "free will." They are born into, and live within, circumstances that they did not choose, and in this sense they are determined by both internal genetic forces and external environmental factors. But they can exercise decision making, exercise their freedom in the new Culture of Insatiable Freedom, and develop and improve themselves throughout their lives.

Additionally, Mill discussed individuality in Chapter 3 of *On Liberty*, stating that it is important because it "comes from, or is identical with, continued effort at self-development. Even eccentricity is better, he held, than massive uniformity of personality and the stagnation of society that would result from it" (Schneewind 1967, 321). Mill, in other words, equated continuous improvement of the individual with continuous improvement of society. They are isomorphic, and both have insatiable potentiality. Without this "driven" character in both, he says that we get "stagnation"—something that no society should have. But what Mill thought might be an unfortunate stagnation could perhaps be a better and more sustainable world in the twenty-first century. The point is therefore to shift our cultural consciousness from thinking about the static state as stagnation to thinking about it as sustainability!

MILL IS US, AND WE ARE HIM

Mill is remarkably contemporary. He was a precocious productivist at an early age. He mentions in his autobiography that his father had him studying Latin at eight and logic at twelve and reading David Ricardo when he was only thirteen. He was clearly raised with the moral imperative to "be all he could be." He states:

From the winter of 1821 [he was fifteen], when I first read Bentham, and especially from the commencement of the Westminster Review, I had what truly might be called an object in life: to be a reformer of the world. My conception of my own happiness was entirely identified with this object. I was accustomed to felicitate myself on the certainty of a happy life which I enjoyed, through placing my happiness in something durable and distant, *in which some progress might be always making, while it could never be exhausted by complete attainment.* This did very well for several years, during which *the general improvement going on in the world and the idea of myself as engaged with others in struggling to promote it,* seemed enough to fill up an interesting and animated existence. (Mill [1873] 1937, 85; emphasis added)

Even though in 1826 he became depressed about his role in facilitating worldly progress, the notion of insatiable improvement for both himself and society is everywhere conspicuous in his *Autobiography*. Later in life he was elected to the British Parliament (1865–1868), and while a member of Parliament (MP), he was also elected rector of the University of St. Andrews. In his address to the university, he talked about education's "vindicating the high educational value alike of the old classic and the new scientific studies." He said that he hoped that this would "not only aid and stimulate the improvement which had happily commenced in the national institutions for higher education, but to diffuse juster ideas than we often find, even in highly educated men, on the conditions of the highest mental cultivation" (Mill [1873] 1937, 188). So for Mill, like his predecessor John Amos Comenius, education's purpose is to foster individual self-development.

The purpose of education is to foster the type of knowledge that allows people to better exercise their freedom and improve the world. In Book VI of *A System of Logic* Mill states that humanity can end up either in a "cycle" or in "progress." He adds, "Progress and Progressiveness are not here understood as synonymous with improvement and tendency to improvement," as there can be necessitated changes in humans over time that aren't exactly improvements, but "it is my belief indeed that the general tendency is, and will continue to be, saving occasional and temporary exceptions, one of improvement—a tendency towards a better and happier state" (Mill [1843] 1967, 596).

He adds that "progressiveness of the human race is the foundation on which a method of philosophising in the social science has been of late years erected" (Mill [1843] 1967, 596). His point is that the whole purpose of "social science" is to improve humankind's ability to improve itself, that is, to improve the improvement process! So people are about being all they can be, and the essential objective of education is to help people be even more. At the same time, although he was optimistic and saw this as human nature, he feared that mass society might have a debilitating effect.

He disagreed with many of his nineteenth-century peers who felt that social science might be able to discover an underlying "law of social progress." In this he agreed with Comte. Moreover, Mill felt that political science's mission was as the "indispensable basis of the theory of social progress." He didn't foresee a " law" but did hold out for a "theory." Social progress, then, could be explained, and the conditions that foster it could likewise be understood and mapped. He argued for a more evolutionary approach to explaining social progress that he called a "consensus of the social phenomena," where all factors are codetermining and mutually reinforcing. This is dynamic, he says, not like the usual, empirical Cartesianism: "The dynamical consideration of the progressive development of civilized humanity, affords no doubt, a still more efficacious means of effecting this interesting verification of the consensus of the social phenomena, by displaying the manner in which every change in any one part operates immediately, or very speedily, upon all the rest" (Mill [1843] 1967, 599).

Mill says that "intellectual activity, the pursuit of truth, is among the more powerful propensities of human nature," and this is what contributes to endless social progress. Yet he was also willing to admit that people have baser intentions most of the time as "the impelling force to most of the improvements effected in the arts of life is the desire of increased material comfort" (Mill [1843] 1967, 604). Of course, these kinds of material improvements can take place only by improving our education, since "the state of knowledge at any time is the limit of the industrial improvements possible at this time" (604). Mill wanted to see an "economy of continuous improvement," or what we have called an "Economy of Insatiable Improvers." For this to happen, according to Mill and all other like-minded progressives to this day, education is the key. He closes his *Logic* on a note of great optimism:

The longer our species lasts and the more civilized it becomes, the more, as Comte remarks, does the influence of past generations over the present, and of mankind *en masse* over every individual in it, predominate over other forces: and though the course of affairs never ceases to be susceptible of alterations both by accidents and by personal qualities, the increasing preponderance of the collective agency of the species over all minor causes is constantly bringing the general evolution of the race into something which deviates less from a certain and preappointed track. (615)

His point? We create our own future; we are in control of our destiny; and we determine our social progress and improvement.

But Mill's best statements about insatiable self-development are found in *On Liberty*. Mill says that the "appropriate region of human liberty" is both about the "inward domain of consciousness" that includes freedom of thought and feeling and the exogenous domain of "liberty of tastes and pursuits, of framing the plan of our life to suit our own character, of doing as we like, subject to such consequences as may follow, without impediment from our fellow creatures, so long as what we do does not harm them, perverse or wrong" (Mill [1859] 1985, 71). His view reduces to the notion of "doing what you want, so long as it doesn't destroy another's ability to do likewise." It's a reasonable idea and a position widely held by most folks today. Yet it is also the basis for his view that humans should pursue Be All You Can Be. In effect, Mill is saying that equal liberty has a purpose: to allow us always to be more. His position on liberty is totally consistent with his imperative of Be All You Can Be.

But Be All You Can Be requires a tolerance of diversity and individuality. He says that "men should be free to act upon their opinions—to carry these out in their lives without hindrance, either physical or moral, from their fellow men" and that "it is desirable, in short, that in things which do not primarily concern others, individuality should assert itself." Diversity is good, in other words, because it is "the chief ingredient of individual and social progress" (Mill [1859] 1985, 120). Diversity can result only from liberty, and its role is to foster our perpetual transcendent element of becoming. He quotes Wilhelm von Humbolt, saying that most people outside Germany don't get Humbolt's message that:

"the end of man, or that which is prescribed by the eternal or immutable dictates of reason, and not suggested by vague and transient desires, is the highest and most harmonious development of his powers to a complete and consistent whole"; that therefore, the object "towards which every human being must ceaselessly direct his efforts, and on which especially those who design to influence their fellow men must ever keep their eyes, is the individuality of power and development"; that for this there are two requisites, "freedom, and variety of situations"; and that from the union of these arise "individual vigor and manifold diversity," which combine themselves in "originality." (Mill [1859] 1985, 121)

Mill is quick to add to this that customary behavior typical of the ordinary person living in mass society is often rather uncritical and unthinking. To conform to it is not progressive, and so "to conform to custom merely *as* custom does not educate or develop in him any of the qualities which are the distinctive endowment of a human being. The human faculties of perception, judgement, discriminative feeling, mental activity, and even moral preference are exercised only in making a choice" (Mill [1859] 1985, 122). Thus, for Mill, people have the freedom under the proper conditions of government and capitalism to make choices about who and what they will become, and, moreover, what they can become in exercising this freedom [liberty] is always more tomorrow than they are today. He adds that "human nature is not a machine to be built after a model, and set to do exactly the work prescribed for it, but a tree, which requires to grow and develop itself on all sides, according to the tendency of the inward forces which make it a living thing" (123). So Mill suggests here that we have inherent within us the power always to be more and that humans are that particular life form that can constantly seek its improvement. This is where the tree analogy stops, as trees are alive but don't live to improve themselves, nor do they grow forever!

Mill suggests that for humans to Be All You Can Be, they must take advantage of their passions and desires. In this he is different from Aristotle, who, as we mentioned earlier, had a notion of the Satiable Self whose desires should be minimized. As a philosopher of the insatiable self, Mill says that "desires and impulses are as much a part of a perfect human being as beliefs and restraints. It is not because men's desires are strong that they act ill; it is because their consciences are weak" (Mill [1859] 1985, 124). Most today would no doubt agree more with Mill than with Aristotle. Mill adds that "strong impulses are but another name for energy" (125). This kind of energy is good and progressive if it is turned toward human perfection—an endless task.

Yet, Mill worried that people were becoming too submissive, conformist, and passive. He attacked Calvinism because it sought to have people surrender to the "authority of God" and repress their "will." Then he says that:

if it be any part of religion to believe that man was made by a good Being, it is more consistent with that faith to believe that this Being gave all human faculties that they might be cultivated and unfolded, not rooted out and consumed, and that he takes delight in every nearer approach made by his creatures to the ideal conception embodied in them, every increase in any of their capabilities of comprehension, of action, or of enjoyment. It is not by wearing down into uniformity all that is individual in themselves, but by cultivating it and calling it forth that human beings become a noble and beautiful object of contemplation. In proportion to the development of his individuality, each person becomes more valuable to himself, and is, therefore, capable of being more valuable to others. (Mill [1859] 1985, 127)

Like Marx, Mill argued for the "fullness of life." Unlike Marx, Mill thought that free markets and a role for government to assure liberty would be enough. Yet Marx would agree with this: "To give any fair play to the nature of each, it is essential that different persons should be allowed to lead different lives" (Mill [1859] 1985, 128). We could read this in any number of popular, self-help books today.

Here is another comment by Mill that the U.S. Army would endorse: "Having said that the individuality is the same thing with development, and that it is only the cultivation of individuality which produces, or can produce, well-developed human beings, I might close the argument; for what more or better can be said of any condition of human affairs than that it brings human beings themselves nearer to the best thing they can be?" (Mill [1859] 1985, 128). Now some might object that the Army does not "cultivate individuality," as it requires all recruits to dress and conform to externally imposed standards, but Army recruiters would suggest otherwise, listing the many options for career development that one can choose from. Although what Mill would think of today's Army is unclear, he was opposed to any form of mediocrity and stated that "the general tendency of things throughout the world is to render mediocrity the ascendent power among mankind" (130–131). The solution to this? Be All You Can Be.

Mill also had another insight dovetailing with Figure 3.6: in the disembedded market economy of capitalism, the insatiable desire to be more is channeled into career productivism. Capitalism directs our ability always to be more into economically useful jobs and careers. This is "career productivism." We should channel Be All You Can Be into something productive: a "career." Mill says that because of the movement toward mass living and uncritical conformity, "already energetic characters on any large scale are becoming merely traditional. *There is now scarcely any outlet for energy in this country except business*" (Mill [1859] 1985, 135). Remarkably, he said this 100 years ago. What's more, "the despotism of custom is everywhere the standing hindrance to human advancement, being in unceasing antagonism to that disposition to aim at something better than customary, which is called, according to circumstances, the spirit of liberty, or that of progress or improvement" (136). For Mill, liberty equals insatiable improvement: "the only unfailing and permanent source of improvement is liberty, since by it there are as many possible independent centres of improvement as there are individuals" (136).

Mill would not say that "improvement is inevitable," however. He continued to worry that although Western Europeans were energetic overachievers, this could degenerate into stagnation if individuality and liberty were not protected. Western Europeans "are progressive as well as changeable: we continually make new inventions in mechanical things, and keep them until they are again superseded by better; we are eager for improvement in politics, in education, even in morals. We flatter ourselves that we are the most progressive people who ever lived" (Mill [1859] 1985, 137). Of course, every American president in the twentieth century said the same to popular audiences. To be "progressive," in other words, is to be on the cutting edge of Be All You Can Be.

Mill argued that the reason for European progressiveness was its "plurality of paths," which created "many-sided development." But, he cautioned, Europe was getting too conformist, too customary, too traditional. It was becoming massified. Therefore, he said, "it is decidedly advancing towards the Chinese ideal of making all people alike" (Mill [1859] 1985, 138). So Mill was worried about the homogenizing effects of mass capitalism. One can only imagine what he would have felt about the Maoist Revolution a century later. There is in Mill's fear something very reminiscent of Martin Heidegger's notion of the "inauthentic we" criticized in *Being and Time* in 1927. Then, too, Mill is presaging the criticism that the Frankfurt school Marxists of the pre– and post–World War II period launched against the Soviet model, German fascism, and mass capitalism's "one-dimensionality." In effect, Mill was worried about the "herd mentality."

But even though Mill was concerned about human slippage, he continued to argue that we are reasonably free agents and can change our ways. In this respect he stated that there are two types of fatalism: (1) pure, or Asiatic, and (2) modified. He rejected both, stating that:

the true doctrine of the Causation of human actions maintains, in opposition to both, that not only our conduct, but our character, is in part amenable to our will; that we can, by employing the proper means, improve our character; and that if our character is such that while it remains what it is, it necessitates us to do wrong, it will be just to apply motives which will necessitate us to strive for its improvement, and so emancipate ourselves from the other necessity. In other words, *we are under a moral obligation to seek the improvement of our moral character.* We shall not indeed do so unless we desire our improvement, and desire it more than we dislike the means which must be employed for the purpose. (Mill 1979, 465–466; emphasis added)

He sounds like Aristotle, but Aristotle held to a simpler principle: just do the right thing when faced with a moral or ethical decision. The idea of "seeking improvement" is not exactly what Aristotle is about. From Mill's perspective, humans must continually strive for improvement, an "improvement" that is never satiated because we can always be more! Mill is clearly concerned with actualizing potential, while Aristotle is not. Aristotle's focus is different. He merely wants humans to make the right choice when it comes along. For Aristotle, being human is not about "seeking" virtue or the self-actualization of potential. But by the time that Mill wrote, almost 2,000 years later, with modernism, capitalism, and the new Culture of Insatiable Freedom, most philosophers were into Be All You Can Be. They were into the insatiable self rather than Aristotle's Satiable Self.

Additionally, from Mill's previous remark, it becomes clearer that he distinguished between the insatiable desire to be more and the insatiable desire to have more. He felt that people should try to be more rather than simply have more, that is, accumulate wealth. But one of the best-articulated statements about material wealth, the environment, and being more is the following:

Nor is there much satisfaction in contemplating the world with nothing left to the spontaneous activity of nature; with every rood of land brought into cultivation, which is capable of growing food for human beings; every flowery waste or natural pasture ploughed up, all quadrupeds or birds which are not domesticated for man's food, every hedgerow or superfluous tree rooted out, and scarcely a place left where a wild shrub or flower could grow without being eradicated as a weed in the name of improved agriculture. If the earth must lose that great portion of its pleasantness which it owes to things that the unlimited increase of wealth and population would extirpate from it, for the mere purpose of enabling it to support a larger, but not a better or a happier population, I sincerely hope, for the sake of posterity, that they will be content to be stationary, long before necessity compels them to it. *It is scarcely necessary to remark that a stationary condition of capital and population implies no stationary state of human improvement.* (Mill 1966, 327–328; emphasis added)

From the foregoing, it should be clear that Mill did not condone the insatiable desire to have more, yet he did see humans as the insatiable improvers (see Hunnicutt 1988, 32–33). His comment would be appreciated by virtually all environmentalists today, by Marxists, and by our culture in general. His point is that limiting the insatiable desire to have more for the sake of the environment and sustainability is the rational course, yet we need not limit our insatiable desire to be more. He favored the stationary state economy and stable population, much like Herman Daly and today's deep ecologists (Daly 1996).

But for all of these thinkers, the stationary state economy and stable population don't imply a stationary state of human improvement. Why? Because the purpose of being human is to improve and insatiably actualize our potential. But like Aristotle, Mill would also say that the unlimited accumulation of wealth can actually drag down human improvement. According to Benjamin Hunnicutt, Mill believed that "excessive attention to economic growth for its own sake gets in the way of real human needs and potential and corrupts life; human needs are finite and can be met; once these needs are taken care of, other human needs— the extra-economic 'graces of life' such as culture and learning—should be cultivated; leisure represents the way to reduce unnecessary production and unnecessary work and make progress possible in other valuable human areas" (Hunnicutt 1988, 33). The idea of "higher" needs beyond material accumulation is implicit in Mill and suggests what Abraham Maslow argued with his "hierarchy of needs" (Maslow 1968).

However, Aristotle was more emphatic, saying that the pursuit of wealth contradicted the pursuit of virtue, while Mill is mostly cautionary. But Mill also says, "I know not why it should be a matter of congratulation that persons who are already richer than anyone needs to be, should have doubled their means of consuming things which give little or no pleasure except as representative of wealth" (Mill 1966, 326).

He didn't say that accumulation was bad, only that it doesn't imply improvement in human character and can be rather unessential to what counts in life. In a similar popularized comment, he said that "hitherto it is questionable if all the mechanical inventions yet made have lightened the day's toil of any human being" (Mill 1966, 328). His point seems to be that the economy is not much good for anything except meeting basic needs. It doesn't do that much to improve our lives. It doesn't save us much labor; it creates unnecessary, wasteful wealth for those who don't need it; and it destroys the environment and natural world. It's hard to argue with any of this. But what Mill would like to see is the diversion of our talents and energies toward improving our ability to Be More, rather than Have More. On an optimistic note he suggests that industrial development, although having not lightened our toil, may be a useful means for our moral and social improvement. Mechanical inventions "have not yet begun to effect those great changes in human destiny, which it is in their nature and their futurity to accomplish" (328).

What does Mill mean that more wealth isn't much good "except as a representative of wealth"? This became *the* issue for Thorstein Veblen a half century later. It is this: more wealth demonstrated by any individual generally sends a message about success to others. So for Mill and Veblen, if one doubles his or her wealth, the additional satisfaction that this increase yields is marginal (as in the neo-classical notion of "diminishing marginal utility") "except as a representative of wealth." What Mill and Veblen mean is that wealth is a measure of one's status and social esteem in capitalism. You can never have too much status, so therefore you can never have too much wealth. This in itself makes the desire to have more insatiable.

Mill saw the insatiable desire for wealth as an impediment for another reason: it gets in the way of making ourselves "a work of art." Mill would no doubt agree with Alan Ryan's assessment that "the goals we aim at can only be described as the freely pursued life of personal nobility—the establishment of the life of the individual as a work of art" (Ryan 1970, 255). Therefore, to make yourself into a work of art, the secret is to Be All You Can Be. Can it ever be completed? Aristotle would say yes, but Mill would say no. Why? The individual-as-work-of-art is insatiable.

Ryan closes his book on Mill saying that:

the good society is one made up of happy people, and Mill's picture of what makes a man happy is not unclear. It is the possession of a character which is self-reliant, rational in its assessment of the world, tolerant, wide-ranging in its interest, and spontaneous in its sympathies. To be a saint or a hero by order is just a nonsensical idea. The whole point of saintliness and heroism is that they establish new goals, new standards of what man can do when he tries. Without freedom there can be no such moral progress as this leads to. And, however much at odds it sometimes is with his determinist universe, Mill's concern with self-development and moral progress is a strand in philosophy to which almost everything else is subordinate. (Ryan 1970, 255)

Karl Marx would enthusiastically embrace this statement. Marx would add that the happy person with wide-ranging interests who chooses to pursue always being more is one who requires very specific material and institutional conditions: socialism. Marx would say that Mill's vision sounds good, but Mill forgets about the conditions that make this possible. So what is the difference between these two icons of Be All You Can Be?

MARX MEETS MILL

Karl Marx was born in Trier, Germany, in 1818, twelve years after Mill. They were contemporaries. These heavyweights were on opposite ends of the political spectrum but shared what became our essential cultural norm: Be All You Can Be. In simple terms, Marx suggested that the material preconditions for a world in which all people are democratically and justly able to Be All You Can Be are not present in, and consistent with, capitalism, while Mill's view is that they are. Mill said that the essential ingredient for insatiable self-actualization is liberty and that this is what capitalism and representative democracy offer, while Marx said that the essential ingredient for insatiable self-actualization is the absence of class society, and capitalism doesn't measure up.

The backgrounds of Marx and Mill are quite different. Marx finished a law degree in Berlin in 1836 and then turned to Hegelian philosophy (Hegel died in 1831). Hegel's predecessor was Immanuel Kant, and consequently Marx was steeped in German speculative philosophy. Therefore, while Marx was more in tune with the traditions of continental rationalism, Mill was the British empiricist. Politically, Mill would be considered a social democrat if not a classical liberal. Mill evolved over the course of his life from his classical liberal roots to a contemporary, social democratic liberal. Marx was a leftist, a socialist, and a communist by nineteenth-century standards. He would have been horrified by the Bolsheviks and Stalinism and what became "Soviet communism." On this point, both Marx and Mill would agree: not only was the Soviet experience a bastardized version of socialism, but its totalitarian character was completely contrary to the principles of insatiable social and self-development.

But with respect to capitalism, there were features of it that Marx appreciated. One of these is capitalism's dynamism, its energy, and its "drivenness." He also understood it to be driven by insatiability. In the *Grundrisse* he says that "the tendency to create the *world market* is directly given in the concept of capital itself. Every limit appears as a barrier to be overcome" (Marx 1973, 408). In other words, capitalism is a system that is constantly searching, continually driven to seek new markets, more profits, more revenue, and more development. It is a system driven by insatiable improvement (at least as its ideologues argue) and the logic of "more is better." It is a system, as Marx realized, that is driven by the insatiable desire to be all it can be. Marx adds that such a system wants and drives "the discovery, creation and satisfaction of new needs arising from society itself; the cultivation of all the qualities of the social human being, production of the same in a form as rich as possible in needs, because rich in qualities and relations—production of this being as the most total and universal possible social product, for, in order to take gratification in a many-sided way, he must be capable of many pleasures, hence cultured to a high degree—is likewise a condition of production founded on capital" (409). According to Marx, capitalism's logic of insatiability requires "a constantly expanding and constantly enriched system of needs," and it likewise seeks "new needs" on an ever-expanding scale (408–409).

The "full and free development of the individual" (and the "individual rich in needs") is Marx's bottom-line value and the standard by which he measures a society. In a limited fashion, as the quotes suggest, Marx knew that capitalism was unique and that it had a dimension within it that fostered both social and individual development on an unlimited scale. He was quick to point out, however, that capitalism's class structure distorted the self-development of capitalists, thwarted and repressed the development of workers, and alienated both classes from the essence of life: unlimited actualization of the individual rich in needs. His critique of capitalism was based upon the fact that it did not allow for *equal* access to the means for self-actualization. In this way it was, for Marx, premised on a fundamental injustice that allowed the wealthier business classes to pursue their full and free development at the expense of the working class' ability to do likewise.

Socialism, and ultimately, communism were supposed to change all of this. He says in the *Early Manuscripts*, "It will be seen how in place of the wealth and poverty of political economy [capitalism] come the rich human being and rich human need. The rich human being is simultaneously the human being in need of a totality of human life activities—the man in whom his own realization exists as an inner necessity, as need" (Marx 1978, 91). Socialism is for Marx the material precondition for the individual to pursue insatiable self-actualization, and such actualization becomes an inner need to which we aspire.

Much of Marx's notion of unlimited self-actualization comes from his understanding of Hegel. Marx says of Hegel's *Phenomenology* that it views the "self-genesis of man as a process." Of course, the process being referred to is that of Be All You Can Be. He then adds that Hegel "comprehends objective man as the outcome of man's own labour. The real, active orientation of man to himself as a species being (i.e., as a human being), is only possible by his really bringing out of himself all the powers that are his as the species man" (Marx 1978, 112). In other words, we are what we become, and we can always become more. But it takes the right material preconditions for this unfolding process. Marx also adds that we actualize ourselves by estrangement from ourselves.

What does he mean by estrangement? Essentially, we are alienated or separated from ourselves in the sense that we are the unique beings that are trying to be something through our self-actualization that at any given time we are not. Our being is divorced from our becoming. We make ourselves, so to speak, out of what we are not. For example, we can aspire to be more virtuous and loving people than we are in the moment, so our vision of perfection causes us to try to be better people. To the extent that we might succeed in this effort, we are more than we knew ourselves to be. We had to recognize ourselves as imperfect in order to become something closer to perfection. We exist as potential to be more than we are in the moment. We are both being and becoming simultaneously. Humans are separated from themselves, as they are always trying to be more than they are. In other words, our immanent being contains a transcendent element. This is common conversation in philosophy and especially phenomenology and existentialism. It means that we make an object of investigation and consideration out of ourselves, and by doing so we become estranged from ourselves but can then try to be more than what we know ourselves to be. To be perfect, one must accept oneself as imperfect, and the only way that this can be done is through a form of estrangement. To actualize your "self," you have to see your "self" as different from that! For Hegel and Marx, this is what it means to be a human being. This is the "self-genesis of man as a process."

Of course, this notion of becoming more tomorrow than you are today is basic to Aristotle and all philosophical thinking since the pre-Socratics. It clearly suggests that people have the existential freedom always to be more, to make choices, and to determine themselves within the parameters of their life conditions. They create themselves out of what they are not. This is "life activity" as Marx understood it. Life is about always becoming more, about insatiable improvement, and that means becoming "rich in needs."

As Hegel says, one of our most basic life activities is "labor." We "produce" ourselves by becoming more and by actualizing ourselves. But much of this life activity is spent working, since to produce ourselves, we have to produce the goods and services that fulfill our basic material needs. For Marx, people are producers in a dual fashion: they produce themselves by working in the economic sense, and they produce themselves off the job through their other noneconomic life activities. We are laborers and producers both on and off the job.

Yet Marx is concerned with the fact that "work" in the economic sense is not adding to our self-actualization, because it is alienated labor that is directed by the dictates of profit maximization and the market. He feels that work should be an outlet for Be All You Can Be; work should be a means for further self-actualization. Work in capitalism, in other words, is about wage labor, getting a paycheck, and performing tasks whose organization is for maximizing profit for business owners rather than for furthering the full and free development of the individual rich in needs. In fact, work in all class societies, including slavery, feudalism, and capitalism, has always been about enriching one group at the expense of the free self-development of the other.

Furthermore, capitalism is even worse than earlier modes of production with respect to thwarting self-development, because in capitalism, as the *Early Manuscripts* argues, wage workers are not able to control their immediate production of products. At least the slave and the serf essentially controlled their direct, day-to-day production in the fields and shops. They were usually allowed the freedom to determine how the goods were produced. They were still exploited, and their personal growth was distorted and repressed, because they had to produce the economic surplus for the dominant class. But capitalism not only extracts the surplus output of the worker but goes deeper into the production process and reorganizes it to enhance profits. The worker pretty much loses control over everything except the decision about whether to stay or leave the job.

In *The German Ideology* Marx says that capitalism doesn't really care about any worker in particular but only labor as a "factor of production." The system and the business owner are indifferent to the individual worker's needs and self-development. Labor "has lost all semblance of self-activity and only sustains [a worker's] life by stunting it" (Marx 1978, 190–191). For Marx, capitalism alienates the individual worker from an essential expression of his or her life activity and self-development: the labor activity of the production process. Wage labor turns one's life activity into a commodity to be bought and sold and used for maximizing business' profits. It is, therefore, no longer meaningful life activity, says Marx.

Unlike its precursors, where slaves and peasants had a measure of control over their labor, in capitalism all productive forces are so alienated from the workers that for the working class to overcome this alienation, they have to carry out a true revolution and "appropriate" the productive forces in order to free themselves for insatiable self- and social improvement. Marx adds that this appropriation is "nothing more than the development of the individual capacities. The appropriation of a totality of instruments of production is, for this very reason, the development of a totality of capacities in the individuals themselves" (Marx 1978, 191). The point for Marx is that the workers have to regain democratic control over the entire economy in order to be able to develop a "totality of capacities" for themselves (191). This means, as well, that, as alienated labor, the working class is the class that gets cheated out of the benefits of technology with respect to its own self-actualization and social improvement (192).

He's a little shortsighted in this last remark from *The German Ideology*, because there is evidence that Marx never understood that the "freedom" or "free labor" of the capitalist economy is a significant experience for many working people. Since his death, in the more developed economies of Europe and North America, average working folks have tended to experience their economy as "freedom" rather than as alienation or exploitation. Consequently, they have never become revolutionary in Marx's sense. They've generally had more to lose than their chains. With decent wages being the norm in the industrial world, many appreciate the freedom to "get ahead" and pursue being all they can be. Existentially, they experience the freedom of the disembedded economy and its Culture of Insatiable Freedom. They haven't felt that they have borne all of the burdens and received none of the advantages. Although Marx probably didn't realize the extent to which people "feel" the freedom of the disembedded economy, he recognized working-class freedom as significantly greater than that of a slave or serf. He says in the *Grundrisse* that in the labor market, a worker does have the choice of changing jobs, changing locations, and obtaining skills compared to serfs and slaves, at least to the extent of one's income and resources. But this is still only "formal freedom" (Marx 1978, 255). In other words, the labor markets of capitalism do two things: (1) they give workers a type of freedom to choose and to get ahead that the absence of such markets in feudal and slave systems denies them, and (2) they simultaneously conceal or reify the unequal dependence (or lack of freedom) that they have upon all business as a whole.

But Marx's definition of socialism is essentially "the absence of alienated labor." This is fairly clear in his *Early Manuscripts*. Such a definition doesn't specify the actual institutional arrangements but leaves that up to the democratic control of the people as they carry out social change. Marx would, furthermore, say that the Soviet experience was one of alienated labor much like capitalism. The purpose of going beyond both capitalism and Soviet society is for Marx to free everyone to Be All You Can Be. He says that "only in community with others has each individual the means of cultivating his gifts in all directions," adding that it is through democratic kinds of community that real personal freedom is achieved (Marx 1978, 197). Of course, Marx meant that people aren't really free to develop themselves in an unlimited fashion unless they are part of a society that fosters this. In capitalism workers' ability to Be All You Can Be is stunted, as he says. It is clearly the case that they don't have *equal* freedom with the dominant classes in this regard. Marx really didn't focus on what freedom workers did have but only what they didn't have.

Yet the *purpose* of having more and equal freedom is what is at issue. Marx's assumption is that there is only one purpose for transcending alienated labor: to Be All You Can Be. In "Wage Labour and Capital," published in the *Neue Rheinische Zeitung* in 1849, he again elaborates the alienated character of labor power in capitalism, because, as a commodity to be sold in markets, the workers lose control over their own activity—the activity of laboring to meet their own basic needs. Labor is a big part of each person's day and, as such, "is the worker's own life-activity, *the manifestation of his own life*." But, says Marx, his vital, self-actualizing, life activity has to be sold in the market to earn the necessities of life. "Thus his life-activity is for him only a means to enable him to exist," so the worker doesn't feel the vitality of this life activity, since it is actually experienced as "a sacrifice of his life" (Marx 1978, 204; emphasis added). The implication of this, if we read between the lines, is that in socialism, absent the alienated labor that stunts our growth, we should "live to work" rather than merely work to live, and working would therefore no longer be a sacrifice of life but life itself. In this respect Marx is a "productivist."

Marx believed that humans are all about "life activity" and that this type of activity is equivalent to the ability of humans always to be more, to develop themselves, to actualize themselves, and to realize themselves in an endless quest for social and self-improvement. To have life activity, in other words, is to be able to insatiably improve. Yet one of the most basic of all life activities is laboring to meet material needs, and to have this particular expression of self-actualization distorted by capitalist relations is therefore contradictory to what it means to be human.

But capitalism does have a "ceaseless striving" for "more"—more profits, more wealth, more investment, more business successes—and this becomes the economic foundation for the "development of the rich individuality" that is "all-sided" in both production and consumption. Consequently, for Marx labor is no longer a means but an end expressed as the "full development of activity itself" (Marx 1978, 249). What is the "full" development of activity? It's never full, because humans have the inherent capacity always to be more tomorrow than they are today. It's insatiable. The problem of capitalism is that it dehumanizes labor, yet its "drivenness" creates the technology and the means of production to allow everyone equal pursuit of insatiable self-development. Of course, says Marx, real wealth is the power of all workers participating in democratic harmony in the socialized economy, and saving labor time means an increase of free time, that is, "time for the full development of the individual, which in turn reacts back upon the productive power of labour as itself the greatest productive power" (290). So communism is humanized labor, freed to be all it can be.

Accordingly, capitalism is unique in its ability to prepare us for communism because it focuses on production itself. Its predecessors didn't do this, because they were systems based upon the Culture of Security and the Satiable Self. They didn't make much of an issue of the production process itself, because they were not into having or being insatiably more. But capitalism focuses on production because it is the means to achieve ever more profit and wealth for the business classes. Everyone is (unequally) free to get ahead and have and be more. Everyone's attention is riveted on production regardless of whether he or she is an owner or not. Production is the key to each person's ability to get ahead, and in precapitalist societies, "getting ahead" was not the goal.

Capitalism has another quality in the preparation for communism. Industrialization, Marx adds, makes it clear to us that "variation of work" is not only possible but essential, because it implies "the greatest possible development" of a worker's "varied aptitudes" (Marx 1978, 413). "Varied aptitudes" are essential for one's self-realization. Thus, industrialism, even it its alienated form, forces us to substitute the "detail-worker of today by the fully developed individual," whose many capacities and multiple skills give "free scope to his own natural and acquired powers" (413–414). Marx is not suggesting that capitalism gives us this "free scope," but only that it creates the modes for this. Basically, what firms want, in other words, are workers who can do all kinds of different jobs within the company—multitalented and skilled workers. The actual reality of this has been challenged by many Marxists, of course, including the classic treatment of deskilling by Harry Braverman in *Labor and Monopoly Capital* (Braverman 1974). But Marx's point is that capitalism has some progressive qualities, all of which lead to a socialist revolution where working people understand that for them really to be all they can be, a new system is in order.

This is because the work process is in the "realm of necessity" for Marx; that is, we have to work to eat. Our livelihood is not handed to us. Although this realm should be humanized and should express our ability always to be more, Marx continues to maintain that the realm of freedom lies beyond necessity and therefore is the space in which humans can truly Be All You Can Be (Marx 1978, 441). It may seem that Marx is saying contradictory things: on the one hand, that work is everything, and, on the other, that it is a means to self-realization. He most likely saw work and everything that we do when we are not working as one large and integrated realm of life activity in which we constantly strive to improve ourselves, our society, and humankind through our insatiable efforts always to be more, to Be All You Can Be.

As Marx states in the *Communist Manifesto*, a communist system "shall have an association, in which the free development of each is the condition for the free development of all" (Marx 1978, 491). This means that there would be equality of access to the means for all of us to Be All You Can Be. Two decades later, he adds in the *Critique of the Gotha Program* that with communism, technology and industrial production will have advanced to where each person has achieved such a level of self-development that we can finally say, "from each according to his ability, to each according to his needs" (531).

How large are "his needs"? For Marx, they are insatiable; they represent "the individual rich in needs." Additionally, Marx suggests that labor will be an end in itself, as it will become "life's prime want." Does this contradict what he says regarding the realm of necessity versus the realm of freedom? No, since for him life activity, work, labor, self-development, self-realization, and self-determination are equivalent to one idea: that to be is to Be All You Can Be. So, it won't be until we transcend capitalism and its alienated labor that we can fully and insatiably appreciate this on an equal and democratic basis. We have to ask ourselves the question, Does Marx mean that with communism (unalienated society) we are finally free from the dictates and alienation imposed by capitalism only to be enslaved by the moral, social, and ethical imperative to be all we can be? More importantly, can our global habitat sustain this?

Marx, like Mill, was a representative of the Culture of Insatiable Freedom. They both believed that the fundamental purpose of being human is to insatiably actualize our potential. They were both "productivists," as well, although Marx had a greater propensity to idealize work and a greater desire to have it be a vital, if not *the* most important, dimension of our self-actualization. Mark Poster says that "Marx had reduced human reality to work, to making tools, to conquering nature, to producing efficient machines that led to automation: what he did not call enough attention to was that human reality also had to create itself, in Rimbaud's words, 'to change life,' not only to satisfy material needs, but to attain the full satisfaction of desire" (Poster 1975, 224).

So Marx was far more focused on production itself than Mill, whose attention was directed at the notion of liberty. Mill was also less concerned with the satisfaction that comes from the "goods life." In his view, as we mentioned earlier, people should pursue being more rather than having more. Hunnicut states that Mill's notion represented a popular "current of thought" in the United States at the turn of the century. People had some interest in moving toward an "alternative vision of human progress based upon work reduction" (Hunnicut 1988, 33). Marx would have applauded this as well, as both he and Mill share the productivist paradigm. Yet this "alternative" hasn't happened. Hunnicut's view is typical of many today: "Work is no longer a means to an end. It's not a road to higher things, such as the mind, the spirit, love and family. Instead of being part of life, work becomes the most important part of life" (A7). Mill would say that work shouldn't be the most important part of life, because we should focus on the "higher" things to actualize our potential. Marx would agree about the focus on the "higher" things but argue that work, if humanized and unalienated, can be "higher" and self-actualizing as well.

Marx was fixated on identifying the material conditions that would make the economy the major vehicle for self-development and being all one can be. Rather than examining what the new society would look like, he focused on the absence of these conditions in capitalism, in an effort to demonstrate why capitalism was inconsistent with them. But his productivism can't be disputed. He saw production as *the* primary sphere of life, and he argued for the "primacy of production." In the *Critique of the Gotha Program*, he said that the distribution of consumer goods and services is no more than a consequence of how the means of production are distributed—and both are very unequally distributed in capitalism (Marx 1978, 531). He meant by this that what people have to spend—that is, their incomes ("means of consumption")—and thus their ability to have all they can have are dependent upon their work, their occupations, and their careers, that is, production. But he also meant, as Figure 3.6 on productivism and consumerism suggests, that to have all you can have, you need to Be All You Can Be.

The Marxist and socialist movement in the twentieth century continued to reinforce the productivist paradigm. Some in the movement maintain that work should be the essential venue for self-development. Others, like Hunnicut and Poster, argue that work should be merely a means to an end. By so doing, it can be humanized, they say, but our real effort should be on the self-actualization that takes place beyond the workplace. Yet both sides of the debate agree that life is about insatiable self-development and social progress.

Any notion that there might be more to life than being more is conspicuously absent in Marxist literature. Virtually every critique of capitalism or blueprint for a postcapitalist society is premised upon the guiding principle that life is about insatiable self- and social improvement. The arguments against capitalism and for an alternative vision of a humanized society reduce to the notion that the market-based, profit-driven system stunts our personal growth and our social development, that we can't be all we can be within the parameters of such a system.

Many of the post–Cold War and new left authors and activists are legacies of the movements of the 1960s and were likewise exposed to both the social activism of the times and the hippie movement. We had a sense that capitalism had an alienating and distorting effect on an individual's personal growth, what one could be, and how one could live. Social activism and the hippie movement were two strands of the same critique. The social activist movement was more producvitist, suggesting that capitalist society stunts our self-determination and thwarts our ability to be what we want to be in life; it stifles our ability to be all we can be. The hippie movement, on the other hand, had two separable criticisms of American society: (1) that consumerist life is vacuous and (2) that our productivist culture of always having to be more is lacking as well. The first is an implicit rejection of the "goods life," and the second is a rejection of productivism. But the social activists, for the most part, continued to embrace productivism while rejecting consumerism. Everyone agreed that the insatiable desire to have more was no longer meaningful. Yet the insatiable desire to be more remained a key value; it was questioned, to be sure, but not rejected. In both Charles Reich's *The Greening of America* (1970) and Theodore Roszak's *The Making of a Counter-Culture* (1969) this is evident. Although these classic statements of, and about, the 1960s have been the object of decades of criticism, one can't help but get their message that the new left and hippie movement embraced the imperative of Be All You Can Be.

Two examples of this are Bowles and Gintis' *Democracy and Capitalism* (1986) and *Liberating Theory,* collectively authored by Michael Albert and a number of prominent leftist scholars associated with South End Press and *Z Magazine* (Albert et al. 1986). These are excellent books that we would today call post-Marxist. But they again exemplify the extent to which our modern culture of freedom has internalized the imperative of insatiable self-development. Both books maintain that the problem with capitalism is that it thwarts our ability to be all we can be. In a new social order, one that Bowles and Gintis call a "postliberal democracy" and what Albert et al. call a "humanist vision," we would be "liberated" to pursue our self-actualization and realize our limitless potential on an equal basis.

Bowles and Gintis say that a postliberal democracy "encompasses a set of human purposes, embracing a broad vision of human development as its guiding principle" (Bowles and Gintis 1986, 178). Also, such a society "represents people as learners for both choice and labor are indispensible means toward personal development." Not coincidentally, they add that "we thus follow John Stuart Mill in celebrating Wilhelm von Humbolt's profession of Enlightenment faith: 'The grand, leading principle, towards which every argument unfolded in these pages directly converges is the absolute and essential importance of human development in its richest diversity'"(178). Their view is that by democratizing the economy, "economic activity [will] be considered not as an end but as a means toward democratically determined forms of human development" (178).

Essentially, the implication of "democratically determined forms of human development" is that development is limitless because we all know that you can always be more. Making the economy a "means" rather than an end also implies that it would be more than a vehicle for meeting insatiable material needs, that is, economic growth. Accordingly, the economy should be used for personal growth rather than economic growth. This, too, is what both Marx and Mill would argue. Bowles and Gintis also add that the legitimacy of their model is based upon the human ability to continuously learn and that learning implies the "continuing deepening of capacities and understandings through a process of personal and social transformation in the interests of human development" (Bowles and Gintis 1986, 178–179). But how much "deepening of capacities" is enough? There's never enough. It's insatiable. So the economy must become a vehicle for continuous improvement of the self and society. This, too, is what Marx and Mill said. The postliberal democracy that Bowles and Gintis outline is one that, although more socially just and democratic than capitalism, is still an Economy of Insatiable Improvers! It is premised upon the imperative of Be All

You Can Be. The problem with capitalism is, then, that it simply is not doing a very good job of this.

What about the "humanist vision" in *Liberating Theory*? It's very similar to the postliberal democracy. Like Bowles and Gintis, Albert et al. are trying to move Marxism beyond the "economic determinism" that so strongly influenced it in the twentieth century, particularly after the Bolshevik Revolution. Albert et al. agree that if we ask most people in our "have all you can have" culture what they want out of life, they are likely to tell us "more stuff, please." They will parrot back the dominant consumerist ideology, in other words. Yet these authors say that "to have confidence in our evaluations we must ask, instead, in what society will people seek and attain the most. Unlike philosophical nihilists who reject value statements or moral judgments and wonder only whether citizens in a society support it, we have to wonder whether citizens also maximally develop and fulfill themselves" (Albert et al. 1986, 116).

This suggests that we need to examine the conditions in which, as Marx maintained, there is the greatest possibility for the "full and free development of the individual." Consequently, "while many different social core characteristics are *possible*, not all equally fulfill human potentials, and while all sets of core characteristics fulfill at least some aspects of human potential, not all sets equally promote all aspects or foster all forms of human development" (Albert et al. 1986, 116–117). They add that "to argue for the desirability of a particular set of core characteristics it follows that we must show that they are compatible with the full expression of all important aspects of human potential. That is, we should determine which core characteristics allow for the fullest development of all important human potentials for all of society's citizens" (117). Like Marx, they want to identify the institutions that "best promote all people's human fulfillment and development" adding, "We also believe that no other logic can generate this kind of 'ethical imperative.' Most simply, a humanist must ask: what characteristics must a society have for people to freely develop to their fullest potentials?" (117).

So like all the Enlightenment thinkers and progressives from the sixteenth century to today, the purpose of a "good society" and humanized economy is to bring out the most in us. How much is that? It, too, is insatiable. Have you ever heard someone try to argue that our full potential is finite and that we can know when we have developed it all? Albert et al. also consider such a humanist vision for Be All You Can Be an "ethical imperative." Why? Because in our Insatiable Freedom Culture, the whole purpose of having freedom is to actualize our insatiable potential always to be more. What else could it mean to be a human being? We are, after all, the insatiable improvers—something that no other life form can call itself.

We can, no doubt, pick any place along today's political spectrum and find commonality on the imperative of Be All You Can Be. Yet there have been skeptics and critics. One was Herbert Marcuse. His *Eros and Civilization* ([1955] 1962) is a very sophisticated treatment of Freud from a critical theory/Marxist perspective. Marcuse, as the intellectual mentor of the new left and one of the twentieth century's most outstanding Marxist scholars, suggested that contemporary capitalism had twisted Freud's notion of the "reality principle" into something that Marcuse called the "performance principle."

Freud had argued that the reality of having to work to eat and survive requires that humans must repress some of their more immediate gratifications, and these gratifications Freud termed the "pleasure principle." In other words, reality means we have to forgo some pleasure in order to reproduce our societies over time. Freud's instinct theory developed in *Civilization and Its Discontents* implies that "civilization begins when the primary objective—namely integral satisfaction of needs—is effectively renounced" (Marcuse [1955] 1962, 11). Of course, this means for Freud that the fundamental drive for humans is not to be all we can be but instead is the "integral satisfaction of needs," that is, the pleasure principle. The reality principle and the struggle for existence both mean the "repressive modification of happiness" (17), and "behind the reality principle lies the fundamental fact of scarcity, which means that the struggle for existence takes place in a world too poor for the satisfaction of human needs without constant restraint, renunciation, delay. In other words, whatever satisfaction is possible necessitates work, more or less painful arrangements and undertakings for the procurement of the means for satisfying needs" (32–33).

But Marcuse argued that capitalism forces people to forgo much more than what is actually necessary. He distinguished between necessary repression and surplus repression. The reality principle of Freud is about necessary repression, but in capitalism, says Marcuse, because the system is driven by insatiability, people—both workers and business owners alike—are compelled to work more and sacrifice free time for the sake of "performance." In other words, the system represses our ability to be lazy and have immediate gratification, so that we then internalize the "performance principle." We are driven to "perform," as the system's logic is all about getting us to accept that production and productivism are what life is all about. Freud's reality principle involves only the most necessary sacrifice of the pleasure principle, while, according to Marcuse, in capitalism the reality principle is replaced by the performance principle, and, in a subconscious fashion, people end up accepting surplus repression as natural.

Marcuse says that "productiveness [is] proclaimed as the goal of the healthy individual" in capitalism (Marcuse [1955] 1962, 236). For Marcuse, the reason that capitalism wants to define us as "productivists" and view our lives as always being more, having more, and achieving more is that capitalism is an inherently expansionary, growth-driven, insatiably driven system. For businesses to have more, get more, and achieve more, it is in their interests to have workers who also identify with these same ambition-based values. What's more, the chief executive officers (CEOs) and top management behave no differently. They see their lives as an unrelenting struggle to make their companies and themselves always more. Consequently, the more that people define themselves as insatiable improvers, the more they will get excited and enthused about working, having careers, moving up the corporate ladder, and enjoying the gratification of their economic "performance." It is in the interests of a system driven by insatiable improvement to have its people also driven by such values. Yet Marcuse does not say that this is a conspiracy of capitalists to get us to enjoy working more than we might otherwise need to. He's not talking about the "work ethic." By applying Freudian ideas, Marcuse suggests that the performance principle—to be is to work, produce, perform, and be more—is internalized and assimilated through the culture itself and through the subconscious. He says:

The restrictions imposed upon the libido appear as the more rational, the more universal they become, the more they permeate the whole of society. They operate on the individual as external objective laws and as an internalized force: the societal authority is absorbed into the "conscience" and into the unconscious of the individual and works as his own desire, morality, and fulfillment. In the "normal" development, the individual lives his repression "freely" as his own life; he desires what he is supposed to desire; his gratifications are profitable to him and to others; he is reasonably and often even exuberantly happy. This happiness enables him to continue his performance, which in turn perpetuates his labor and that of the others. Repression disappears in the grand objective order of things which rewards more or less adequately the complying individuals and, in doing so, reproduces more or less adequately society as a whole. (42)

Therefore, the reification in capitalist culture and the extent to which we don't feel our own alienation imply that we can become happy little robots who see ourselves as "economic performers" and productivists. Moreover, we don't feel repressed, and we come to believe that getting out there in the world, primarily out there in the economy, and getting as much accomplished as possible are the essence of life. To be is to perform, to produce, to achieve and accomplish. Drawing on Freud, Marcuse's theory is that this type of acceptance and internalization of productivist values is embedded in the nature of capitalist relations of production. This notion also draws from Marx's idea of the "fetish character of commodities" in volume 1 of *Capital*. So the successful internalization of productivist values implies the "organization of the human existence into an instrument of labor" where "man is evaluated according to his ability to make, augment, and improve socially usefully things" (Marcuse [1955] 1962, 140). The bottom line is that we ultimately define being human as the insatiable ability always to be more.

Marcuse developed these ideas in the context of industrialism and capitalism, as if this social and economic system causes us to assimilate productivist values. Yet capitalism and modern life are as much a result as they are a cause. So the insatiable desire to be more and, with it, the internalization of Be All You Can Be are a deeply embedded part of our Culture of Insatiable Freedom, which itself has been evolving for 10,000 years and ultimately became our cultural norm with the birth of capitalism. With capitalism and the disembedding process, we transitioned from the Culture of Security to that of Insatiable Freedom.

It is not because capitalism or capitalists want us to define ourselves as insatiable improvers that we do this. In fact, it is just the reverse: capitalism and industrialism are the logical consequences of a culture that has come to define being human as being always more and as insatiable self-actualization. Capitalism is an effect, more than a cause, of our definition of what it means to be human. Capitalism channels our insatiable desire to be more down economic avenues, like careerism, and sublimates our insatiable desire to be more into the insatiable desire to have more. Thus, to be more, is to be more *in the economy*. The social process whereby we work more and forgo more than we should have to (to live decently, with little hardship, minimal needs, and basic security) is what Marcuse calls the performance principle. It means that if we aren't out there trying to Be All You Can Be or getting settled in a career, then we are supposed to feel guilty, and Marcuse said that it is the system that is imposing this productivist logic.

Yet it is the Culture of Insatiable Freedom that's doing this. It's a moral and social imperative. Consequently, capitalism reinforces this imperative and channels it into careerism and having more possessions. The difference between Marx and Marcuse is that Marx didn't *blame* capitalism for the imperative of Be All You Can Be. He embraced the imperative. Like Marx, Marcuse opposed capitalism but was more radical by suggesting that it imposed an unnecessary form of repression on us by getting us to internalize productivism. However, Marcuse also said that the performance principle "glorifies repressive productivity as human self-realization" (Marcuse [1955] 1962, 199). The implication is that human self-realization is good but requires "nonrepressive productivity" instead. Perhaps Marcuse's problem with capitalism is merely that it repressively channels our self-realization into the economic process rather than allowing us the freedom to be more in other spheres of life.

Finding a correct interpretation of Marcuse is not the point. He clearly made a contribution in *Eros and Civilization* to a better understanding of today's cultural imperative of Be All You Can Be. Another critique of orthodox Marxism and its embrace of productivism is Jean Baudrillard's *The Mirror of Production* (1975). Baudrillard's issue with Marx is that Marxist thought has acted like a mirror, reflecting much of the same productivism that it set out originally to criticize.

In effect, says Baudrillard, capitalism puts the economy and production at the center of life, and when Marx set out to attack capitalism, he inadvertently did the same thing. He critiqued capitalist production and by so doing correctly revealed its exploitative relations, but, in criticizing capitalism, he accepted the primacy of production. Marx didn't go far enough, in other words. He criticized "capitalist" but not "production." Capitalism wants people to define themselves "in the identity that man dons with his own eyes when he can think of himself only as something to produce, to transform, or bring as value" (Baudrillard 1975, 20). Baudrillard accuses Marxism of "failing to conceive of a mode of social wealth other than that founded on labor and production" (29). Much like Marcuse, Baudrillard's argument is that Marxism has traditionally been as productivist as classical liberalism. On the other hand, Marcuse's attack was aimed more at the dominant social order and our culture of productivism that is perpetuated by capitalism. Baudrillard's attack is aimed at Marxism itself. But both have raised this issue: is it true that what we humans are supposed to be about is the insatiable desire to self-develop, self-actualize, and self-realize?

Baudrillard argues that Marxism "convinces men that they are alienated by the sale of their labor power, thus censoring the much more radical hypothesis that they might be alienated *as* labor power, as the 'inalienable' power of creating value by their labor" (Baudrillard 1975, 31). To be "alienated *as* labor power" means that if we conceive ourselves as insatiable improvers, then we are alienated, because this definition of humans is culturally determined. Baudrillard, in effect, accuses Marx of being a productivist, of uncritically accepting the Enlightenment notion, like Mill, that to be is to be always more. Unfortunately, Marx says, labor power, that is, our ability to actualize and realize ourselves through economic and artistic activity, constitutes our human essence. But if this is the case, then socialism means that "the individual finds himself 'liberated' as labor power while work continues as the principle of reality and rationality, as axiomatic" (140–141). Do we want work to have this role? It means that to be is to work and that to be more means to work more. Of course, this is a broad definition of work that equates to improvement activity.

Is there a bottom line in this? Yes. What is, in fact, "axiomatic" today is the norm that to be is to Be All You Can Be. Mill said this; Marx said this; most leftists today say this; and they say this because it is an assumption about our natures that is deeply ingrained and embedded in our Culture of Insatiable Freedom. While some, like Mill, Marcuse, and Baudrillard, say that the economy shouldn't have to be the primary outlet for this, others say that it should, once work is humanized in a postcapitalist society. But they all reflect the dominant cultural norm and have elevated to the status of a moral imperative the idea that humans are fundamentally about insatiable improvement, unlimited self-actualization, and realizing our infinite potential. All have embraced the insatiable self.

Yet, Paul Wachtel states in *The Poverty of Affluence* (1989) that he:

was attracted to the idea that personal growth might be an alternative to economic growth. Personal growth, moreover, seemed to have fewer harmful side effects. After a while, however, I began to feel uneasy. Gradually my thinking began to shift, and a notion almost the opposite of what I originally intended took hold. I began to see that in many respects the idea of personal or psychological growth was but one more manifestation of a growth-obsessed society. The emphasis on growth, change, and self-betterment that one sees in much of Western psychology, at least since Freud's time, seemed to me part of the very thrust that had created our environmental crisis and our endless discontent. (Wachtel 1989, 111–112)

A "growth-obsessed society" is basically another label for a culture, like ours, that says that improvement is not only insatiable but what we must continuously encourage.

Wachtel says that the personal growth movement might have been a well-intentioned effort at an alternative to the insatiable desire to have all you can have but that it was sidetracked or co-opted. He criticizes Reich's *The Greening of America* (1970) as an example of our cultural fixation on personal growth. Wachtel's argument is essentially that our personal growth (i.e., Be All You Can Be) fixation is a function of our economic growth obsession. In other words, our insatiable desire to be always more is a by-product of our economy driven by the insatiable desire to have all you can have. But the causation is exactly the opposite: our insatiable desire to have all we can have is a function of our cultural norm of Be All You Can Be.

The issue of which came first notwithstanding, Wachtel is on the right track in questioning the personal growth fixation. One of his chapter subheadings is titled, "Is 'Self-Actualization' an Alternative?" He then mentions the "human potential movement" that was popularized in the 1960s, suggesting that it became a third force in psychological thought along with behaviorism and psychoanalytic schools. Carl Rogers, Abraham Maslow, and Fritz Perls are examples of the human potentialists from this earlier period, but Wachtel's criticism is not aimed at their Be All You Can Be imperative. His concern, which is also legitimate, is that their notion of personal growth is too individualistic, as if the person can grow and become more regardless of the social conditions that surround him or her. Like Marx, Wachtel emphasizes the fact that people don't self-develop in a vacuum, that is, that we can develop ourselves only in fully humanized society. The "self," in other words, is "social." It takes society for any personal development, and the more alienating and dehumanized the society, the more stunted and distorted the personal growth is going to be. This is a valid point, but what's at issue is the imperative character that our society has given to personal growth, self-development, and the insatiable desire to Be All You Can Be.

Wachtel's critique is not radical enough. However, he does criticize our culture for its fixation on the *innate* character of Be All You Can Be, that the more inherent this drive is, the more people can actualize themselves regardless of their social environment. But Be All You Can Be is a cultural artifact. So we have to agree with him when he says that "throughout the human potential movement, emphasis is placed on such concepts as the *natural urge to grow,* innate self-actualizing tendencies, and other notions which present change as a spontaneous upswelling of something from within the organism" (Wachtel 1989, 132; emphasis added). There's nothing natural about the desire to personally grow and develop. Even Jacob Bronowski ruled this out and maintained that imagination and creativity might be natural but nothing else. Abraham Maslow's argument is the apex for human potentialists: a person's highest need is to self-actualize. The fact that this view was, and still is, so widely accepted and popularized testifies to the fact that our culture has assimilated the imperative of Be All You Can Be.

Wachtel concludes his case against the "goods life" by stating that he "would like to see less emphasis on the economic dimensions of our lives—growth, productivity, the creation of needs for more and more goods, the 'bottom line'—and more on the psychological: the richness of subjective experience and the quality of human relationships" (Wachtel 1989, 141). This sounds good and appears to be something that Marx, Mill, and the American Left would accept. But if we assume that the "richness of experience" and the "quality of human relationships" are insatiable and that our purpose in life is to pursue these, then the shift from the goods life to the psychological dimension is merely a shift from one treadmill to another. If these two dimensions of our lives are insatiable and if we argue that they should be what we strive for, then they become merely another way to talk about insatiable human improvement—they are two ways to talk about Be All You Can Be. We get off the "have all you can have" treadmill only to get back on the Be All You Can Be treadmill. We'd be stuck in the cultural milieu of insatiability, as we have for the last 500 years.

Still, with respect to Abraham Maslow, Wachtel is right on. By 1968, when Maslow published *Toward a Psychology of Being*, there were few dissenters from this view that to be is to actualize yourself. The popular consciousness in the industrial capitalist world was by then that freedom is what life is about, because freedom is what we use to insatiably improve ourselves and our world. Maslow, in other words, popularized what Mill had said a century earlier.

Maslow is best known for his idea that humans have a "hierarchy of needs" in which physical needs are at the base, and rising above this most basic need are the needs for safety (like order, predictability, and dependability of one's environment), love, affection, belongingness, self-esteem, and, finally, self-actualization. Maslow's critics over the past few decades have largely attacked the idea that a "hierarchy" of needs exists, in which certain ones have to be fulfilled before others are satisfied (Leiss 1976). But the issue of an inherent hierarchy of needs is not the point. The point is that Maslow's notion of self-actualization is viewed as biologically driven and innate. The implication of Maslow's notion is that what humans are ultimately all about is the insatiable desire always to be more tomorrow than they are today—to strive insatiably to fulfill their potential.

In the Preface to the first edition of *Toward a Psychology of Being*, Maslow says that he had trouble deciding on the title to the book and that "psychological health" is what it is about. But then he adds that "self-actualization" is the message. To be healthy, humans must be able to self-actualize. Why? Because it "stresses 'full-humanness,' the development of the biologically based nature of man, and therefore [this] is (empirically) normative for the whole species rather than for particular times and places, i.e., it is less culturally relative. It conforms to biological destiny, rather than to historically-arbitrary, culturally-local value-models as the terms 'health' and 'illness' often do" (Maslow 1968, vi). Maslow's view is that people are about "growth"—personal growth, primarily, but actualization of this is also coupled with social growth as well. The two work together, just as the Enlightenment scholars Mill and Marx said.

Toward a Psychology of Being is his explanation, in part, for how we humans in the twentieth century became aware of our innate propensity to pursue our self-actualization. After a thorough treatment of personal growth issues, Maslow then discusses "Some Basic Propositions of a Growth and Self-Actualization Psychology." This is essentially a testimony to the concept of the insatiable self. He says that "when the philosophy of man changes everything changes," including the philosophy of personal growth, which is "the theory of how to help men become what they can and deeply need to become" (Maslow 1968, 189). He suggests that "we are now in the middle of such a change in the conception of man's capacities, potentialities and goals. A new vision is emerging of the possibilities of man and of his destiny, and its implications are many" (189). Maslow adds that "self-actualization is defined in various ways but a solid core of agreement is perceptible. All definitions accept or imply, (a) acceptance and expression of the inner core or self, i.e., actualization of these latent capacities, and potentialities, 'full functioning,' availability of the human and personal essence. (b) They all imply minimal presence of ill health, neurosis, psychosis, of loss or diminution of the basic human and personal capacities" (197). The "ill health" results when this inner nature is repressed or frustrated, of course.

But more importantly, self-actualization, for Maslow and for most folks in the capitalist world, is much like our view of human potential: it's insatiable. His point—the point of the personal growth and human potentialists—is that we have finally realized that our ability to self-actualize is limitless. This is clearly quite different from what Aristotle, Seneca, and St. Augustine were driving at. In the Culture of Security that prevailed until capitalism's arrival, the philosophy was that of the Satiable Self. By the twentieth century the philosophy of humankind shifted, with the transition to the Culture of Insatiable Freedom, to the philosophy of the insatiable self, and Maslow became in the 1960s its mentor.

Accordingly, Maslow states that "we have, each one of us, an essential inner nature which is instinctoid, intrinsic, given, 'natural,' i.e., with an appreciable hereditary determinant, and which tends strongly to persist" (Maslow 1968, 190). This inner nature is composed of basic needs, capacities, and talents, among other things. Then, he adds that "these are potentialities, not final actualizations. Therefore they have a life history and must be seen developmentally. They are actualized, shaped or stifled mostly by extra-psychic determinants (culture, family, environment, learning, etc.)" (190–191).

This widespread acceptance of Maslow's ideas suggests that insatiable potentiality is a given of our culture. That this manifests itself as an inner need to be actualized is Maslow's point. Maslow says, "Man demonstrates *in his own nature* a pressure toward fuller and fuller Being, more and more perfect actualization of his humanness in exactly the same naturalistic, scientific sense that an acorn may be said to be 'pressing toward' being an oak tree" (Maslow 1968, 160). Marx and Mill were saying the same thing 100 years ago, and it was no doubt Marx's mentor, Hegel, who first made this clear to the young Marx. Their view was that people exist as potentiality to be actualized, and that a "good and just" society is a precondition for this to happen. They felt that it should happen—that people should actualize themselves and that they would if they were allowed to. Mill said that capitalism was the best of all possible worlds for this, and Marx disagreed. Unlike Maslow, however, Marx and Mill didn't go so far as to argue that there was an "inner drive" for this that, if thwarted, would lead to all kinds of psychological difficulties. So Maslow goes another step beyond Marx and Mill: Be All You Can Be is not only a good thing but so deeply rooted in our being that to repress it causes us harm.

Marx, Mill, and Maslow agree that "the person, insofar as he *is* a real person, is his own main determinant. Every person is, in part, 'his own project' and makes himself" (Maslow 1968, 193). This defines, in fact, the essence of the Culture of Insatiable Freedom. Consequently, we are free, in this existential sense, to determine ourselves, yet not equally so, because some have external conditions of poverty, lack of education, the dysfunctional family, and, for Marx, the alienation and oppression of capitalist relations. Maslow's words, we should notice, are also suggestively "productivist," as Baudrillard would be quick to point out. We "make ourselves" by our choices, says Maslow, and he would surely agree with Marx that these choices are socially and economically determined by the social relations around us. But, argues Maslow, "if this essential core (inner nature) of the person is frustrated, denied or suppressed, sickness results" (193). Marx thought that a revolution would result. A century earlier, workers were enough aware of the source of their frustration that Marx thought that they would carry out a revolution rather than become so "alienated from their alienation" that they'd be sick instead!

Mill, Marx, and Maslow—they all embrace Be All You Can Be. But they also imply that it's natural. However, the reason that people in the industrial world have been so willing to accept this notion is that capitalism's fundamental insecurity and its accompanying freedom predispose them to this. With capitalism we became both insecure and free, and Be All You Can Be became something that we can, should, and must do if we are to be a winner in the *economic* game. It just makes sense. But there is another reason that we are predisposed to the idea that to be is to be always more: there is a *social* game, as well. Thorstein Veblen, at the turn of the nineteenth century, was one of the first to articulate the *social* game that also makes us believe that being always more is natural to our species.

THORSTEIN VEBLEN AND INVIDIOUS SELF-DEVELOPMENT

Veblen is important because he understood that capitalism had a peculiar way of dealing with people's need for self-esteem. A century ago Veblen argued that capitalism makes having more a measure of being more. Much of what Veblen was getting at in his now classic piece, *The Theory of the Leisure Class* ([1899] 1945), was an answer to the question of *why* capitalists always want more profit; why is it that they never seem to be satisfied no matter how much money they make?

If we ask them how much is enough, we already know the answer: there's never enough! Marxists, at the turn of century when Veblen wrote, were not troubled by this question. They mostly relied on the assumption that one can never have too much money or too many of the things that money can buy. Period. Yet Veblen's basic premise is that much of what capitalism is all about is not just making money in order to have more immediate gratification. It's about status. People buy, own, and accumulate ever more things because this is a measure of status or social esteem.

Veblen calls status comparisons "invidious" comparisons, as what the individual is doing is trying to arouse the envy of another. It's like saying, "Hey, look at me; see what I've done; see what I own; see what I've achieved. Aren't I better than you?" In other words, the more I own, the more status I achieve. The more status I have, the more esteem I get, and since one can never have too much esteem and must always work to maintain it (since it is always relative to what others may achieve), then one can never have too much status. Veblen says that "the invidious comparison can never become so favorable to the individual making it that he would not gladly rate himself still higher relatively to his competitors in the struggle for pecuniary reputability" (Veblen [1899] 1945, 32). He then adds that "since the struggle is substantially a race for reputability on the basis of an invidious comparison, no approach to a definitive attainment is possible" (32). This leads to the existence of an economy, capitalism, that is driven by a type of insatiablity that is psychologically based. It suggests that having all you can have is insatiable because it's driven by the psychological need for self- and social esteem. We need the esteem of others, as Maslow argues. The best way to get it is to Be All You Can Be, or to perform, as Marcuse argues. But capitalism says to us that the best way to demonstrate our success at being all we can be is to have all we can have. The economy serves two ends then: to meet material needs and to meet insatiable psychological needs. In Veblen's words, "the propensity for achievement and the repugnance to futility remain the underlying economic motive" (33).

Capitalism, in Veblenian terms, is a very elaborate game of "I am better than you." Most of what it is about, beyond being the means for satisfying material needs, is this. Its drivenness, for Veblen, comes from its character as a status-chasing or status-seeking game. So capitalism for Veblen is driven by the insatiable quest for status, rather than the desire to accumulate ever more wealth for the sake of more immediate gratification. Having more is a visible and demonstrable way to show others how successful we are at life.

But having more is merely a surrogate for being more, and being more was, and is, the basis for achieving self-esteem, social respect, and reputability. As Veblen says, "in any community where such invidious comparison of persons is habitually made, visible success becomes an end sought for its own utility as a basis of esteem," and "esteem is gained and dispraise is avoided by putting one's efficiency [*that is, performance*] in evidence" (Veblen [1899] 1945, 16, 181, 69, 26–28; emphasis added). Or, in different words, "the usual basis of self-respect is the respect accorded by one's neighbors" (30). A continuous theme in the discipline of psychology has been that people don't live in a vacuum. Consequently, since self-respect is, in part, a function of what others think of us and since humans do not live well without it, then we are compelled to give consideration to what others think. In fact, belongingness and self-esteem are two of Maslow's natural inner needs that rank just below self-actualization in his hierarchy. Maslow even states that, with respect to his hierarchy of needs, "the needs for safety, belongingness, love relations and for respect can be satisfied only by other people, i.e., only from outside the person" (Maslow 1968, 34). Implicit in Veblen's *Theory of the Leisure Class* is the premise that respect and status are socially accorded to those who demonstrate their self-actualization and self-development.

Yet the easiest way to demonstrate our achievements and accomplishments (what Veblen meant by efficiency), which themselves indicate progress toward greater self-actualization and being more, is to do so through financial ("pecuniary") means. Thus, people need self-esteem, and some of this is socially constituted. To obtain social esteem, people must demonstrate their self-actualization. To do this, people must demonstrate their accomplishments and achievements. Finally, capitalism offers us the convenient avenue of demonstrating our accomplishments through the conspicuous display of financial power, wealth, and consumption, and this is insatiable, because it is by relative comparison that we measure ourselves against others.

Veblen does not argue that our need for esteem is new or a product of the disembedded economy of capitalism. He suggests that since the beginning of settled populations and the Agricultural Revolution, people have been competing for status because there have been economic and social classes since that time. Marx would agree about the existence of economic classes but wouldn't make much of the status issue. "The propensity for emulation—for invidious comparison—is of ancient growth and is a pervading trait of human nature. It is easily called into vigorous activity in any new form, and asserts itself with great insistence under any form under which it has once found habitual expression" (Veblen [1899] 1945, 109; see also 148, 186, 189).

We have to keep in mind that between the Agricultural Revolution and the emergence of capitalism, the Culture of Security prevailed. Consequently, the competitive struggle for status was latent. Status existed, as we are aware, because we see it proudly demonstrated in royal dress, the privileges awarded to the ruling classes, and even the regalia of royal courts and battlegrounds. But it wasn't a "struggle" as it is today. Why not? Because these were embedded economies in which security was their essence. There was little freedom to self-develop, to achieve, and individual freedom was not their basis. These were not economies driven by insecurity and the freedom to have and be more. But with the birth of capitalism all of this changes. The competitive struggle begins, and no one is assured of esteem or economic status. Everything is up for grabs. The standard of esteem keeps rising over time as capitalism evolves, and it is fed by an economy that knows no limits. Having more is the way to demonstrate being more. Being more, by Veblen's time, had become the way to achieve social esteem and respect.

To the extent that any of us can impress others and arouse their envy, then, as Veblen said, this becomes "invidious." What has happened since Veblen is "invidious self-development." The point is that we feel compelled to develop ourselves, and now there is social recognition for nonpecuniary development. Today we have broadened the range of skills that show how good we are. We can arouse others' envy by letting them know how much we have developed ourselves in noneconomic ways. Even Veblen would admit this: "The propensity changes only in the form of its expression and in the proximate objects to which it directs the man's activity" (Veblen [1899] 1945, 33). Veblen was aware of the widespread assimilation of Be All You Can Be. He says that "all extraneous considerations apart, those persons (adults) are but a vanishing minority today who harbor no inclination to the accomplishment of some end, or who are not impelled of their own motion to shape some object or fact or relation for human use" (94).

For example, college teachers can impress others by the number of articles and books that they have published regardless of whether or not they have become rich and famous. The professors receive the esteem of colleagues through a nonfinancial avenue that still communicates that they are being all they can be. This is what impresses others, both in and outside the academic community, and the public can say that "they are ambitious self-actualizers." Additionally, by demonstrating their "continuous improvement," they can keep their jobs.

Veblen's contribution is his suggestion that capitalism is driven by the insatiable self's need for more than basic necessities. The economy becomes a useful tool to pump people up, and people need to be pumped up. But there is no limit to how high we can go—except the limits of our earthly habitat. The insatiable self is compelled by our need for esteem, and it is pressured by the logic of capitalism that forces us to struggle for security. Thus, there are continuous cultural demands to Be All You Can Be.

One of the hallmark platitudes of the corporate world today is "continuous improvement." Every manager exposed to the trendy theory of "quality management" is increasingly fatigued by having to respond to the imperative of "continuous improvement." Naturally, there is no end to it. Improvement is always possible. Since the self has become defined as insatiable, there is no excuse for not continuously improving something—ourselves, our jobs, our lives, our companies—everything of value in life is subject to the imperative of "more." Improvement of everything that is good in life has become a cultural norm because it is a by-product of the social embrace of the insatiable self. Because the self can insatiably improve, then everything associated with it that is "good" should do likewise. Finally, what happens if we don't buy into this insatiable improvement culture? What happens to those who resist the productivist treadmill of Be All You Can Be? We have to recall that, first of all, our economy is motivated by our insecurity and the possibility of using our freedom to become and have more. If we fail to adopt productivist values, that is, ambition, goal orientation, self-directed achievement, then Veblen says that we are like "a hornless steer [which] would find itself at a disadvantage in a drove of horned cattle" (Veblen [1899] 1945, 263). So Be All You Can Be or risk being a "hornless steer" in an economy of competitive bulls.

Chapter 5

From Being More to Having More: *Today's Economy of Insatiable Improvers*

We have assessed the development of the Culture of Insatiable Freedom as it unfolded throughout the nineteenth century. Now, we need to survey today's global economy. One of the conclusions drawn from the end of the Cold War and the marketization of much of the world is that not all capitalisms are the same. It used to be the case that we compared capitalism with socialism/communism, as if each was a monolith of unique, system-based features. In other words, there was "capitalism," and there was "the Soviet model." Using this dichotomy, it was largely assumed that there were few cultural or institutional nuances that needed to be compared. The Cold War suggested that the only comparison needed was between these big systems. Now with most of the world going capitalist, we have begun to scan the economic landscape for the many features that make one nation's capitalism distinguishable from another's.

The imperative of Be All You Can Be is affected by both the dominant Culture of Insatiable Freedom and by remnants of the previous Culture of Security. In Europe security has played a much more visible role than in the U.S. A survey of the evolution of social democracy suggests that the insatiable self has been constrained by Polanyi's notion of "the protective response." The protective response is an expression of the human need for social assurances of security. Likewise, in the Asian economies there has been a continuous concern for security. Since security and freedom are a trade-off, we can explain the trade-off better by comparing these economies with that of the U.S. Clearly, freedom and laissez-faire capitalism have been more pronounced in the U.S., while security has been more important in both social democratic (like the U.K., Sweden, and Germany) and corporate paternalist economies (like Japan).

The trade-off between security and freedom is also a conclusion made by Bowles and Gintis in *Democracy and Capitalism* (1986). Paul Piccone, editor of the critical theory journal *Telos*, has stated it this way: the basic need for security "explains the lure of any socialism, from the mildest forms of social democracy to the most oppressive versions of Stalinism," and it is "one of the most important preconditions for human happiness" (Piccone 1988, 9). He adds that "freedom as such will never effectively compete with more fundamental economic preconditions if the first excludes or curtails the second. A well-fed Socrates could self-assuredly claim that the unexamined life is not worth living while freely philandering with the acolytes after sumptuous meals" (9). But the argument that security has been a fundamental need results, in part, from the fact that, before capitalism, it was *the* norm. For over 1 million years prior to the sixteenth century, security was the norm, and freedom was an aberration. Bowles and Gintis suggest that in a "postliberal democracy" we should "regard the access to a socially acceptable standard of living as a right; depriving people of their livelihood would thus be as contrary to social norms and legality as depriving them of their liberty or violating their physical person" (Bowles and Gintis 1986, 206). They are arguing that security is fundamental to being human.

Yet in capitalism, security is generally something that is not assured but "earned" through the pursuit of productivism, that is, realizing our potential and being ambitious and goal-directed. Bowles and Gintis share Michael Walzer's view that we owe each other an assured level of material security if we want to have stable communities. For "members" in a stable, political "community," the "first thing they owe is the communal provision of security and welfare" (Walzer 1983, 64–65). Bowles and Gintis add: "A mutual commitment to securing each person's conditions of life builds the respect and communal identification upon which a democratic culture must rest, but it also raises economic problems. We have emphasized the problem of inducing people to work and stressed the manner in which *capitalist societies rely heavily on economic insecurity as a major if often implicit disciplinary and motivational device*" (Bowles and Gintis 1986, 207; emphasis added). In other words, capitalist societies have relied upon insecurity to motivate both production and insatiable improvement.

But as the post–Cold War period has shown, not all capitalisms are alike. The Europeans, the Japanese, and other industrial economies as well (e.g., Mexico) have had substantially productive economies with less reliance on insecurity. Their provisioning through corporate (Japan) and state programs (social democratic nations in Europe) has created a richer appreciation for the extent to which security can actually motivate people, if they feel, in turn, a greater sense of belonging and membership in a political and economic community, whereas the laissez-faire capitalism, more characteristic of the U.S. system, has mainly relied on insecurity and personal freedom to motivate people. To the degree that security is universally vital to us, then we should recognize that one difference between U.S. capitalism and other capitalisms today is that in the former, it is "earned," while in the latter, it is at least partially assured through the welfare state or corporate paternalism. We can't say that the Culture of Security has survived outside the U.S., however (except in enclaves of indigenous people). But the sense and appreciation for an assured form of security clearly run deeper in these other capitalisms.

Of course, the concern for provisioning security through welfare programs and such has not diverted the priority of insatiable improvement. The Culture of Insatiable Freedom still rules in these European and Asian nations as well. Yet there is merit to the idea that an emergence of a Satiable Self and a new twenty-first-century Culture of Sustainability might be more likely in these parts of the world. The cultural holdover of security might provide the springboard for a new norm of sustainability. The felt need for sustainability on the part of individuals in any nation is likely to arise from the positive experience of assured security. The needs for security and for sustainability, in other words, dovetail. So is it more likely that the Satiable Self will begin to emerge from the social democratic and corporate paternalistic nations than from nations more like the U.S.? This is debatable, because one can also argue that if the "struggle" for security that drives competitive capitalism in the U.S. proves to be too stressful and exasperating for many folks, then it may foster a felt need for a sustainable, satiable, and secure alternative. It could go either way perhaps.

This leads to an examination of the recent events in the former Soviet Union. Here we can see the security–freedom trade-off very easily. The Culture of Insatiable Freedom has only recently been experienced since it comes into being with the collapse of the Soviet model, that is, the institutionalizing of both economic and political freedom. Until the last decade, the Culture of Security continued to dominate despite the norm of the insatiable self. Now Russians in particular are undergoing the transformation from their security culture to their freedom culture. There is mounting evidence that many are disillusioned with the competitive struggle and the awareness of "you're on your own, pal." Many are wondering whether the sacrifice of assured security is worth the freedom that it creates. Perhaps the Satiable Self is more likely to emerge from this experience than from either the social democratic, corporate paternalist, or individualistic experiences of other parts of the world. Many Russians want to "have it all" but find the requirement of "be it all" too stressful.

Finally, we must examine that part of the world that has had the most experience with victimization by the Economy of Insatiable Improvers. Which way might they go or be going? The Southern Hemisphere has been subjected to the economy of the insatiable self as capitalism has spread worldwide over the last 400 years. Here there is also the ongoing tension between the Culture of Security and that of Insatiable Freedom. Indigenous peoples have been subjugated and/or assimilated to the Culture of Insatiable Freedom, so we must examine the extent to which the Satiable Self might emerge from this tension. Clearly, there is need for "improvement" in the lives of peoples in this part of the world. Human suffering must be eliminated to the extent that it is humanly induced.

The issue is whether or not the have-nots of the world are in a position to look beyond the insatiable economy of industrial capitalism, weather the storm of the global economic free-for-all, and come up with an agenda for a sustainable economy. Like the Russians, they are experiencing the transition to the Culture of Insatiable Freedom and must contend with the insecurity that this entails. With overuse of their habitat as an operative feature of their social and physical landscape, is it possible for them to desire anything but "more"? Still, isn't it also possible for them to realize that it is the global economy of "more" that is victimizing them?

Sustainable development has become a trendy cliché embraced since 1988 by both corporate leaders and the poor nations. This is, in part, a response to overuse issues and the awareness that the usual growth prescriptions cannot possibly work anymore. Relying on business-led foreign investment and the remedy of economic growth has been the twentieth-century approach to all problems of Third World poverty. Yet we now realize that to bring the Third World up to the Western industrial standard of living is environmentally impossible (without a major technological fix).

The bottom line for this part of the world is that, instead of growth, the solutions that are sustainable and consistent with the Satiable Self require redistribution of global resources and power. What may have increasing appeal to those victimized by globalization is not the Culture of Insatiable Freedom but the demand for a type of redistribution that promotes economic security, self-sufficiency (bioregionally and nationally), simplicity, equality, and justice. Yet these values are essentially what describe the Satiable Self. Will the poor of the Southern Hemisphere (and related regions) get exasperated with the compete-or-die logic of the global system? They can resist; they can jump in and try to compete successfully (like the Pacific Rim nations); or they can acquiesce and submit. Resistance is, and will be, based upon a vision of redistribution, sustainability, and the Satiable Self.

In effect, what the have-nots are up against is the culmination of three historic forces: (1) white Europeans, (2) who like to work hard, and (3) who don't mind taking advantage of others. Whether it is colonialism, imperialism, or the new global economy, the Culture of Insatiable Freedom and its Economy of Insatiable Improvers have been a freedom-driven wealth machine, moving around the world, pushing and shoving, plowing and pirating. It is the offspring of a peculiar European culture where "more" has become the essence of being. For example, in 1500 only 9 percent of the world's land surface was controlled by Europeans, yet by 1800, they controlled 35 percent, and by 1878, they had 67 percent. Ultimately, by World War I, they controlled 85 percent of the world's land surface, and they weren't accommodating to the indigenous peoples whom they encountered along the way. Daniel Quinn suggests in his novels that we should call this aggressive European culture the "takers," while the subjugated indigenous peoples, whose lifestyles are those of the embedded economy and the Culture of Security, he calls the "leavers" (Quinn 1992, 1996, 1997; see also Quinn 1999). With respect to the Spanish conquest of the Americas, Quinn mentions in *Beyond Civilization* (1999) that in 1540 the takers were up against

25 million indigenous leavers in Mexico alone. Yet by 1680 these leavers had been reduced to only 1 million.

Because the "taker" culture of insatiable improvers is an exported and imposed culture, there is a greater chance that its victims in the Third World can see beyond it. The evidence for this becomes clearer with the situation of the world's have-nots. The have-nots need to have more. But can this demand arise from other than the imperative of the insatiable desire to be more? Can it arise from a notion of the Satiable Self?

THE CULTURAL NORM OF BE ALL YOU CAN BE
IN U.S. CAPITALISM

Today, the culture of Be All You Can Be applies at both the individual and personal level and also the institutional and organizational level. Consider the multitude of prefixes that are currently attached to the word "development." This is only a partial list at most but is characteristic of the discourse in the United States today. In academe, there's *career* development, *management* development, *student* development, *corporate* development, *business* development, *course* development, *program* development, *strategic* development, *economic* development, and, of course, *professional* and *faculty* development.

The list is probably as insatiable as our being. We hear about personal growth and personal development constantly. Anything that is skill-related usually can be associated with development, too. There's writing development, math development, and skill development. There are development centers, development funds, development programs, and development strategies. But what does "development" actually mean? The etymology of the word reveals that it is of French origin, dating to 1656, that is, the beginning of capitalism and the Culture of Insatiable Freedom and the insatiable self. Its earliest meaning in French and also English is that of "unfolding" or "unwrapping." The word "development," as an English word, was first used in 1756. Today's dictionary definition says that development means "to cause to become gradually fuller, larger, better," "to build up or expand," and "to bring something latent or hypothetical into activity or reality" (*Webster's New World Dictionary* 1974). With the possible exception of "unwrap," there is nothing in the word "development" that suggests satiability.

The word, by its very nature it seems, signifies insatiability and unlimitedness. We use the word, as the previous list clearly demonstrates, because it is premised upon the assumption of insatiability. Development implies, in our current discourse, unlimited development. If you examine the list of prefixes, are there any that are not insatiable? Career development, faculty development, economic development, social and political development, skill development—are any of these associated with a final, satiable outcome? Hardly. They are integrally tied to the notion of continuous improvement. Because we have assumed that the "self" is insatiable, we assume that anything that the self does, both individually and collectively, is insatiable as well.

Recalling Mill, Marx, and Maslow, we know that the ultimate in insatiable development is *human* development: Be All You Can Be.

UNLIMITED DEVELOPMENT IN THE CORPORATE WORLD

In the corporate world of U.S. capitalism, development and continuous improvement go hand in hand. The language of the competitive, driven arena of corporations is all about Be All You Can Be. It's about insatiable development, compete or die, and continuous improvement. We apply these terms both to the individual and to the corporation. If you examine Figure 5.1, the context for insatiable development is clear.

Figure 5.1
The Insatiable Improvers and Endless Development

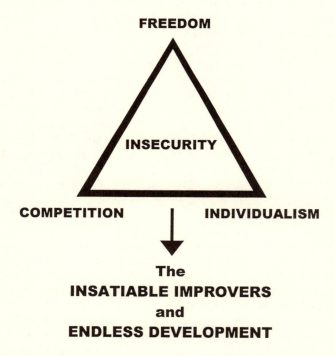

As the triangle suggests, our culture today is premised upon a configuration of three forces: (1) freedom, (2) competition, and (3) individualism. All three are necessary to create the norms for insatiable improvers and endless development. Corporations work under competitive market conditions that create, as we know, a coercive force—they must exercise their economic freedom and pursue their development. But they also act in a climate of individualism; that is, they are individual corporations afloat in the competitive ocean, free to sink or swim. More importantly, they have to learn how to swim and swim very well if they are to succeed. In other words, in the middle of the diagram is the fundamental condition of insecurity. They start out insecure. But they have freedom, their individual initiative on which to act, and they are stuck with a competitive environment. What's the outcome? A corporate world of insatiable improvers pursuing their endless development.

An excellent example of this is the popular 1994 book by James Collins and Jerry Porras, *Built to Last*. It tells it like it is. It's had over seventy printings, has been translated into seventeen languages, and was fifty-five months on the *Business Week* best-seller list (Collins 2000, 135). Collins and Porras examine numerous Fortune 500 corporations that have been financially successful over the last half century. Their list of visionary companies that are the "best of the best" includes 3M, GE, Ford, American Express, HP, IBM, Wal-Mart, and Disney. They say that "the essence of a visionary company comes in the translation of its core ideology and its own unique drive for progress into the very fabric of the organization—into goals, strategies, tactics, policies, processes, cultural practices, management behaviors, building layouts, pay systems, accounting systems, job design—into *everything* that the company does" (Collins and Porras 1994, 212). Additionally, "a company must have a core ideology to become a visionary company. *It must also have an unrelenting drive for progress*" (216; emphasis added). In effect, they are describing the logic of compete or die. Firms need to have a set of beliefs that all workers can not only understand but embrace and be committed to, and they must develop themselves in the same way that we talk about self-development—"an unrelenting drive for progress." How much is enough? There is never enough progress—never enough development. Success, in other words, requires drivenness, because the climate of insecurity coupled with competition and the knowledge that "you are on your own, pal" (individualism) means develop or lose. This is the insatiable self transposed into the corporate arena. The "self" is the corporation.

Of course, these companies are not exclusively profit maximizers. They are not about simply making the most profit. That makes sense to us, as we realize that, like individual self-development, there is more to life than money. Many people in the advanced capitalist nations, surely in the U.S., are now aware of the fact that Be All You Can Be need not exclusively focus on having all you can have. In this respect, the "visionary company" is no different from the individuals who constitute it. The corporation is into Be All You Can Be, and to do so suggests that profits don't always come first.

Collins and Porras also debunk various myths about corporate success, and one corollary to profit maximization is the myth that to be successful, the firm must focus on beating the competition. Yet the authors argue that "visionary companies focus primarily on beating themselves. Success and beating competition come to the visionary companies not so much as the end goal, but as a residual *result* of relentlessly asking the question 'How can we improve ourselves to do better tomorrow than we did today?' And they have asked this question day in and day out—as a disciplined way of life—in some cases for over 150 years. No matter how much they achieve—no matter how far in front of their competitors they pull—they never think they've done 'good enough'" (Collins and Porras 1994, 10). This speaks for itself. These corporations exist within the Culture of Insatiable Freedom and the insatiable self. No amount of achievement is ever enough—a business, just like an individual, can always be more tomorrow than it is today. Both personal and corporate success comes to those who are productivists, who embrace the values of limitless improvement. This is broader than profit maximization.

In fact, Chapter 3 in *Built to Last* is entitled "More than Profits." It begins with several quotes from top CEOs, all of whom insist that their companies are about "improvement" and "development" rather than profits. The Merck and Company's (pharmaceuticals) *Internal Management Guide* says, "We are in the business of preserving and improving human life. All of our actions must be measured by our success in achieving this goal." Also, John Young, a former CEO at Hewlett-Packard says, "We've remained clear that profit—as important as it is—is not *why* the Hewlett-Packard Company exists; it exists for more fundamental reasons" (Collins and Porras 1994, 46).

Today's corporations emphasize development that is clearly insatiable. Collins and Porras say, "Indeed, a visionary company continually pursues but never fully achieves or completes its purpose—like chasing the earth's horizon or pursuing a guiding star. Walt Disney captured the enduring, never-completed nature of purpose when he commented: 'Disneyland will never be completed, as long as there is imagination left in the world'" (Collins and Porras 1994, 77). Clearly, imagination as part of our human being is something that we, along with Bronowski, would agree is unlimited. But Bronowski did not, like Walt Disney, suggest that insatiable improvement is what we are about. Disneyland, after all, is not the realization of imagination but a commercial enterprise whose quest is to insatiably develop, improve, and progress.

The "core ideologies" of these visionary companies attest to the embrace of Be All You Can Be, as well. For Nordstrom department stores, the four components of its core ideology are (1) service to the customer, (2) hard work and productivity, (3) *continuous improvement, never being satisfied*, and (4) excellence in reputation, being part of something special (Collins and Porras 1994, 70; emphasis added). If we think about it, this is exactly what we teach in business colleges and what we say individuals should also practice. If you replace the word "customer" in the preceding statement with "humanity/community," then this "core ideology" fits nicely with a prescription for individual success in today's world. Clearly, Nordstrom would be very gratified if its employees professed this personalized version of its core ideology. It's a core ideology for the insatiable self. John Stuart Mill and Karl Marx would both embrace it.

In drawing their conclusion that continuous improvement and insatiable development are key values, Collins and Porras also add: "Boeing can never be done pushing the envelope in aerospace technology; the world will always need a corporate Chuck Yeager. HP [Hewlett Packard] can never reach a point where it says, 'There are no more contributions we can make.' GE can never complete the task of improving the quality of life through technology and innovation" (Collins and Porras 1994, 77).

The fourth chapter in *Built to Last* is entitled, "Preserve the Core: Stimulate Progress." Under this chapter's subheading, "Drive for Progress," the authors say: "Core ideology in a visionary company works hand in hand with a relentless drive for progress that impels change and forward movement in all that is not part of the core ideology. *The drive for progress arises from a deep human urge—to explore, to create, to discover, to achieve, to change, to improve.* The drive for progress is not a sterile, intellectual recognition that 'progress is healthy in a changing world' or that 'healthy organizations should change and improve' or that 'we should have goals'; rather, *it's a deep, inner, compulsive—almost primal—drive*" (Collins and Porras 1994, 82–83; emphasis added). Their point, as the statement above clearly demonstrates, is that our desire to insatiably improve, to be all we can be, is part of our human nature. The extent to which the Enlightenment value of self-development has been assimilated into our Culture of Insatiable Freedom is evident in the authors' remark. They are clearly focusing on the notion that *to improve, to progress, and to achieve* is essentially what it means to be a human. It is a deep, inner drive or urge, because it is integral to what constitutes our being in the world. Yet, this is not the way that humans lived for the million and a half years prior to the Agricultural Revolution. To say that to improve and relentlessly drive for progress is to act on deep, inner urges merely affirms our contemporary cultural imperative of Be All You Can Be. What, in fact, Collins and Porras are saying is that successful (i.e., visionary) companies succeed because they understand that "to be" is always to "be more." The degree to which the corporation and its employees internalize the imperative of Be All You Can Be ultimately determines success.

Collins and Porras then describe the "drive for progress." They say, "Indeed, the drive for progress is never satisfied with the status quo, *even when the status quo is working well*. Like a persistent and incurable itch, the drive for progress in a highly visionary company can never be satisfied under *any* conditions, even if the company succeeds enormously: 'We can always do better; we can always go further; we can always find new possibilities.' As Henry Ford said, 'You have got to keep doing and going'" (Collins and Porras 1994, 84). These remarks speak to the insatiability of development. It is presumed to be insatiable, and, thus, a company that comprehends that development is unlimited and insatiable is more likely to succeed in the long run. We are not talking about development, growth, success, or achievement that at some point terminates and is satiated and complete but the insatiable desire to be always more: the incurable itch!

In effect, success is a function of internalizing productivist values. This is the essence of what it means to be *built to last*. As Collins and Porras say, "Like core ideology, the drive for progress is an *internal* force. The drive for progress doesn't wait for the external world to say 'It's time to change' or 'It's time to improve' or 'It's time to invent something new.' No, like the drive inside a great artist or prolific inventor, it is simply *there*, pushing outward and onward"

(Collins and Porras 1994, 84). This statement fairly well sums up the ideas of the Enlightenment philosophers, the modern education philosophers, Mill, Marx, and Maslow. It's a corporate spin on Maslow's *Toward a Psychology of Being*.

Some dispute Collins and Porras' thesis that corporate success is premised upon internalizing productivism. In fact, Collins has recently written an informative article in the edgy, New Economy business magazine *Fast Company* (Collins 2000, 131–140). He responds to critics who suggest that in the New Economy, driven as it is by high-tech industry, success is not about being built to last but built to "flip." That is, today's financial success is based upon a new game that's related not to stability and longevity but to fast bucks. Collins takes issue with this but says that "the point of this new game was *impermanence*: Startups flip their stock to underwriters, who flip the stock to individual buyers, who flip the stock to other individual buyers—with everyone looking for a quick, huge financial gain" (135).

Regardless of whether or not financial success is based upon long-term goals and the ideology that there's more to life than money, both the "built to last" as well as the "built to flip" advocates would agree that business is about productivism and Be All You Can Be. Collins is rightly concerned that today's "fast buck" approach to business is producing excessive greed, financial instability, and a growing social divide between the new rich haves and the have-nots. Collins is a very astute observer of the business scene, and his view that the New Economy may not be built to last correctly states that it, too, is driven by greed, immediate gratification, and profits-first. Still, we have, as *Built to Last* demonstrates, defined ourselves, as both individuals and organizations, as the insatiable improvers.

Collins and Porras have examined companies that have been successful over decades, and their conclusion is that success comes from the attributes associated with Be All You Can Be. Maybe their success comes from something else. Maybe these corporations are actually far more pragmatic than they are "ideological." Yet, as the CEOs have stated, with regard to *how they see their companies*, success has much to do with a commitment to Be All You Can Be. What these authors suggest is that the ideology of productivism, the awareness of the insatiability of improvement, and the actualization of unlimited potential have a great deal to do with longevity, and with this comes something else: the "achievement" of a measure of security. But, of course, in the global, competitive market today, security can be achieved only by "continuous improvement" and insatiable development.

This logic is not unique to profit-motivated or private sector organizations. All organizations, private or not, profit-driven or not, are caught up in the culture of unlimited development. For example, at my university the college of business was recently reaccredited with the Association to Advance Collegiate Schools of Business (AACSB International). One of the self-evaluation reports submitted to AACSB International had a cover page entitled: "Achieving Quality and Continuous Improvement through Self-Evaluation and Peer Review." The essential content of this report, like so many others in nonprofits and nongovernmental organizations (NGOs), is to demonstrate to the accrediting agency or any other group for which the organization is held accountable that we are trying to Be All You Can Be.

"Achieving quality" means to demonstrate your ability and enthusiasm to set the highest standard for yourself that you can possibly achieve. Then demonstrate achievement of this standard. We can apply this idea to an organization, and we can apply this to individuals. It means to demonstrate productivism: set your goals yourself, set them as high as you possibly can and still be able to meet them, and finally demonstrate to others that you have achieved these goals. Then make up new goals and keep going. In other words, say what you are going to do; make it as much as you possibly can; then do it. But don't quit there. There are always more goals and more potential to actualize. Hopefully, others will recognize your accomplishments and applaud your success. This holds true for you and me in our jobs, for our organizations, for our communities, and for our society. Everybody and everything are caught up in the insatiability of continuous improvement. Whether this is a good thing or whether it is bad is not the issue. The point is that this is how we now define ourselves and our collectivities, that is, our businesses, our economy, our government, our social organizations. In our Culture of Insatiable Freedom all things good and worthy are about insatiable improvement and unlimited development.

UNLIMITED DEVELOPMENT OF THE INDIVIDUAL: THE CASE OF CAREERISM

Although today's New Economy is faster, more accelerated, change-driven, and immediacy-oriented, it hasn't altered the fact that Be All You Can Be is ultimately behind these changes. In fact, the speed of the economy has no doubt also intensified the coerciveness of productivism. It becomes even more important today to get out there in the world and make something of yourself, because if you don't, you'll be left behind that much sooner. When we shift the focus of the insatiable desire to be more from business organizations to the individual, the concept of "career" becomes pivotal. The insecurity of the disembedded market economy compels people to perform (as Marcuse said), to hustle, to get educated, to pursue goals, to be self-directed, and to actualize their unlimited potential. The capitalist economy also has the effect of channeling this energy to be more into economically useful activities, that is, careers. We've gone from "you *can* be more," as Aristotle understood, to "you *should* be more," as Marx and Mill understood, to "you *must* be more," as the New Economy dictates. How does one go about this? By getting a "career."

Over the last 200 years, "career" has become a household word. It was first used in 1803 in its contemporary meaning by the duke of Wellington. A career, which originally meant a "race course" in Middle French (1534), now means "an occupation or profession through the course of one's life" (Barnhart 1988, 145). But for our purposes a career is an occupation that is one's chosen outlet for Be All You Can Be. This meaning is implicit in all of the related literature. For example, IBM's Web site has a page targeting the 1999–2000 bachelor's degree business graduates (www.ibm.com/whywork). The caption reads, "In choosing a place to take your talent, what do you care about most?" The text then adds, "You've been absorbing a lot of knowledge these past few years. Now, it's time. Time to show the world what you've learned. *Time to channel your enthusiasm into great work.* In Project View you can investigate opportunities to spend your days with others who value good work as much as you do, and who will benefit from your enthusiasm and fresh ideas. It's your time" (emphasis added). Of course, IBM is one of Collins and Porras' visionary companies. What they and every other corporation are looking for are employees who embrace the basic productivist ethic, who enthusiastically embrace the imperative of Be All You Can Be. The corporate world is looking for a "few good women and men" to come on board, and say, "You know, this job is not a just a job for me; it is a career; it is what I've been wanting to do all of my life; I want to love working here, doing this job and expressing myself and realizing my potential right here in this firm!" Naturally, the college graduate or any other applicant, for that matter, who demonstrates ambition, self-directedness, and a desire to achieve and accomplish good things through his or her career is exactly what the company wants. A "career" is that occupation in which the individual can enthusiastically pursue Be All You Can Be.

Careers are those occupations in which it is easy, meaningful, and gratifying to actualize one's potential and self-development. This dovetails with what the firm is looking for in a "good" employee. The firm wants a dedicated, excited, energetic worker. If you want this job, you know that displaying this is important. *Computerworld* magazine has a publication called "Careers," and in the fall 1999 issue the editor states to the senior-year college student: "You're hearing it from your professors, parents, and campus career advisors. Be aggressive, start looking for a job NOW—this fall. No one would blame you for wanting to tune them out. You've been back in school for only a couple of months. Plus, you think you've got it made because you've almost completed a highly coveted degree in information technology [IT]. But if you don't want just any job, you'd be smart to heed their advice. There are tremendous opportunities in the world of IT, but those who find the best jobs are those who start looking early" (Malloy 1999, 1). The editor is right, of course. The charge is to be aggressive, get out there, be enthused, and demonstrate the proper productivist attitudes: Be All You Can Be and perform to the max!

There are essentially two kinds of jobs in our capitalist economy: (1) wage labor and (2) career labor. The difference between them is something that everyone knows. Wage labor is the traditional kind of labor that Marx talked about. The company pays you a "fair day's wage for a fair day's labor." It is not necessary to embrace productivist values to be a wage worker. The company is not asking this much of you. These kinds of jobs have been typical of the industrialization period of capitalism in which basic manufacturing is the foundation and an industrial labor force exists. Most of these jobs are skilled to some degree but require little formal education. They may or may not pay well, and this has historically been dependent upon the extent of unionization. Most wage workers in U.S. basic manufacturing industries associated with mining, steel, railroads, cars, and automobile-related products historically did similar work, got similar pay, lived pretty similar lives, for example, Henry Fords' River Rouge plant in the 1920s, five-dollar-a-day period. This is traditional wage labor. No one thought to call these jobs "careers." One worked the assembly line, the mill, or the mine, got paid, and didn't have to "buy into" the company's ideology about progress, improvement, and being all that one or the company could be.

Wage labor, in other words, was about doing what the company told you to do and getting paid for it. These have not been attractive and glamorous jobs. Wage labor is a "means to an end." It is what one does to get a paycheck and usually qualifies as "aliented labor" in the Marxist sense. It is alienated because the company controls the work process (see Braverman 1974; Edwards 1979). The advantage to this is that the worker doesn't have to profess productivist values and embrace the corporate ideology. Why not? Because with wage labor the productivity of the worker can be effectively measured by the company. The assembly line does this, for example, because the output per worker hour is determined by the pace of the line. But any job in which the worker's output per unit of time can be monitored, controlled, or measured by the employer is generally a job that doesn't require the worker to embrace productivism. Either one does the job or doesn't. The worker's attitude is not important to the bosses, because what counts is simply doing the job as directed by the work process itself.

We can think of many jobs that we either have had or know about in which attitude is not very important. Showing up and doing what's required are critical to keeping the job. For these jobs, most don't apply the word "career." They are frequently low-paying service jobs in today's economy. One doesn't have much "say" on the job. You do it and go home. You don't care about the job beyond the paycheck that it fetches. There may or may not be job security. But that's not the pivotal issue. Wage labor is not about your attitude. The employer doesn't normally care. You need to be responsible, for sure, and hard working, diligent maybe. But what's fundamental is that it is not generally viewed as the major outlet for you to "develop yourself." Wage labor is not career labor because it is not what folks think of as the avenue for channeling your insatiable desire to be more. It is not where you go to Be All You Can Be. That much is understood. The fast-food, franchise, burger bar, naturally, would like the prospective short-order fry cook to say, "This job is me, and I am it. This is what I've always wanted to be, and is where I wish to express myself. In fact, you don't need to pay me much, because the job is its own fulfillment for me." But that doesn't happen often.

On the other hand, the job applicant for a career position is supposed to say exactly this. Substitute "accountant" or "marketing director" for fry cook. It makes sense then. Career labor is the avenue for Be All You Can Be. It is about professing productivist values to the employer. With a career it's important that one cares about it beyond the paycheck, that it is an outlet for self-development and the realization of human potential. But the bosses want to hear this, too. It may or may not be your special place to insatiably realize your potential. But your employer is not likely to hire you or promote you if you don't fake a good line of productivism. If you hate the job, even though it is a career, or if you don't care about it beyond the pay, don't let the supervisor know. As we all know, to get and keep a career job, one must play the game and profess productivism. One must embrace the ideology of the corporation. One must act *as if* this is *the* avenue for Be All You Can Be. You don't have to do this with wage labor. That's the difference.

But why does career labor focus on the employee's attitude? Because it is labor where productivity is difficult to measure. With career jobs the output of the worker is simply hard to assess, measure, and monitor. Obviously, with many jobs, like managers, teachers, and motel front-desk clerks, the actual "output per worker hour" is hard to measure. These are jobs where the "control" over productivity tends to reside with the employee. Productivity is hard to see and not very observable. The worker may or may not be giving it his or her "best effort." Maybe productivity could be higher, but it is hard to determine if it is not visible.

If the employer can remove control over productivity from the worker, much as what assembly lines do, then none of this matters. But what has happened over the past century, especially in the last two decades with the new globalized, high-tech economy, is that there are more and more jobs being created where productivity is hard to measure. Service jobs, high-tech, information tech jobs, managerial jobs—this is the growth of career labor. If the employer can't measure your output very easily, in part because you have "greater responsibility" and flexibility on the job, then your attitude becomes very important. Obviously, an effective manager is not going to hire you for such a position if you act as if you don't care about it beyond the paycheck. To hire such a person runs the risk that the employee will slack off, and what's more, you, as the boss, wouldn't know it! So what happens? Bosses, human resource managers (doing the hiring), supervisors all look for the worker to demonstrate productivist values. They want an employee to say, "This is my career; it is what I want to do; it is me, and I am it." By this demonstration the employer can be reasonably assured that workers are actually working and hopefully giving it their all.

So with jobs for which productivity is easily measured we have "wage labor." With those for which there is more responsibility, thus better pay, more flexibility, more employee control, more worker participation and decision making, and, finally, little productivity measurement, we have "career labor."

In effect, career labor, by virtue of there being more and more of it in our high-tech economy, adds another dimension to the imperative of Be All You Can Be. With more of these jobs, there is more effort by companies to hire workers who have internalized productivst values and who demonstrate that they want the career in order to express their insatiable desire to be all they can be. So if one wants to avoid the drudgery of wage labor and pursue career labor, then it is imperative to find that niche in which the job is *the* outlet for self-development. If the individual can find this niche in the new global labor market, he or she doesn't have to fake the line, "This is me, and I am it!" The company is delighted, because the genuine expression of this by the worker means that he or she is giving it his or her all and that productivity will be maximized. The company might, in turn, become a visionary company.

Do companies really want employees who profess productivist values and who demonstrate that the career position is their outlet for self-development? Of course they do, and this is obvious regardless of whether or not the position is career or wage labor. It's important for career labor only because these tend to be positions where there is an element of trust involved. When productivity is hard to assess, the company must trust that the worker is actually working up to maximum potential. To the extent that Marcuse's notion of the performance principle has been internalized throughout the culture of capitalism, then it is easier to trust employees. To the benefit of bosses and owners in today's disembedded economy of insecurity and insatiable freedom, the insatiable desire always to be more has been largely internalized.

The performance principle has been assimilated, in other words. The performance principle, that is, the imperative of Be All You Can Be, has an element of rationality and universality to it once it becomes part of our culture, as Marcuse said thirty years ago. Our culture has reached the point where, if we don't devote our life to finding a career, to always becoming more, then we are judged by our peers as losers or slackers; we feel guilty about not continuously trying to actualize potential. Surely, corporations want this norm to be internalized and act like an "external objective law" on behavior. Consequently, corporations would like to believe that Marx was correct when he suggested that to be human is to be a producer, a doer, a worker—that to be is to work.

In this regard, Jim Collins, however, warns that the New Economy may be eroding what we have called the performance principle or productivism. He says that "when it emerged in the early 1980s, the new economy culture rested on three tenets: freedom and self-direction in your work; purpose and contribution through your work; and wealth creation by your work. *Central to that culture was the belief that work is our primary activity and that through work we can achieve the sense of meaning that we are looking for in life*" (Collins 2000, 139). This sounds like Marx, and it clearly reflects the extent to which Be All You Can Be has been channeled into economic activities and has captured the concept of "career." Collins adds that this new economy was driven by the ambitious,entrepreneurial spirit (as Joseph Schumpter argued fifty years ago) of people who asked the question, "How can I create work that I'm passionate about, that makes a contribution, and that makes money?" (140). Essentially, what this reduces to is the question, fundamental to career labor and entrepreneurialism, How can I find an economic niche in which I can be all I can be, feel good about it, and then have all I can have? Or, How can I find an economic outlet for the full realization of my insatiable potential?

Finding this niche is not that easy, as most of us know. But the corporations continue looking for those "few good men and women" who want to be all they can be. Bill Allen, Boeing's CEO between 1945 and 1968, said: "Boeing is always reaching out to tomorrow. This can only be accomplished by people who live, breathe, eat and sleep what they are doing (I am) associated with a large group of knowledgeable, dedicated (people) who eat, breathe, and sleep the world of aeronautics. Man's objective should be the opportunity for greater accomplishment and greater service" (Collins and Porras 1994, 81). To get employees in career labor as motivated and dedicated as possible requires that the company build a "culture" represented by a "core ideology," according to Collins and Porras. They say that "visionary companies more thoroughly indoctrinate employees into a core ideology than the comparison companies, creating cultures so strong that they are almost cult-like around the ideology" (71). The idea is to have a company where workers "buy into" the productivism that drives it. This is, historically, the capitalist counterpart to what we in the West accused the communist regimes of doing with their "propaganda" during the Soviet period. *Built to Last* has a list of the basic tenets of various visionary corporations. For example, for 3M there are "respect for individual initiative and personal growth"; for American Express there is "encouragement of individual initiative"; for GE there are " individual responsibility and opportunity"; and for Marriott we have "people are number 1—treat them well, expect a lot, and the rest will follow" (68–69). Of course, the list continues with the litany of corporate growth and development expectations. The point is that corporations that are successful work hard to build a culture where their careerists can link their own personal development with the mission of continuous improvement for the corporation.

The examples are endless. At my college's 1999 Leadership Forum, Kathryn Munro, the CEO for the high-tech firm Bridgewest L.L.C., spoke to the business students about leadership in the corporate world today. She stated to them that "leadership equates to competitiveness" and that this is the key to success. Additionally, Munro says that "there is no doubt in my mind that the world will belong to passionate, driven leaders—people with enormous energy who can energize the people around them. It will be up to these prospective leaders to understand the company's culture and values before they join it. They need to associate with a company with values that they want to follow." She also says that "companies have to care about the personal lives of their employees. They have to do everything they can do to encourage their workers to be productive. It has been shown that companies that do this are among the most profitable and admired companies in the world" (Munro 1999, 3).

In effect, she is parroting much of what Collins and Porras say in *Built to Last*. This makes sense to us, because it essentially states what, in fact, is the essence of our Culture of Insatiable Freedom: to win in the competitive game both as an individual and as a business, we must be all we can be, make this an internalized imperative, and actualize our insatiable potential. Moreover, the culture of Be All You Can Be, to achieve unlimited self- and business development, must be at the heart of leadership, the core ideology, the visionary company, top-level management, and ingrained in the career employees along with the wage workers (if possible). The point is to be a team, embrace each other, cheer one another ever onward, and join in the chorus of commitment to continuous improvement of the company, each other, and all good things in life. It's simply a statement of the performance principle and productivism.

In the April 2000 issue of *Fast Company*, a special feature on "The Best Practices of the Best Companies" reinforces Collins and Porras. One article concerns Ford Motor Co. and the degree to which Ford sees itself as building a cutting-edge culture of performance, in part, based upon the kind of leadership that Kathryn Munro describes. One of Ford's new "grassroots leaders" is Tom Iseghohi, director of global pricing. He says, "I was convinced that Ford's top leaders were serious about change. They understood what it took to attract someone like me. Talented people don't want an easy slam dunk; they want a challenge. They're passionate about winning, and they want the people around them to share that passion. To be a successful entrepreneur, you must accept risk. You have to be comfortable standing on the precipice, asking, 'Why not?'" (Hammonds 2000, 143–146). The successful companies are looking for folks who want to be all they can be and are effective at demonstrating it to everyone. The company itself, to be a winner, must want the same thing.

But accepting the challenge and winning on a never-ending treadmill of compete or die is not easy, nor does it offer much security, and companies know this. Each individual careerist, each wage worker, each CEO, each "grassroots leader," and each corporation must submit to the fundamental insecurity that underlies the disembedded Economy of Insatiable Improvers. Insatiable improvement is, in part, an imperative because we have created a culture that prescribes it as integral to being human. Improve or die! Because capitalism, especially in the new, globalized economy, requires this for success in the compete-or-die game of buying and selling.

In the popular career, self-help book *What Color Is Your Parachute?*, the twenty-second edition describes the environment of the new global economy of the 1990s. It is referred to as a "workquake" occurring below the surface of the marketplace. This book is a manual for helping people find that career niche where they can genuinely feel good about being all they can be at their jobs. *Parachute*'s author, Richard Bolles, says that the 1990s involved a "major and profound restructuring of the whole workplace." The restructuring included "downsizing everywhere, pessimism, more hours, lower paychecks, lower standard of living, more part-time work, and less job security" (Bolles 1994, 11).

More specifically, he says:

The consequence is that nobody's job is safe anymore. You may find yourself thrown out of work at any time, *due to another "workquake" aftershock.* Your firing or termination may be precipitated by: a "downsizing," or a "rightsizing," or a "restructuring," or by your employer going out of business, or by a personality conflict with your supervisor or boss, or by some form of prejudice: age discrimination, racial discrimination, sex discrimination, and the like. In many cases you can be laid-off or fired *totally without warning.* You are *out of there.* Also, with so many unemployed people, many employers have new and higher standards for employee performance, and if you don't measure up, there are plenty of others they can find to take your place. Even CEOs of large corporations—General Motors, IBM, etc.—can be suddenly out on the street, these days. (Bolles 1994, 12)

Of course, one of his key points is that companies are expecting a lot from their employees—"perform or else" is the bottom line. Surely, there is greater probability for a measure of security if one embraces productivist values and internalizes the performance principle. Ultimately, the best shot at security is to find that career niche, then go out there in the corporate world and insatiably develop yourself with the tandem goal of contributing to the company's self-development in the process. Harmonize your development with that of the company—this is what it means to have a career today!

BE ALL YOU CAN BE MEANS HAVE ALL YOU CAN HAVE—MAYBE

As the productivism-consumerism diagram (Figure 3.6) suggests, one of the payoffs for self-development in the economy is consumerism—have all you can have. One of the rewards for careerists is higher pay, even if it is not enhanced job security. In *U.S. News and World Report*, James Lardner wrote the feature article, "The Urge to Splurge" (Lardner 1999). His conclusion: "Since the 1970s, most of the income growth in the United States has gone to those who were already making the most. According to the Commerce Department, more than 8 million households have annual incomes over $100,000, and about half that number are estimated to have $1 million or more in assets. America can now lay claim to what conservative critic David Frum has aptly called 'history's first mass upper class'" (48). For example, the top 20 percent of the population accounted for 55 percent of new car purchases in 1996, while in 1980 they bought only 42 percent of the total. But everyone is going deeper into debt to emulate the rich, just as Thorstein Veblen argued in 1899. The Harvard economist Juliet Schor calls today's status-seeking, invidious consumerism a "national culture of upscale spending" (Schor 1998).

Lardner mentions the book *The Millionaire Next Door*, the 1996 best-seller by Thomas Stanley and William Danko. Stanley and Danko found that in the pre–New Economy period (post–World War II) the rich lived in reasonably modest houses. But today that's history. "To Stanley, the turn toward bigger cars and bigger houses represents a wave of 'hyperconsumption'—much of it, he argues, by 'under-accumulators' who are basing their financial decisions on 'the best year they've ever had'" (Lardner 1999, 51). As Federal Reserve chair Alan Greenspan and others have publicly stated, the longest expansion in the history of American capitalism, that is, the expansion that started in the mid-1980s and continues today, has been fueled by consumer debt and the "wealth effect"—the consumer buying spree due to the growth in paper wealth that many have experienced since the stock market boom started in the late 1980s.

Many Americans have gotten rich on the rise in stock values associated with the NASDAQ composite of high-tech companies. Feeling richer, they go on spending binges; that is, the "urge to splurge" has grabbed many of the newly rich. To the extent that many of these big spenders are, at the same time, yuppies who have also been focusing their Be All You Can Be self-development on their careers, they surely feel justified in having all they can have. Having more and being more went hand in hand in the American expansion of the 1990s. Productivism and consumerism continued to reinforce one another. This is today's Economy of the Insatiable Improvers. All of this is justified by assuring ourselves that it results from the drive for continuous improvement of life itself.

Yet as Scott Adams, creator of *Dilbert*, says, "If all the people who were buying things that have no utility whatsoever realized they have no utility, the economy would collapse" (Lardner 1999, 52). But this is not likely to happen. The product may not have direct use in our daily lives, as, more importantly, its utility is frequently found in the status that it either begets or helps to maintain. As Veblen said, much of the buying and the attachment to consumerist culture is driven not by our material needs but by our need for self- and social esteem. Because the need for esteem is always present and, in effect, insatiable, so is the consumption that results from it. But is it sustainable?

OTHER CAPITALISMS TODAY

Even casual observers of the global economy understand that the United States has what, in fact, is a unique version of capitalism, as the U.S. system has not only a 200-year history of reasonably stable representative democracy but one of the longest-standing laissez-faire economies. The extent to which the "protective response" (Polanyi) took hold in the U.S. is far less than in Europe and Asia. Therefore, outside the U.S. we see capitalist economies that have assured a much greater degree of security. For a variety of reasons in Europe and Asia, the disembedding of the economy from society was accompanied by a much stronger assertion by the people and businesses of their intuitive need for security. These efforts, which have frequently been directed at the state, are a reaction to the market's effort to make all incomes (wages and profits), employment, and basic material security determined by the competitive and impersonal forces of supply and demand. Everyone's security is a function of being able to sell goods or labor in markets on a steady and determinable basis.

The protective response is the grassroots, felt-need reaction of those stuck in the precarious position of having to meet their basic needs by selling things in markets that they don't directly control. They try to get control by forming unions, cartels, trade organizations, and industrial lobbying associations and finally by going to their respective governments to ask or demand legislation that will give them a measure of protection from "market vagaries." There are essentially two ways to deal with the insecurity that comes from the market-driven process: (1) work individually to "earn" (achieve) it, that is, the U.S. case, or (2) organize and use the state as a way to "assure" it, that is, the European and Asian case. If you look at Figure 5.2—the Mixed Economy Matrix—the differences in these approaches to security are more visible. Also, the matrix title, the Mixed Economy, is typical economics textbook language for most twentieth-century capitalisms in which there is a mix of public and private ownership, a mix of market and planning, and a mix of profit and non-profit industries. But it has to be noted that the approach of "earning" security in the

U.S. has not been a failure, and neither has the "assuring" of security in Europe and Asia.

We tend to think in the U.S. that people need insecurity to be motivated and that without the fear of economic hardship and the lure of getting rich, nothing gets done. Yet these economies elsewhere in the world are interesting counterexamples. We also tend to think that institutionalized insecurity creates a greater dynamism for both individual and social improvement. Compared to what preceded capitalism, this is true. But in looking at the European and Asian cases, it is also clear that a measure of assured security has not been an observable disincentive on their individual and social development. They, too, have been successful at actualizing their insatiable potential in the last 200 years. The Culture of Insatiable Freedom does prevail in these economies, too. They are also driven by the desire to have all they can have and be all they can be. But their capitalist economies have evolved differently than in the U.S. What does the matrix suggest?

Figure 5.2
The Mixed Economy Matrix

	Government	Business	Labor
Japan	Industrial Policy MITI	Keiretsu Conglomerates Zaibatsu J-Management	Corporate-Sponsored Employment Security
France	Dirigiste Colbertism Statism = State Ownership Nationalizations Indicative Planning Welfare State Industrial Policy	Government-Sponsored Protectionism	Autogestion Strong Radical Unions Unions = CP + SP
Sweden	Government-Sponsored Welfare State Strong Social Safety Net	SAF and LO Negotiate Contracts Nationwide Collective Bargaining	Social Democrats = Unions Solidaristic Wages Meidner Plan
Germany	Welfare State Social Democracy	Social Market Economy	Codetermination Unions and Factory Councils Social Democrats

The four nations listed on the left are all successful capitalisms that have followed, although not necessarily intentionally, an approach of "assuring" significant security. The three main sectors of their economies are listed in the columns to the right: *government, business,* and *labor.* The policies, agreements, and other economic features that distinguish their systems are stated in the middle of the matrix. All of the items in the matrix not only have something to do with how they differ from the U.S. model but, more importantly, indicate a feature that addresses the assurances of security.

If we start with Japan, under *government* you see industrial policy and MITI. The Ministry of International Trade and Industry (MITI) is the main vehicle of Japan's industrial policy (Rosser and Rosser 1996, 139). Industrial policy is, loosely, an arrangement between government and the various industrial firms that involves working together and collaboration not only between the government and business but among firms in various related industries as well. Its purpose is to "plan," that is, "strategize" for a smoother and more stable economic future. Industrial policy is not at all like the material balance planning of the Soviet experience, but it is used to bring economic players together to move forward in unison. It has been successful, yet there has never been a similar U.S. experience, except for the National Industrial Recovery Act, passed during Roosevelt's first term in office in 1933 but later declared unconstitutional (1935). "Working together," that is, cooperation among firms and the government, is an indicator of Japan's recognition of protection and security afforded to the big producers. In the U.S. security can be earned through competitive success, while in the Japanese model security can be assured through cooperation.

Under *business,* Japan is characterized by giant conglomerates known as *keiretsu* and *zaibatsu.* These organizations not only are big but involve interlocking directorates, cross-holding of stocks, and vertical and horizontal collaboration and cooperation between subsidiaries and branches. This, too, is unlike anything in the U.S. experience and is a measure of security considerations in Japanese business culture. The *keiretsu* and *zaibatsu* would be considered trade restraint under Federal Trade Commission (FTC) legislation. Even the J-management style in Japan refers to "joint" management between workers and managers and among various units within a given firm. The U.S. style is referred to as H-management, that is, hierarchical management in which decision-making control is more top-down, frequently more alienating for workers, less democratic, and more competitive and involves more supervisory labor than in Japan.

Under *labor* we have corporate-sponsored employment security. The Japanese model involves a minimal role for government implementation and administration of a "welfare state," but corporations have taken up the slack. It is a corporate paternalist model in which the firm has provided a measure of security for workers in lieu of the state. Lifetime employment, although under attack and involving only about half of the workforce, is still an observable indicator of corporate-created protectionism and paternalism. It is clearly not anything like the U.S. experience. But it has worked because it has increased loyalty by and for workers. There have been few strikes in the Japanese post–World War II period, yet it also has to be admitted that the corporate paternalist ethic has preempted not only strikes but militant unionism as well.

Under France and *government*, a list of terms (dirigiste, Colbertism, and statism = state ownership) speaks to the extent of government involvement in the French economy. Its history as a capitalist system since the end of the French Revolution suggests that there has been a climate of legitimacy for government ownership and government direction that is unheard of in the U.S. model. Why? In part, because the French government has been seen as a stabilizer and protector of security for both business and workers. It has had a stronger welfare state than in the U.S. and, like the Japanese, has had variations of industrial policy. The French have been known for "indicative planning," too. Again, this shares some commonality with the Japanese system and is not like the Soviet planning experience. Indicative planning is used to collaboratively indicate future goals and expectations for businesses and means that they work together to help "secure" their collective future. It has not been done in the U.S., except to a certain degree during World War II.

Under *business* we see government-sponsored protectionism. In the French experience the government has assured far more security for big firms than in the U.S. Businesses in the post–World War II period have frequently been subsidized when their revenues don't cover costs. Under *labor* there is autogestion, strong radical unions, and unions = CP + SP. Over the last two centuries in France there has never been the kind of culturally based harmony between workers and employers that is common in Japan. *Autogestion* was a key demand made by French unionists during the radical, 1968 nationwide demonstrations and general strikes. It hasn't been implemented in a fully coherent manner, but the demand, the interest, and the significance placed on this by workers and their unions indicate yet again something much different than in the U.S. Autogestion is really about worker self-management and the desire to democratize company decision making. It involves giving workers a greater say on the job, has been at various times a bargaining issue for the nation's strong radical unions, and represents a link between the unions and the Communist Party (CP) and Socialist Party (SP) (Unions = CP + SP), at least as they influenced unions before the 1980s. The connections between leftist political parties and unions are not common to the U.S. experience except to a limited extent during the depression of the 1930s. But with the passage of the Taft-Hartley Act in 1947 and the upshot of the McCarthy red scare in the early 1950s, the link between radical political parties and unions was severed in the U.S. The role of unions in the French economy not only has been greater and more radical than in the U.S. but has been motivated by, and indicates a measure of, the security that informs French work life.

Sweden is another example of the protective response in Europe. Under *government*, you see government-sponsored welfare state and strong social safety net. The Swedish have had less government ownership and government direction of the economy than the French. They have had little industrial policy, unlike the Japanese and French, but the government has played, in part through their strong unions, a major role in financing their welfare state and safety net. Rather than being a planner, owner, or director of the Swedish economy, the government has been a spender to assure security concerns. Although this makes for high taxes, as we often hear, the Swedes have had the attitude that, like buying a consumer product in the U.S., if you pay money and get something in return, then it's all right. Yet over the last twenty years, the Swedish model has been under attack by both the competitive requirements of globalization and Swedish citizens who don't want to pay the taxes. But their model has been successful since the 1940s. Under *business* it says SAF and LO negotiate contracts and nationwide collective bargaining. The SAF is the business organization that bargains on a national level with the LO, the Swedish labor federation. This practice has been in place since 1938 yet is something unheard of in U.S. experience. Sixty percent of Sweden's workers participate in this process, and it would be like the American Federation of Labor/Congress of Industrial Organizations (AFL-CIO) negotiating wages with the U.S. Chamber of Commerce or the Business Roundtable, if such organizations were ever to represent U.S. firms. It makes for more "solidaristic wages," as stated under *labor*. Of course, the point of this is to reduce wage disparities within and across the nation's industries. It reduces competition between workers and assures a greater level of security than otherwise. The Swedish Social Democratic Party (SAP) was formed in 1889 and not only has been the leading political party since World War II but has strong ties to the unions. In U.S. terms, this would be like the Democratic Party's becoming a party of organized labor while at the same time having most American workers join unions and vote Democrat. The closest that the U.S. ever came to this was the brief period during the second New Deal administration between 1936 and 1940. Also we should mention the Meidner Plan, because it represents a proposal, still not fully implemented, that would gradually allow workers to *collectively* own most Swedish firms. Under this proposal, a portion of profits is used each year to buy back company stocks for worker ownership. Unlike individual ESOPs (employee stock ownership plans) in the U.S., the Meidner Plan would turn over ownership to the workers as a whole so that decision making would eventually be more democratic. This is clearly more socialistic than anything in the U.S. but suggests another way in which workers can obtain more "assured" security.

Finally, the matrix describes Germany's system. We have under *government*, the welfare state and social democracy, and under *business*, social market economy. This means that, like many of the other Western European nations, Germany has had an experience of governance by the social democrats, whose politics have been generally leftist, and with this there have been a greater role for unions and a strengthening of the welfare state. All of this has given workers greater protection from the vagaries of impersonal market forces of supply and demand. The market in Germany has been influenced by social forces. Under *labor* you see codetermination, unions and factory councils, and social democrats. Codetermination is a German term for giving workers, through their unions and independent factory (shop-floor) councils, a greater say in determining workplace policies along with management. Again, this has been enhanced by the fact that the German unions have close ties to the Social Democratic Party. Codetermination is similar to autogestion in that both are designed to forge a closer and more cooperative link between labor and management. The intent, if not the result, is to move the economy over the long haul closer to a cooperative, rather than competitive, system. By doing so, there is greater "assured" security, as this makes for a less adversarial model.

If the European Union (EU) continues to have harmonizing and unifying effects, the possibilities for security are even greater. One of the purposes of the EU, as a nested series of agreements between nations, is to provide a climate of stability, fairness, and, eventually, security. It is well intentioned but must come to terms with the security–freedom trade-off if it is to have lasting benefits. In general, the matrix suggests that many of the successful capitalisms have been so either because of, or even despite, the "assuring" security approach. We have to appreciate this.

Yet as the last two decades have borne witness, the globalization process has brought the welfare state and the social democratic commitment to security under attack. Many nations have been forced to reduce their spending on the welfare state, job security, and other pro-worker policies because of the corporate threat that anything leading to higher costs will harm their competitive position in the global arena. This corporate logic has had significant effects in Europe and the United States, and the threat is very real, indeed. William Greider says that the competitive struggle that leads all nations in a downward wage and environmental spiral is a result of the fact that "the chase must continue because there is no finish line. The competitive imperative is sure to intensify not only for the Americans and for the Germans but also for the Japanese" (Greider 1997, 111). This notwithstanding, a future Culture of Security and economy based upon the Satiable Self can draw on these kinds of security-based capitalist reforms and policies already experienced in capitalisms outside the U.S. *A sustainable economy is one that assures security*. We can look to these successful experiences that are available today in building it.

THE TRANSITION ECONOMIES

What about Russia, the former Eastern European economies, and China? Their experience with security, relative to the mixed economies that we've examined, is different. The disembedding process is now under way. They have been embedded economies since the Soviet model was implemented almost a century ago. These populations are in the midst of having their first taste of insatiable freedom but are struggling with the sacrifice of security. They are now into a decade of anguish over the trade-off of security for freedom. This loss of security that was a vital dimension of the Soviet system is now being reevaluated. The freedom is great, many are getting rich because of it, the inequality is growing, and the majority is questioning whether the newfound freedom is worth the sacrifice of security.

In general, these former Soviet states are undergoing in a couple of decades what took well over 100 years in the older capitalist nations. No one ever said that capitalism comes easily. These new transition economies are struggling with the disembedding process not only very quickly but also in the midst of the broader globalization of capitalism taking place around them. This makes their situation even more difficult. Additionally, there are no historical precedent and no blueprint for the transition from a planned industrial economy to a market economy. So they have several strikes against them in the transition: they are going about it fast, at a bad time, and without a map. For the existing capitalist nations and corporations, which have some experience with the market, the globalization process is scary enough. Imagine what it is like for those with no experience with either capitalism or its globalized form. One thing is for sure, however: the appreciation for security is heightened by all of this.

Their story starts with the Bolshevik Revolution, because this earlier transition was informed by what were perceived as major drawbacks with capitalism, that is, the capitalism of the nineteenth century. In many respects, the socialist revolutions a century ago were knee-jerk reactions to some fundamental problems with capitalism revealed by Marx: (1) its exploitative character and (2) its cyclical volatility.

Marx's criticism focused on the fact that if one group of people owns all of the means of production, then everyone else becomes unequally dependent upon this class of business owners, the capitalists. In other words, "you don't get a job, unless they find it profitable to hire you." That makes the workers' security dependent upon the profit interests of the business class. When it comes to a showdown, it is true that capitalists need workers and are dependent upon the working class, just as the workers are dependent upon the capitalists. But Marx essentially said that workers have one thing to rely on—their labor—while capitalists have two things—their labor and their capital. Who is likely to hold out longer in a showdown, a strike? Naturally, the class with the greater wealth. So the point is not that workers are dependent upon capitalists but that they are *unequally* dependent. What happens next? The property-owning class can take advantage of the workers and not only alienate them by controlling the production process but make them work longer than they would otherwise have to. This is the exploitative part of Marx's critique.

But another problem that Marx had with capitalism is the fact that it is totally unplanned, what he called the "anarchy of capitalist production." Who will have a job next year? Will there be enough demand to buy all of my business' supply at profitable prices? Will wages fall or rise next season? Will we be in a recession or depression soon? In capitalism, as we know, there are no answers to these questions beyond the logic of "trust in the market, in the invisible hand, and all will be well." The business cycle has been endemic to capitalism and has caused the anguish of economic hardship, insecurity, and unemployment, affecting the lives of workers and capitalists alike. The invisible hand that Adam Smith trusted has not eliminated the cyclical movements of capitalism, nor has the neo-classical theory that all cyclical movements can be ameliorated, if not eliminated, by competition and the self-correcting mechanisms of flexible wages, prices, and interest rates.

Cyclical volatility and the unequal dependency factor contribute to the insecurity that drives capitalism. So if one were to create an alternative to capitalism that would overcome this insecurity, what would an activist, influenced by Marx, logically come up with? First, eliminate the private property dimension of capitalism that allows one group legally to own all of the property at the expense of the majority. Therefore, statize or nationalize the means of production in the name of everyone in general so that no one group can monopolize it. Second, plan the economy and resource allocation instead of relying on the impersonal forces of the market. By planning the economy, you can effectively obviate the business cycle and the unemployment that results from it.

Thus, Lenin and the Bolsheviks were predisposed to a form of socialism that involved, for logical reasons, state ownership and central planning. It didn't happen right away, of course, and took Stalin's authority to be implemented in the 1930s over the protest of many peasants and workers alike. But what became known as the Soviet model is essentially a reaction to the insecurity that stems from the disembedding of the economy from society, just as Polanyi maintained. The point is to understand that this effort to have industrialization without market insecurity is unprecedented as well. There are two generalizations to make. One is that security has been a truly pivotal piece for the legitimation of the Soviet model. The provisioning of jobs, the fact that there was a "full-employment" economy in the Soviet Union before 1990, and the fact that one couldn't really be fired and that basic education, housing, and health care were assured made it a livable system for most of the Soviet population. It lacked freedom but provided security. It may have been the "security of the barracks," but it was the type of security that existed in precapitalist societies and within the earlier Culture of Security—people were taken care of by the state and the party. Prisons provide this kind of security, of course. The state and the party were paternalistic in this way. To some it was a prison.

The second generalization is that the sovietizing of these economies is essentially a "reembedding" of economy into society. The Soviet model is a reembedded economy. There is little personal and individual freedom; one doesn't have the freedom to Be All You Can Be, although by playing the political game, many were afforded opportunities to self-develop—to be professionals in various occupations. This was self-development that, rather than being compelled by the insecurity of the market—that is, "you're on your own, pal"—was compelled by obligation, command, and the desire to avoid being a redundant wage-worker for the state. Therefore, the Soviet economy is an embedded economy that shares more with all of the precapitalist systems (feudalism and slavery) than with the modern market system. In fact, some have called it "industrial feudalism." But it spoke to the basic need for security that people have continued to value since the sixteenth century. It is security that gave this system any energy and life at all. But also like capitalism, it was based upon alienated labor. Instead of working for profit-maximizing capitalists, workers in the Soviet economy worked for the "output-maximizing" state—both systems of alienated labor are also driven by the desire to have all you can have. Both have been "driven" systems based upon insatiable growth and the logic of "more is better."

One fundamental difference between capitalism and the Soviet model concerns the insatiable desire to Be All You Can Be. Capitalism, as it emerged, also transformed the cultural terrain from that of Security to that of Insatiable Freedom. The disembedding effect of marketization made insecurity the driving force, so with capitalism people had the *freedom from* state and cultural restraints accompanied by the *freedom to* pursue economic gain. This has given capitalism a "drivenness" and dynamism that were lacking in the Soviet model. For example, the individual enterprises in the Soviet planning system were extremely risk-averse, because if they experimented with new technologies, they might have jeopardized their directive to "fulfill the plan." They were not driven by the imperative to Be All You Can Be but by the "command" to "fulfill the plan."

Stated differently, the lack of dynamism in the Soviet model is partly a function of the prevailing culture. Their system, as output-maximizing and growth-oriented as it was, existed within the old Culture of Security, not within the capitalist Culture of Insatiable Freedom. Besides this, it was very undemocratic. Because authoritarian security is what kept this system together and gave it any coherence at all, their efforts to motivate work or improve performance were obstructed. To try to grow your way past capitalism and create a middle-class standard of living worth emulating on the basis of a very undemocratic Culture of Security is not possible. In other words, it's hard to capitalize on people's ability to actualize unlimited potential when they are constrained by both the Culture of Security and authoritarianism. The Soviet population eventually came to realize that what they wanted was the capitalist freedom to get rich. The Soviet citizenship witnessed the West's observable success at having it all on the basis of being it all. Yet they watched this from the outside, from behind the barracks walls, and increasingly became aware of the fact that their embedded economy and Culture of Security were the obstacles.

The point is that it is improbable that people can have all they can have without being able to be all they can be, and it is hard to Be All You Can Be within the parameters and confines of the Culture of Security. If the Soviet population was going to pursue have all you can have, they had to have the freedom to Be All You Can Be. For this to happen, the totality of the system and its security culture had to go. Thus, we get the dismantling of the old and the leap into the new. Once folks in this part of the world saw their security leave and yet hadn't been able to operationalize their potential to be more and to insatiably self-develop, they were caught without assured security and without having "gotten ahead." Some entrepreneurs, mostly escapees from the older bureaucratic planning class, have been able to get ahead and capitalize on their new freedom to be more. As we often hear, corruption was endemic to the old system and has been instrumental in the new one.

What the transition is leading to is not so much either the social democratic, mixed economy of Western Europe or the laissez-faire system of the U.S. but a hybrid form of capitalism that we might label Mafia Capitalism. It's not fascist; it has certain features of immature representative government, but it's not fully functional. If the former Soviet populations understood that what they are dealing with is the historical trade-off between freedom and security, it would help clarify the predicament, and this may happen, considering the fact that the transition in the former Soviet Union has seen industrial production fall by 50 percent in the last decade (Hertsgaard 1998, 151). But we can't lump all these economies together and make blanket generalizations. Poland, the Czech Republic, Hungary—these nations have begun this debate to some extent. But most do continue to embrace the norms of having it all and Be All You Can Be. Their concern is more about how to get more and be more than on finding that mix of freedom and security that will maximize human and environmental sustainability. The paradigm of sustainability has not surfaced in the arena of public debate at this point.

Then there is China. Surely one of the most penetrating analyses of this country is that by Mark Hertsgaard in *Earth Odyssey* (1998). Imagine, he says, a country the size of the continental U.S. in which all of the people west of the Mississippi move east of it. Then take this population all living in the East and multiply it by five. That's China. The western half of it is largely unpopulated, while the east is congested to a degree that most Americans don't want to imagine. Now take this population, give them some incentives to get rich ("to get rich is glorious," said Deng Xiaoping), and suggest that to emulate the West is best. To Hertsgaard, what you get is the most congested and polluted place on the planet. China combines two enormous problems: the world's largest population that historically has been very poor and a new, market-driven pattern of mass consumerism. Lots of people consuming lots of goods. As Hertsgaard says, it's an "environmental superpower in reverse" (223). The world cannot sustain a standard of living in China that matches that of the West, yet at this point the Chinese are committed to just that. The Three-Gorges Dam project on the Yangtze River is the biggest construction project ever undertaken by humankind! It is the icon for the Chinese insatiable desire to have all you can have. Their effort brings to mind Gandhi's remark that if it took the British the whole planet to create their standard of living, how many planets would be required for India? Now we can add China's 1.2 billion people to India's 900 million and estimate the results on the earth's carrying capacity, the recuperative powers of the biosphere, and the sustainability of the rest of humankind. It's a dark prospect, of course.

It's apparent that there are many people in the world for whom have all you can have is *the* operative phrase, and if it takes being all you can be to achieve this, then they are prepared to undertake both. But the Chinese post-Mao experience is very different from what we've said about the former Soviet Union and Central/Eastern Europe. The Communist Party still directs the Chinese economy, and the planning system has not been completely dismantled. They have not chucked the principle of security, they have not transitioned to any form of representative democracy, and they have not done their marketization reforms uncritically, unthinkingly, and hastily. This suggests that the Chinese watched the "all or nothing" or "all at once" approach of the Soviets and said, "No thanks."

The Soviet Union reached an impasse in which economic reforms without political reforms were ineffective. Gorbachev knew this and wanted to slow down the process. But he couldn't. The Chinese, on the other hand, have been extremely successful at maximizing their mileage with economic reforms without giving up the party's political control. So far they are able to have their cake and eat it, too. The Chinese leadership has been sensitized to what happened in the former Soviet Union and doesn't want the anarchic effects of the post-1990 Russian experience to occur in China, where 1.2 billion people's lives are at stake. A Russian-style transition on a Chinese scale would be unthinkable. We should appreciate this awareness on the part of their leadership. Yet to compensate for the lack of political reform, the economic magnitude of the marketization reforms could undermine global sustainability, and after the government's crackdown message with Tiananmen Square in 1989, the political–economic trade-off is clear. The party conveys in no uncertain terms that in return for accepting its monopolization on political representation, the people are free to make all of the economic gains that they can. To the extent that this works, the people can forge ahead with have all you can have while sacrificing political democracy. If the leadership can continue to grow the economy and if the standard of living continuously rises, then the party's legitimation is stabilized. If environmental, resource, or other political constraints interfere with economic growth, the stability of the world's largest nation is threatened.

There is a disembedding process going on in China, however. What is happening is that a separate economic sphere is being allowed to emerge very carefully under the watchful eye of the party. The profit incentives and privatization in agriculture have been largely successful. The Chinese leadership initiated the town and village enterprises (TVEs), which are something like rural cooperatives, run and managed by the farmers for their own profit. There is also the success of the Household Responsibility System in agriculture after 1978. The reforms are significant and have led to China's remarkable growth rates over the last twenty years. China has had about the highest gross domestic product (GDP) growth rates in the world since the mid-1980s (Rosser and Rosser 1996, 373–381). The Chinese economy is now the seventh largest in the world, and incomes there have doubled since 1979, yet five of the ten most polluted cities in the world are in China (Hertsgaard 1998, 5). As long as the people are content with their efforts to have all you can have, then it works. As Greider says, "Commerce became an island of freedom within a land of stern control and suppressed politics" (Greider 1997, 157). There is an element of freedom to pursue economic gain that has also been significant for the special economic zones (SEZs), enclaves of capitalism begun in certain cities along the southeast coast after 1979. Also Hertsgaard says of Hong Kong that if mainland

China wanted the capitalist experience, then Hong Kong was it in its "most insatiable consumeristic variety" (Hertsgaard 1998, 234).

China has not allowed itself to go the way of the former Soviet Union. The disembedding is partial; the shift from security to freedom as a cultural norm is partial, as well. But the growth is substantial, the inequality is worsening by the year, and the environment is drifting toward overuse, serious degradation, and ultimately threatening a meltdown. Here are a few examples of what the rest of world needs to consider (we say "the rest of the world" because, if things are going to change, redistribution from the advanced capitalist nations to China and other Third World nations is a must):

- Approximately 75 percent of Beijing's air pollution is caused by coal burning.
- Coal accounts for 75 percent of China's energy use.
- 100 million peasants still live without electricity.
- Only 7 percent of households had refrigerators in 1985, but now 62 percent have them.
- China is now the world's largest refrigerator producer.
- Acid rain affects 20 percent of the land and causes $5 billion in damage each year.
- China is responsible for 50 percent of Japan's acid rain problem and 80 percent of South Korea's.
- Only 4.5 percent of China's sewage is treated, as most is dumped directly into its rivers.
- Eighty percent of China's rivers are so polluted that they no longer support fish.
- In Hong Kong, Victoria Harbor receives 1.7 million tons of raw sewage per day, with 70 percent of it untreated.
- Only 20 percent of China's coal gets washed.
- Water and air pollution are killing more than 2 million Chinese each year.
- Suburban sprawl and erosion have eliminated 35 million hectares of farmland since 1950 (which equals all of the farmland combined in Germany, France, and the U.K.!).
- China plans to build more than 100 new power stations during the next decade, adding 18,000 megawatts of capacity every year (approximately equal to the entire state of Louisiana's power grid).
- China's coal production is projected to double, if not triple, by 2020 (see Hertsgaard 1998, 156–188, 221–259).

Of course, these few statistics don't, and shouldn't be expected to, present the full picture of what the world must confront with China's growth and the impending environmental crisis. Right now the Chinese people are more into growth and consumerism than into the environment. Hertsgaard interviewed Ma Zhong, the director of the Institute of Environmental Economics at Renmin University. During this conversation, Ma mentioned that an average Chinese citizen was asked on television what his number one dream was. He said, "Money." His number two dream? Also, "Money!" Then Ma remarked that in order for outside environmentalists to get anywhere with Chinese policy, they need to understand this economic mentality first (Hertsgaard 1998, 179–180).

On the other hand, if China installed the latest and the best of alternative methods and equipment, they could actually cut their energy consumption by 40–50 percent (Hertsgaard 1998, 184). Ultimately, if the world cares about what happens as a result of China's population growth and economic growth, then here is an excellent opportunity to help through programs of redistribution. Perhaps the other, more affluent nations might consider funding programs to help China shift to alternative energy sources and to produce with cleaner and greener technologies. It's possible that the global community might offer the Chinese a deal: if you foster and promote the democratization of both your economy and your polity, we will help you in the transition to a more sustainable culture. So China is a transition economy with problems that are vastly different from what they hope to avoid by examining their Russian neighbors. Yet they, too, are embracing the Culture of Insatiable Freedom and turning away from that of Security. They, too, are being driven more and more by have all you can have. The global capitalist system driven by Be All You Can Be and Insatiable Improvement has swamped both the former Soviet Union and China.

Lastly, what about the remainder of the world, particularly Africa and Latin America? Africa is often called a basket case. It is the poorest continent in the world. There are almost 800 million people on this continent, and its problems are very much different from those of both China and the former Soviet Union. Africa's problems are not about the consequences of rapid growth, rapid marketization, and economic transition. Like China, Africa faces an environmental crisis. Unlike China, it is not due to rapid growth but the overuse that results from no growth, that is, that results from abject poverty.

Consider these facts:

- One out of every eleven African children dies before his or her first birthday (Hertsgaard 1998, 21).
- One out of every seven children alive at one year dies before the age of five (Hertsgaard 1998, 76).
- According to the United Nations' (UN) Food and Agriculture Organization (FAO), the number of chronically malnourished people in sub-Saharan Africa increased from 96 million in 1970 to over 200 million by the early 1990s (Hertsgaard 1998, 25).
- Sub-Saharan Africa's debt nearly doubled in less than a decade, from $210 billion in 1984, to $352 billion by 1991 (Greider 1997, 283).
- The yearly $12 billion that Africa pays in debt service to Western banks would cover the immediate food, health, education, and family planning needs for the entire continent (Hertsgaard 1998, 26).
- Forty-two million Africans are likely to die from starvation in the next year (Hertsgaard 1998, 25).

- In Sudan the civil war has left 1.5 million dead, while 85 percent of the southern inhabitants are now refugees (Hertsgaard 1998, 45).
- Twenty-seven of the sixty-one low-income ($785 per capita income or less) nations in the world are in Africa (Schnitzer 2000, 313).
- Thirty-two of the forty-four UN "low human development" nations are in Africa (Schnitzer 2000, 313).
- The lowest fifteen of the forty-four UN "low human development" nations are in Africa (Schnitzer 2000, 313).
- Africa has the lowest life expectancy of any continent (Schnitzer 2000, 313).
- Africa's literacy rate is less than 50 percent (Schnitzer 2000, 313).
- Eighteen of the African nations had negative growth rates between 1980 and 1997 (Schnitzer 2000, 313).
- Population growth rates are the highest in the world (Schnitzer 2000, 313).

The statistics are, of course, overwhelming. The only outlier in the otherwise gloomy African scene is Botswana. Just ahead of China, it had the highest growth rates in the world between 1980 and 1992. Why? Diamonds, the De Beers company, and a fairly honest government. But Botswana is an anomaly in Africa (Rosser and Rosser 1996, 471). Africa will be the biggest challenge for poverty-driven environmental crisis, while China will be the biggest challenge for growth-driven environmental crisis. Between the two, we are looking at over a third of the world's population of 6 billion. Yet, it will be much harder for the haves of the world to ignore China than it will be to ignore Africa.

Latin America is somewhere in the middle. There are twenty-eight nations in this region. Except for Brazil (and a few others), all of them are former colonies of Spain. The economic gains that these nations made in the 1960s were largely canceled out in the debt-burdened performance of the 1980s, so much so that for most of them, the 1980s were negative growth years (Schnitzer 2000, 292). Also, "Income inequality is greater in Latin America than in other areas of the world. Incomes received by the top 10 percent are 50 times greater than incomes received by the bottom 10 percent. In the United States it is 19 times; and in Sweden it is 5.5 times" (Schnitzer 2000, 294). What about poverty? It is clearly less than in Africa and Southeast Asia, but it has been, in part, aggravated by the out-migration of peasants from the rural to the urbanized cities. "In Chile, which is one of the richer nations of Latin America, 38.5 percent of the population live on less than $2 a day. One of the poorest countries in Latin America is Guatemala, where 77 percent of the population lives on less than $2 a day" (Schnitzer 2000, 295). Additionally, as Hertsgaard points out, the infant mortality rate in Brazil, typical of Latin American nations, is actually *five* times higher than that of the average industrial nation (Hertsgaard 1998, 195).

There is no end to the alarming statistics that we can assemble to describe the Third World nations today. We often talk about them as the "developing" nations, but the case of Africa contradicts the notion of "developing." In the broader scope of the Culture of Insatiable Freedom we have to admit that, for example, the migration to the cities, a phenomenon occurring worldwide, is driven by the prospect of "having more" and "being more." The have-nots of the world today, for the most part, have been influenced by the global economy, and this is the Economy of Insatiable Improvers. What motivates the have-nots, like the haves, is the desire to improve. Their migration both to cities and around the world is driven by improvement. Yet as the World Bank's *World Development Report* states, this doesn't necessarily happen, and naturally the exception is Africa. "Between 1970 and 1995 the average African country's urban population grew by 4.7 percent annually, while its per capita GDP dropped by 0.7 percent a year" (World Bank 2000, 130). Still, the drive is there, and these folks are desperate yet also motivated by a legitimate urge to end their suffering.

The two most pressing problems that pose the biggest challenges for global sustainability are inequality and the environment. We have traced our human odyssey from the Culture of Security and the Satiable Self to our present predicament, precipitated by our dominant Culture of Insatiable Freedom and the insatiable self. We have evolved during the course of the last 400 years to an Economy of Insatiable Improvers bent on the unthinking commitment to improve, develop, actualize, and realize our unlimited potential always to be more and have more. If we examine the world around us (see, e.g., the Worldwatch Institute's annual *State of the World*), human inequality and what this is doing to the carrying capacity of the earth are glaring contradictions to sustainability.

Even the World Bank says that "the broad picture of development outcomes is worrisome." With respect to growing inequality, it adds that:

the average per capita income of the poorest and middle thirds of all countries has lost ground steadily over the last several decades compared with the average income of the richest third. Average per capita GDP of the middle third has dropped from 12.5 to 11.4 percent of the richest third and that of the poorest third from 3.1 to 1.9 percent. In fact, rich countries have been growing faster than poor countries since the Industrial Revolution in the mid-19th century. A recent estimate suggests that the ratio of per capita income between the richest and the poorest countries increased sixfold between 1870 and 1985. (World Bank 2000, 14)

Schnitzer adds that "not only in the United States, but elsewhere, the rich of the world are getting richer, and the poor of the world are getting poorer. In 1960 the 20 percent of the world's population who lived in the rich countries had 30 times the income of the poorest 20 percent of the people. By 1980 the ratio between the richest 20 percent and poorest 20 percent had increased to 45 to 1, and by 1995 the ratio between the richest 20 percent and poorest 20 percent was 82 to 1. It is estimated that the world's 225 richest people have a combined wealth of over $1 trillion, equal to the annual income of the poorest 47 percent of the world's population" (Schnitzer 2000, 370; see also United Nations Development Program, *Human Development Report 1998*). The one fact that we have to admit is that economic growth is not eliminating the divide. The have nations of the world and their privileged classes, since the birth of capitalism and the imperative of Be All You Can Be and have all you can have, have always said to the poor that capitalist-driven economic growth will solve the have-nots' problem. This has not worked.

Not only is the world becoming more unequal, but the grinding poverty that defines the bottom is not being lifted. For example, in Latin America the proportion of people living on less than one dollar per day (a frequently used poverty statistic) rose from 22 percent to 23.5 percent between 1987 and 1993. In Africa it went from 38.5 percent to 39.1 percent, that is, from 180 million to 219 million people. Even in Europe and Central Asia those living on less than one dollar per day increased from 2 to 15 million, mostly as a result of the failure of the capitalist transition to provide security. In South Asia, the number of poor increased from 480 million to 515 million (World Bank 2000, 25). "With the recent East Asia crisis," reports the World Bank, "poverty rates have risen again, even in this successful developing region. If the poverty level is set at $2 per day, Thailand is projected to see poverty increase by 19.7 percent between 1997 and 2000" (World Bank 2000, 25). Every day 11,000 children die of starvation, while in the Third World as a whole, 40 percent of the people live in absolute poverty. The UN's FAO says that 841 million people (about one-fifth of global population) are malnourished, that is, constantly hungry (Hertsgaard 1998, 46). The bottom line is that global poverty is not being eliminated and that the gap between the haves and the have-nots continues to widen. We would be foolish to say that global capitalism's drivenness and its insatiable dynamic of "more is better" are solving the problem.

What about the environment? It is, as one would expect, worsening. David Orr begins his book *Ecological Literacy* (1992) with the following: "If today is a typical day on planet earth, humans will add fifteen million tons of carbon to the atmosphere, destroy 115 square miles of tropical rainforest, create seventy-two square miles of desert, eliminate between forty to one hundred species, erode seventy-one million tons of topsoil, add twenty-seven hundred tons of CFCs [chlorofluorocarbons] to the stratosphere, and increase their population by 263,000" (Orr 1992, 3). Not only was this an ugly picture when he painted it in the early 1990s; but it has gotten only uglier. The production of man-made chemicals, for example, increased 350 times between 1940 and 1982, and the U.S. alone produced 435 billion pounds of them in 1992 (Hertsgaard 1998, 8–9).

What about global warming? Carbon dioxide concentrations in the air have increased 50 percent since the Industrial Revolution. Carbon emissions are increasing 1 percent per year, so that by 2100 there will be twice as much in the air as before the Industrial Revolution (Hertsgaard 1998, 11–12). Carbon dioxide emissions are up 30 percent since the beginning of the nineteenth century, yet they were stable for the previous 2 million years. After reporting these simple statistics, Hertsgaard adds that "like the captain of an oceanliner who has to turn the helm miles ahead of where he actually intends the vessel to change course, humans will have to alter their environmental behavior years in advance of seeing much positive effect" (12).

For Hertsgaard and many other observers of the global environment, like the World Watch Institute, the car is one of the major causes of our atmospheric decay. Population has doubled since 1945, but cars have grown by ten times that amount. Cars and gasoline are the two biggest industries in the world, and in the U.S. the two biggest corporations have been GM and Exxon. What we created in the twentieth century and partly what made capitalism grow and prosper in the advanced world is "car capitalism." It's not likely that, in the current transition to the New Economy, cars will be any less significant for driving the system. They are a pivotal part of the Economy of Insatiable Improvers. Hertsgaard mentions that in Bangkok there are 500 cars and 700 motorbikes added to the streets each *day* (Hertsgaard 1998, 97). The rest of the world, in assimilating the have all you can have culture, wants more cars. They have facilitated our mobility for sure, therefore contributing to our Be All You Can Be actualization. Yet 80 percent of the cars are owned by the wealthiest 20 percent of the world's population (103). The distribution of cars reflects the distribution of income, in many respects.

The developing nations want to have more cars and everything else that demonstrates the "goods life." For example, in Thailand per capita income in 1991 was U.S. $1,570, which is six times higher than it was in 1971 (Hertsgaard 1998, 87). It has been considered a financial success, of course. But at what price? The Chao Phraya River, south of Bangkok, is virtually dead. The luxury hotels along the waterfront dump their raw sewage into it. There are no treatment plants here. Thailand's tree cover fell from 60 percent to 18 percent of total land area between 1950 and 1991. Forty-four days a year the Thai workforce sits in traffic jams while the CFC emissions in Thailand doubled between 1986 and 1989. With all of this exemplary growth, the income inequality worsened such that now the richest 10 percent have over half of all of the income, and Thailand now is among the top five in the world for worst income disparity. Lured by the have all you can have culture, a third of Bangkok's 6.5 million people are rural immigrants and squatters in its shantytowns. If they can get ahead, they do, like everywhere else. While in 1992 the average Bangkok commuter spent three hours a day in traffic, by 1996 it was up to five hours a day for total commuting time. Also for this average commuter, the commute absorbed 30 percent of his or her income (89). For most this is the price of insatiable improvement, and it is considered worth it.

But along with cars, congestion, and atmospheric stress, there are many other signs that the Economy of Insatiable Improvers is not working. Timber cutting, for example, is hard on the atmosphere as well. Global deforestation contributes to 25 percent of all carbon dioxide emissions, and we have now lost half of the earth's prehistoric forest cover. Also, about half of today's deforestation is caused by slash-and-burn agriculture. Then there's the water issue. Water use worldwide quadrupled between 1940 and 1990, with half of this increase due to higher per capita consumption and the other half due to population growth (Hertsgaard 1998, 212). As we know, the world's population doubled from 3 billion to 6 billion in this same half century.

To feed the continually growing population, the FAO estimates that food production will have to double again in the next thirty years as population continues to grow (Hertsgaard 1998, 213). Yet we are simultaneously losing 25 billion metric tons of topsoil a year.

So with the Culture of Insatiable Freedom spreading around the world and the assimilation of Be All You Can Be and have all you can have, inequality grows, and the environment deteriorates. It is hard not to draw the conclusion that *the trajectory of this driven world is in the wrong direction. Both the logic of insatiability and the insecurity that grounds it, as well as the competitive struggle that drives it, are not toward sustainability.* Insatiability—the uncritical acceptance of continuous improvement and the unthinking belief that to be human is to be always more—has to be rethought.

I use bumper stickers in all of my economics classes. There have been three, and each student gets one of these three stapled to his or her syllabus. They sum up the situation and look like this:

Bumper Stickers, Environmental

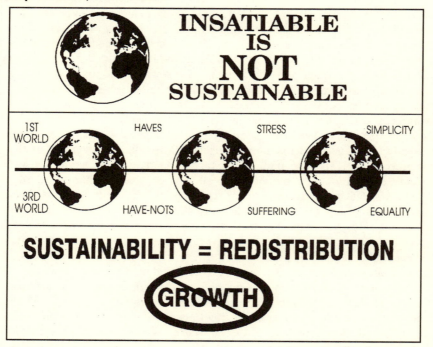

The first is obvious. It is the theme of this book. The second suggests that the world is increasingly divided among the haves and have-nots. The problem for the haves is "stress," having to live by the imperative of Be All You Can Be and to feel locked onto the productivism-consumerism treadmill in which one's compensation for the continuous self-development that this entails is have all you can have, that is, consumerism and the goods life. What's the solution for these folks? A life of greater simplicity. For the have-nots (mostly in the Southern Hemisphere) the problem is essentially suffering—economic deprivation and hardship. What does their solution involve? Global redistribution from the haves to the have-nots, from the North to the South, that is, equality in the world. The haves might support this if they buy into the simplicity and sustainability lifestyle. The redistribution of economic resources and political power, coupled with empowerment of the people, workers, peasants, women, and kids, will allow them to ameliorate their suffering through sustainable practices that offer an alternative to the Culture of Insatiable Freedom and, especially, have all you can have.

Finally, the last bumper sticker suggests that redistribution, rather than the old, but unworkable, remedy of economic growth, is the key to sustainability for humankind. The glaring problems of inequality and the environment are destroying the prospect for human sustainability. It should also be remembered that the industrial nations of the First World are about 20 percent of the global 6 billion population but account for 80 percent of resource use and an equivalent percentage of the world's pollution, for example, greenhouse gases and acid rain. The U.S. alone is only 6 percent of the total population but creates 30 percent of the world's pollution and uses 30 percent of its resources. In fact, in the last fifty years the U.S. has used more resources than all of humanity did in all of its previous history! Redistribution toward a more just and egalitarian world holds the answer. Bill McKibben mentions in his recent *Mother Jones* article on Gandhi that "the debate is pretty clear. Rich countries, and therefore rich people, need to use less fossil fuels, thereby costing themselves some money. And they will have to transfer money and technology to poor countries, to help them build alternative energy systems. If you have to take care of more people, and if endless growth is becoming less desirable—well, then, the problem might become how to share" (McKibben 1999, 71). We will have to put security, justice, sustainability, and equal participation ahead of insatiable improvement. To do this requires the building of a new culture. There are precedents for this, and the reforms to make it work have been used in a piecemeal fashion. To build a truly novel Culture of Sustainability, we can return to the Satiable Self that Aristotle advocated. We can commit to eliminating suffering rather than obsess over insatiable improvement. The two are very different.

PART THREE

Where Should We Go—
The Culture of Sustainability

Chapter 6

The Satiable Self:
Zorba Meets Gandhi

For cultural change of the magnitude that we've suggested, there needs to be both a clear vision and knowledge that it is possible. Such a vision cannot be a utopian pipedream. In what follows there are no proposed reforms that are particularly novel. We have heard about them; politicians and activists have debated them; many countries have experimented with them. David Brower was asked, when interviewed in the spring 1998 issue of *Wild Earth* (1998, 37–38), "Should conservationists acknowledge that sanding the rough edges off the existing paradigm is inadequate, and that we need to move beyond industrial growth culture if we are to fully protect Earth's biological diversity?" Brower said, "Yes. There is a simple answer. We will have to rethink the industrial age. It puzzles me. Where did we get this addiction to growth? Why do we think it necessary to keep growing, and growing, and growing? Our devotion to constant growth has done nothing but cause trouble. Nature doesn't work that way."

The answer to Brower's question is that we have defined ourselves as the species that by its nature must always grow (personally, socially, developmentally, spiritually, institutionally, physically, mentally, and in every other "good" fashion), that is, be more tomorrow than we are today—Be All You Can Be. Brower is right that nothing else in the natural world is like this. No other life form conceives itself or behaves insatiably. Only humans insist that to be is to be always more.

What would a sustainable *culture* look like? Certainly not like our existing paradigm. Robert Theobald says about the situation today: "You gradually realize that you are merely the tiniest of tiny cogs in a global machine with no one at the helm, and that your culture, your life, and even your own private beliefs are products of economic forces that you cannot comprehend" (Theobald

1997, 37). What does it mean to rethink the value of insatiable improvement and infinite self-actualization? Is it possible to go beyond the imperative of insatiable self-development? It is *not* hard to find a sympathetic audience for limiting human wants, for controlling our wants in a socially just manner, and for reeling in our appetites for the "goods life."

But to go beyond the insatiable desire to have more means rethinking, if not actually transcending, the insatiable desire to be more. We think we are unique because we can insatiably self-actualize. But without rethinking this, the sustainability prospects are grim. However, to suggest that there is more to life than improvement outrages most folks. Most want to retain the idea of unlimited self-realization and reconcile it with limited consumption. Even the Hoover Committee, seventy years ago, said that since "wants" may be insatiable, we should focus on nonmaterial wants rather than material wants: "[Our] survey has proved conclusively what has long been held theoretically to be true, that wants are insatiable; that one want satisfied makes way for another. The conclusion is that economically we have a boundless field before us; that there are wants which will make way endlessly for newer wants as fast as they are satisfied" (Rifkin 1995, 23).

Because "being more" is considered our sacred feature, many think that we need to rechannel our insatiability toward being more virtuous, being more spiritual, being more enlightened, being more sustainable. If that's all we do, contrary to David Brower, then we are stuck within the existing paradigm and the Culture of Insatiable Freedom. If we stay the course of Be All You Can Be, we can embrace our sacred value of insatiable self-realization, legitimate social and self-improvement, and maintain our imperative to be always more tomorrow. To think otherwise, according to conventional wisdom, is to think of humans as stagnating, as lazy, as impotent creatures—goin' nowhere, doin' nothin.

On the other hand, Mahatma Gandhi and Zorba the Greek are alternative role models that take us beyond Marx, Mill, and Maslow. How so? First, consider that there are essentially three types of life activities:

1.   taking care of each other
2.   having fun
3.   self-development

Whether we examine the social, political, economic, or spiritual spheres of life, or whether or not we examine the infinite variety of cultural spheres that have existed, life activities of individuals can be classified loosely into one or more of the three areas. There is overlap, but they are separable.

For example, a family might cook dinner together, and the individual members might participate in such a way that they are taking care of each other, having fun, and one or more might be experimenting with a unique recipe that involves self-development directed at being a gourmet cook. On the other hand, they might be cooking a dinner that none want to do except for getting the meal prepared and the task completed, in which case, the activity would serve only as taking care of each other. Additionally, caring for each other can be authoritarian, democratic, sexist, or exploitative depending on institutional conditions, the role of the state, and the type of economy.

So with respect to Gandhi and Zorba, we can see how their lives related to these three categories and demonstrate that the Satiable Self is one in which the first two are paramount and the last, self-development, is subordinate. First, the Culture of Security preceded capitalism. For the first 3 million years of human existence, life was organized around number *1*, taking care of each other, which was the guiding principle. Certainly, people had fun, but self-development was not a thematic concern. People lived, had some fun, and took care of each other. The Satiable Self ruled. But with the Neolithic Revolution and the emergence of the insatiable self, it was possible to have more fun *and* pursue self-development. Yet this was restricted to the ruling classes.

Taking care of each other continued to be the principal theme of slave and feudal societies. Then with the emergence of capitalism and the Culture of Insatiable Freedom, two things happen: (1) the opportunities and social legitimacy for having fun mushroom and (2) self-development becomes an economic and moral imperative. Capitalism suggests to us that fun and various forms of immediate gratification and self-indulgence are acceptable. It also mandates continuous self-actualization. You can Be All You Can Be and have fun along the way. Taking care of each other is relegated to the magic of the market. Of course, the family continues to be a crucial center for caring for each other, but the market is supposed to function on the basis of self-interest to assure economic provisioning.

This is simply a twist on Adam Smith's invisible hand doctrine. The market mechanism is supposed to be self-correcting, self-adjusting, and equilibrium-oriented, so that by trusting in the market, that is, in the impersonal forces of supply and demand, *we will be taken care of.* All that is needed to make this function is for us to be willing to "earn" our security. If we work hard and pursue our self-development, the system will be like a paternalistic father and take care of us. If we simply devote ourselves to our economic self-interest, under the market's competitive conditions, we will be provisioned and will have "achieved" the security that we all know we need. The point is that we aren't expected to focus on caring for one another, because the invisible hand of the market does this for us.

Yet we realize that it can't do it all. In addition to the market, there are government, the extended family, neighbors, and friends. For example, what happens when our parents get old and need our help? We like to think that we do take care of them, yet the growth of the nursing home industry suggests that even here we rely on the market. Of course, someone has to pay for this, and it is frequently our tax dollars channeled through Medicare/Medicaid, or it is us directly. Again, I may pay my parents' nursing home costs. This allows me to pursue my insatiable self-development through my career. By being all I can be in the economy, I can have all I can have; that is, I can have a bigger income that will finance my life and that of my elderly parents. So the Culture of Insatiable

Freedom and the Economy of Insatiable Improvers makes activity *3* a priority. Consider the pre-Neolithic peoples. The order of life activities was number *1*, then *2*, and virtually no *3*. Then with the emergence of the insatiable self and the Culture of Insatiable Freedom, the priorities are actually reversed! Capitalism is about self-development and having fun. The market and pursuit of self-interest will provide for us and therefore free us for these other activities. Capitalism does not make number *1* a thematic concern. *The "purpose" of capitalism is not to take care of each other. Its purpose is to maximize wealth creation through the channels of individual freedom and competition.* To the extent that people have their needs taken care of in capitalism, it is not because the system makes this an intentional principle.

So if we look at Gandhi and Zorba, we can get an idea of how the Satiable Self might operate in a Culture of Sustainability. There are obviously other real-life figures on whom we could draw for this example, yet these two individuals capture the character of the Satiable Self, and they are contrasting cultural images. Gandhi is a giant in the twentieth century whom almost everyone knows something about, and Zorba, although not a global powerhouse, has a flare and a responsible enthusiasm for life that is worthy of admiration. Nicos Kazantzakis met Zorba in the 1930s and was so captivated by him that he wrote the book *Zorba the Greek*. Many readers may also recall the movie, *Zorba, the Greek*, starring Anthony Quinn. Many of us could clearly come up with other historical figures, or people we know or have known who fit the image of the Satiable Self. Mill and Marx don't fit it, yet Aristotle probably does. Thomas Merton, the Trappist monk and theologian, comes to mind. Maybe Jesus, Mohammed, Buddha, the Dalai Lama, Lao Tzu, and Thich Nhat Hanh are or were Satiable Selves worthy of emulation. They might be. The world's religious leaders have never been known for material indulgence. Many, however, have been into insatiable *spiritual development*. We can go beyond that as well.

Many working people in our lives who, when we consider what it means to live more simply, less compulsively, and with less "drive," are simultaneously committed to both caring for others and having fun. My mother qualifies. Then there is Edward Abbey, whose life, compared to those we've mentioned, was no doubt the closest to that of Zorba. Yet one of the difficulties in our culture today is that if one wants to live the Satiable Self life, it is not easy, because this pits you against the overwhelming cultural influences of our Be All You Can Be world.

Some have found the right niche, however. The niches are out there, but generally, without an independent income that allows you to live satiably, you are thrust into the productivist milieu and must pursue your self-development to "earn" your security.

Yet people who want to avoid wage labor and career labor are seeking the "noncareer lifestyle." This is a niche that can provide family security, maybe an outlet for social activism, and is a stress reducer. In a Culture of Sustainability and an economy that fosters, rather than penalizes, the Satiable Self, the "noncareer lifestyle" would be a viable and respectable alternative to Be All You Can Be. Dropping out can work for some today; the price is higher than it needs to be since the dominant culture is against you. Many who want to bail out on the "goods life" frequently get creative. For example, there are self-help books like *Your Money or Your Life* by Joe Dominguez and Vicki Robin (1992), Duane Elgin's *Voluntary Simplicity* (1993), David Shi's *The Simple Life* (1985), and Juliet Schor's *The Overspent American* (1998) and *The Overworked American* (1992). Additionally, Duane Elgin's book was inspired by the original article by this title published by Richard Gregg in 1936 in the Indian journal *Visva-Bharati* (August 1936). Gregg was one of Gandhi's students. His article eventually appeared in the humanist journal *Manas* in 1974 (4 September issue) and then was republished in *CoEvolution Quarterly* (Summer 1977). So we can, in effect, trace "voluntary simplicity" back to Gandhi, himself.

What many call "downshifting" and "voluntary simplicity" are today's creative efforts to get off the productivist-consumerist treadmill and live the Satiable Self lifestyle. But this is frequently accompanied by the need to pursue some serious self-development in order to make it work in a culture that opposes it.

But for many of those seeking voluntary simplicity and such, their focus is not on avoiding the imperative of Be All You Can Be but only on the rejection of have all you can have and the stress that this has caused them. The "noncareer lifestyle" that should be part of the Culture of Sustainability is about letting go of both Be All You Can Be as well as have all you can have. The Satiable Self—and my choice of Gandhi and Zorba as representatives of it—is not simply a self that works less and lives a less consumerist lifestyle. It's about a self that doesn't see the meaning of life in the imperative to be always more, to "make something of oneself," or to "accomplish" goals.

GANDHI'S CULTURAL MESSAGE

Gandhi devoted his life to number *1*, the principle of taking care of each other. His philosophy of simplicity, equality, and justice is postcapitalist and fixated on the concept of "sufficiency" in all things. He realized that Indians needed to have an "improved" life and was clearly militant about their efforts to overthrow British domination and clear the way for social progress. Yet he was not into greed, insatiability, technology, or the logic of "more is better." He did not see "progress" as the meaning of life or as the fundamental attribute that distinguishes us from other life forms, that is, that humans are different because they have to "progress." Gandhi did spend much of his life advocating a basic improvement for his people: free yourselves from British rule. He did this not because he believed in improvement but because he believed in taking care of one another. Thus, from his point of view, for Indians to take care of each other, they had to be independent and autonomous.

By his life and ideas, it is obvious that Gandhi was focused on taking care of each other. There is little evidence in Gandhi's writings of an embrace for the imperative of self-development. As he said, "Truth is God." By this he meant that truth is primordial; truth comes first, not God. If there is a god, Gandhi would say, then it must be in the form of truth. Truth, Gandhi was certain about, and if we can be content with calling God the truth, then God exists. Gandhi's truth is that if people practiced selflessness, it would all work. The world required only this one principle. His principle of selflessness is not about being all we can be. It is not about insatiable improvement or about the notion that humans are constituted by their unlimited potential. His principle is consistent with Aristotle's view of virtue. Be selfless; be virtuous; nothing more is required to make humanity sustainable!

Surprisingly, Gandhi's religion was more secular humanist than what would be otherwise expected from this very religious man who grew up a Hindu. His "religion" shares something with Mills' belief in a "religion of humanity." Mill's *Three Essays on Religion* (1874) contains several statements that suggest that the essence of religion, if it is to have any "utility" for humans, is to point people in the direction of perfection and excellence. So, he says that "the essence of religion is the strong and earnest direction of the emotions and desires towards an ideal object, recognized as of the highest excellence, and as rightfully paramount over all selfish objects of desire" (Schneewind 1967, 322). Regarding this, Schneewind adds that "the 'religion of humanity' would cultivate our unselfish feelings and would free us from any need for intellectual juggling or willful blindness with regard to its tenets, since it would rather point out than deny the evil in the world and urge us to work to remove it" (322). Although Gandhi would no doubt embrace this view along with Mill, and even though their religious views are quite similar, they would disagree about the role of human self- and social development. Gandhi would say that our purpose as humans is not to continuously develop ourselves but simply to act selflessly.

Gandhi, in other words, was not into "continuous improvement," nor did he like continuous economic growth. He was not an advocate of Be All You Can Be. He also stated, "A time is coming when those who are in a mad rush today of multiplying their wants, vainly thinking that they add to the real substance, real knowledge of the world, will retrace their steps and say: 'What have we done?'" A major contrast with Mill, Marx, and Maslow.

Time magazine voted Gandhi its runner-up for "Man of the Century" (*Time*, 31 December 1999). Although it gave this award to Albert Einstein, this suggests Gandhi's stature in the twentieth century. The feature article on Gandhi is revealing. Its author, Johanna McGeary, states that most us of know little of his life (1869–1948) beyond what Americans saw in the movie *Gandhi*, starring Ben Kingsley. She adds that "a strange amalgam of beliefs formed the complicated core of Gandhism. History will merely smile at his railing against Western ways, industrialism and material pleasures. He never stopped calling for a nation that would turn its back on technology to prosper through village self-sufficiency, but not even the Mahatma could hold back progress. Yet many today share his uneasiness with the way mechanization and materialism sicken the human spirit" (McGeary 1999, 88). Of course, those who are today seeking a way to jump from the productivist treadmill and reading *Voluntary Simplicity* and are "downshifting" their lives also share this uneasiness with Gandhi. As McGeary says, Gandhi was into neither technology nor insatiable progress.

On the contrary, Gandhi was not an advocate of "dropping out," nor was he an ascetic. He was totally engaged in life, in its emotions, its passions, and its injustices. He was a fighter. He fought for Indian self-rule (*Hind swaraj*) all of his life. "More than independence, it meant a utopian blend of national liberty, individual self-reliance and social justice" (McGeary 1999, 90). His leadership in the struggle for social justice through nonviolent resistance has influenced many activists in the last half century, including Martin Luther King, Nelson Mandela, Lech Walesa, and the Dalai Lama. Gandhi was, above all, a true activist. "Action is my domain," he said. "It's not what I say but what I do that matters" (90). But Gandhi's social activism and his struggle for Indian independence were not inspired by the imperative of self-development and Be All You Can Be. It was his way to express the first life activity of "taking care of each other." In other words, what motivated Gandhi and informed his struggles was not the insatiable desire to Be All You Can Be but the simple, age-old activity of caring for one another.

Nelson Mandela's essay in the *Time* "Man of the Century" issue praises Gandhi's life work and also suggests that Gandhi was a believer in the Satiable Self. Yet, as Mandela states, Gandhi wasn't unequivocally opposed to the use of armed force. It was a last resort, for sure, as active nonviolence in pursuit of social justice was always his preference. Gandhi did admit, however, that "where choice is set between cowardice and violence, I would advise violence. I prefer to use arms in defense of honor rather than remain the vile witness of dishonor" (Mandela 1999, 93). Gandhi would have supported the use of violence, in other words, only in defense of certain principles, and the principles would have to do with the fundamental value and activity of "taking care of each other."

Mandela comments on Gandhi's political economy as well. Gandhi wrote few self-contained books, but his correspondence was voluminous. His one book on economics is *Hind Swaraj* (1938). These thoughts and principles constitute the economics of just and sustainable simplicity. As Mandela says, many of the economic problems faced by poor Third World nations are due to the same market and imperialist forces that Gandhi struggled against in India's independence movement. Economic dependency, the undermining of local economies, and the accumulation of enormous foreign debt are but a few of the problems mentioned by Mandela that are traceable to the lack of self-sufficiency Gandhi knew India needed. "Gandhi's insistence on self-sufficiency is a basic economic principle that, if followed today, could contribute significantly to alleviating Third World poverty and stimulating development" (Mandela 1999, 94). Gandhi was a leftist, to be sure. What he witnessed in both India and South Africa was a type of dichotomy between the wealthy and the poor that paralleled Marx's labor-capital class analysis. Yet Gandhi had a moral vision of collective and common ownership of capital that resulted from a notion of trusteeship. The world's resources should be held in trust by and for all of humanity, and therefore redistribution and equalization of our common natural and produced capital was essential (94). Gandhi believed in collective and cooperative production and empowerment of working people. To this extent he was a socialist.

He was as convinced as Karl Marx that capitalism is a system of injustice based, in part, on the exploitation of labor. To this extent he was a Marxist. As Mandela states, Gandhi didn't accept Adam Smith's laissez-faire notion that we should trust in the magic of the market and the invisible hand. Neither did he accept a Stalinist type of state-owned and directed communism. He didn't favor the Soviet model or the capitalist model but a model of worker- and community-based and -empowered production that should be used to meet basic needs in as democratic and grassroots a fashion as possible. In this respect, he shared much with the American pragmatist and socialist, John Dewey (Brown 1996). Gandhi was a pragmatist and an experimenter. In fact, Gandhi's autobiography, published in 1948 shortly before his death, is subtitled *The Story of My Experiments with Truth.*

He did not like the idea of using an economic system either to confer and demonstrate status or to be an engine of insatiable wealth creation. He would have agreed with Veblen that capitalism is driven by both invidious distinction and insatiability. Gandhi and Veblen shared one very basic idea about what an alternative economy should look like: simple and people-driven. What was needed, said Gandhi, is to harness the "self." Gandhi comments that "Western nations today are groaning under the heel of the monster-god of materialism. Their moral growth has become stunted in so far as we have made the modern materialistic craze our goal, in so far are we going downhill in the path of progress. I hold that the real progress in the sense I have put it is antagonistic to economic progress" (Gandhi 1990, 97). But although Gandhi says in this passage that "real progress" exists, his view about what that means is tempered with satiability. He's not talking about insatiable progress but a form of improvement that moves the world toward sustainability and satiability.

Mandela says that "Gandhi remains today the only complete critique of advanced industrial society. He is not against science and technology, but he places priority on the right to work and opposes mechanization to the extent that it usurps this right. He adds that, given the degrading poverty that inflicts a fifth of our global population, the issue of jobs, inequality, exploitation, and despair might just force us to "ponder the Gandhian alternative" (Mandela 1999, 94). Gandhi's economics is about democratic decision making, subordinating profits to people's basic security (like jobs), and shaping and molding the corporation to fit the needs of the people. Today, he would insist that what the world needs is not "free trade" but "fair trade." He would have joined in the "battle in Seattle" against the World Trade Organization on 30 November 1999. He would have been there in Washington, D.C. to protest the International Monetary Fund (IMF) and World Bank on 16 April 2000.

He was never an enthusiast of growth for improvement's sake or for insatiable betterment. Gandhi would have suggested that for "real progress" to occur, we must get off the productivist-consumerist treadmill. He says that people should reject the "evils" of capitalism and should "strive to attain a juster distribution of the products of labour. *This immediately takes us to contentment and simplicity, voluntarily adopted.* Under the new outlook multiplicity of material wants will not be the aim of life, the aim will be rather their restriction consistently with comfort. We shall cease to think of getting what we can, but we shall decline to receive what all cannot get" (Gandhi 1990, 107; see also Brown 1996; emphasis added). He was not into Be All You Can Be or have all you can have. He was a committed believer, like Aristotle, in the Satiable Self. A just and sustainable economy should conform to the requirements of simple and satiable living.

But the reason for choosing Gandhi as a role model in our vision of a Culture of Sustainability is not his economics in particular. His economics is completely consistent with what we outline as an Economy of Sufficiency within a new cultural paradigm, but there is so much more to Gandhi than his economic ideas. It is about how he lived more than about what he said about an alternative economic system. Gandhi presents us with an individual whom few fail to admire. He lived a life of simplicity, spoke out against social injustice, fought hard for a better world, and lived the best life he could. He was in this world, the world of insatiability, but was not of it. He would have preferred a world of satiability and simplicity. But his alienation from the industrial, consumerist, and capitalist world did not cause him to "drop out" or withdraw from it. He was engaged.

Bill McKibben's article on Gandhi in the last 1999 issue of *Mother Jones* shares much with Mandela's article in *Time*—both also appeared at the same time (McKibben 1999, 68–95). McKibben is impressed with Gandhi's ability to be engaged in this world yet rise above it. He says that this "lightness, of course, did not come from playing; it came from the hard work of renunciation. Gandhi gave up the passion for sex, for money and possessions, for distraction, for comfort. He renounced, at root, the right to put himself first, choosing instead to live for others. An American journalist once asked him, 'Can you tell me the secret of your life in three words?' 'Yes,' chuckled Gandhi, 'Renounce and enjoy'" (McKibben 1999, 70). Renunciation is a problem for many when they consider Gandhi as a possible role model. He didn't renounce the world as a monk might. He renounced the materialist consumer culture, of course, but he never tired of efforts to sacrifice all pleasures that either feed one's ego or obstruct our selflessness.

Renunciation of the consumer culture of capitalism is less problematic because a Culture of Sustainability would be a compensatory alternative. Within this new culture, if it ever comes to pass, such fulfillments as more meaningful, participatory work, quality of all kinds of social relationships, and a less stress-ridden, more relaxed and more secure lifestyle would serve to compensate us for the sacrifice of the "goods life." But renunciation of as many earthly pleasures as possible, that is, Gandhi's form of renunciation, may cause most folks to balk. It doesn't sound like a lot of fun. Gandhi was a true minimalist in all life activities excepting those that served either the cause of social justice or the minimalization of selfishness in all forms. McKibben questions whether or not regular people would accept Gandhi's form of renunciation. He suggests that they might, "but only if it actually makes people happier than the alternative, the consumer culture we all grew up in. Renunciation seems like such a joyless word." "But remember," says McKibben, "that Gandhi's secret for living was

'Renounce and enjoy!'" (McKibben 1999, 94). Gandhi was unique, however. For most of us, the "joy of renunciation" lacks something. Only Gandhi and a handful of monks and nuns are able to conceive this as other than an oxymoron.

Gandhi's kind of renunciation and his extreme minimalism are exceptional, inspiring, and a model of the Satiable Self. Yet Gandhi was not much for having fun. His concept of "joy" was clearly genuine. It was, for him, different from what most of us consider "fun." Gandhi, in other words, put almost exclusive priority on number *1*— taking care of one another. He found this to be an irreplaceable source of "joy." On the other hand, it's important to see, if you can, that he was not a person, like Mill, Marx, and Maslow, who viewed humans as insatiable improvers. Self-development, that is, number *3*, is not Gandhi's message to us. But what about number *2*, having fun? There is little in his writings, his autobiography, or life activities to suggest that "fun" was something that he cherished. "Fun" is a human activity, and it may be one, like taking care of each other, than we share with other life forms. At least, it appears that some animals (and dolphins come to mind) are quite capable of it. We see this behavior in our pets, of course, too. Yet as Zorba proves, we can have a Satiable Self, be minimalists, live simply, and have fun, too. We can take care of each other *and* have fun, as well, and, naturally, we can develop ourselves insatiably or otherwise. But the vision of a sustainable alternative is one that reprioritizes *1*, *2*, and *3* in just that order. In today's Culture of Insatiable Freedom the priority is the opposite: *3*, *2*, and *1*! We think today in terms of development, of insatiable improvement, then of having fun as a compensation for the stress of it, and finally, we hope that everyone gets taken care of. But to understand this, as Gandhi surely did, you have to be able to see the difference between self-development and fun.

Self-development can be fun, just as, with Gandhi, taking care of each other can be a joy—and fun. But, on the other hand, there are all manner of fun activities that *can* have little to do with self- or social development: golf, fishing, running, swimming, watching stars and clouds overhead, walking downtown, or whatever. It is "play" that should come to mind when we talk about having fun. "Just go out and play," we tell our kids. It doesn't have to lead to anything better or anything more. It doesn't have to lead to anything at all. It's immediate gratification. It is what comes to mind when we think of Freud's "pleasure principle." But this type of "play" or having fun is not what Gandhi considered essential to his life. Yet there is in the educational development and child development literature a rich source of thought on the need for play. If we are getting the job done in taking care of each other and we are living in a sustainable and just world, then why not? It is a feature that, as the pleasure principle suggests, we humans have a gift for. It is clearly one of the more beneficial by-products of the reflexivity of consciousness, that is, of being able to be conscious of our consciousness. We can play, feel it, and know that we are playing and feeling it!

But Gandhi's stature is huge. He wasn't much into having fun, to be sure. That's what is missing when considering him as a model for a Culture of Sustainability and the Satiable Self. We know that we don't have to be insatiable about having fun. "Just go play," as we were told, doesn't mean to "play forever, be obsessed about it, and make it everything at the expense of being responsible"—our parents didn't say that. Satiable fun is a valid concept in an alternative society. But Gandhi might have said that it would be a fine idea in the right world or that it might be fine for others to do when the work is done (like at his ashram), but for him, his experiments with denial and renunciation were enough. He set himself so much work to do; fun would not be a part of *his* life—maybe for others.

McKibben's assessment makes sense; however, "sooner or later we will face the problem of status. Having grown as large as we can both in numbers and in appetites, we will need a different idea to balance our economies, our politics, our individual lives," and "we've barely begun to chew over Gandhi's advice. It may be too strong for us in the end" (McKibben 1999, 95). It probably is too strong for us. It's too much renunciation. This is where Zorba adds something special.

ZORBA'S ZEST FOR LIFE

Unlike Gandhi, Zorba was into fun, that is, number 2. Nikos Kazantzakis was so impressed with Alexis Zorba that he made Zorba into a larger-than-life figure. Zorba took the idea of taking care of each other seriously, but having fun held a special place for him as well. For this reason, when we think of the "zest for life," Zorba frequently comes to mind. Renunciation, like that practiced by Gandhi, was not Zorba. But Zorba was not needy, did not embrace the "goods life," and was a minimalist, much like Gandhi. Alexis Zorba provides an excellent contrast to Gandhi because he demonstrates that life can be simple, exciting, and fun simultaneously.

There was purpose in Gandhi's renunciation, but for the Culture of Sustainability and an Economy of Sufficiency, Gandhi's renunciation is not necessary. Gandhi made renunciation into a virtue, and Zorba shows that this is unneeded. An alternative economy and culture that prioritizes sustainability requires renunciation of the "goods life," of insatiability, and unlimited accumulation and multiplication of wants. And Gandhi's example is inspiring, to be sure. But a Culture of Sustainability doesn't require absolute selflessness. If it did, it would be unrealistic—a utopian pipedream.

To clarify Gandhi's concept of renunciation and Zorba's lack of it, we can distinguish between "necessary" and "surplus" renunciation. This distinction, going back to Marx's concept of labor and Herbert Marcuse's concept of Freudian repression (which he borrowed from Marx as well), suggests that there is logically a measure of renunciation in the transition to a Culture of Sustainability; we renounce the "goods life" and consumerism because they are not sustainable. This is necessary renunciation. But Gandhi, in his "experiments with truth," was attempting to renounce more than what would be necessary for sustainability. Gandhi's selflessness was in the domain of "surplus renunciation"—beyond what it necessary. Zorba, on the other hand, by virtue of his zest for life and playful spirit, was more inclined to accept the minimum necessary. For sustainability, Zorba is an important model because he suggests to us that what matters is groping our way to the degree of necessary renunciation and then having fun.

But additionally, like Gandhi, Zorba was not into self-development. Neither one was a "productivist." For Zorba, pulling your weight with social obligations was a priority, justice was a priority, but beyond that having fun was what counted. The point is that neither Gandhi nor Zorba reconciles with today's Economy of Insatiable Improvers, yet these are people whom we surely admire. They demonstrate by their lives that there is more to life than self-actualization—that life can be worthy without being fixated on Be All You Can Be. They are prototypes of the Satiable Self.

Alexis Zorba was a real-life individual. He became something of a philosophical icon for living life to the fullest, in part, because of Nikos Kazantzakis' autobiography, *Report to Greco* (1965), *Zorba the Greek* (1952), and, finally, the Hollywood movie by that title. Kazantzakis was born in 1883 in Crete and studied in France with the eminent philosopher Henri Bergson, after receiving a law degree from the University of Athens. He traveled widely, wrote many novels, and is no doubt Greece's most important writer in the twentieth century. In 1945 he was also Greece's minister of education. He died in Germany in 1957. Kazantzakis made Zorba into a legendary figure, and he wanted to do this. When describing his initial passion to express Zorba's life to the world, he said, "Our many days together crossed in front of me like graceful white doves, full of gurgles. The memories ascended a story higher than truth, two stories higher than falsehood. Zorba metamorphosed gradually and became a legend" (Kazantzakis 1965, 461). He also said that along with Homer, Buddha, Nietzsche, and Bergson, Zorba had the most influence on him. "Zorba taught me to love life and have no fear of death," he said (445).

In his autobiography, Kazantzakis says of Zorba, "If it has been a question in my lifetime of choosing a spiritual guide, a *guru* as the Hindus say, a *father* as say the monks at Mount Athos, surely I would have chosen Zorba" (Kazantzakis 1965, 445). Zorba had, adds Kazantzakis, "the sureness of hand, freshness of heart, the gallant daring to tease his own soul, as though inside him he had a force superior to the soul; finally the savage bubbling laugh from a deep, deep wellspring deeper than the bowels of man," which was able "to demolish all the barriers—morality, religion, homeland—which that wretched poltroon, man, has erected around him in order to hobble with full security through his miserable smidgen of life" (445). It was not Zorba's commitment to self-development or Be All You Can Be that made Kazantzakis feel this way; instead, it was Zorba's ability to see life as both a responsibility to others and a playful adventure simultaneously.

Kazantzakis tells the story of how he met Zorba. It was in the 1930s, and they encountered one another in a bar waiting for a boat to Crete. Zorba was sixty-five. He then tells Kazantzakis how he learned to play the *santuri*, and through their dialogue it is clear that Zorba did not learn this stringed instrument out of a need to develop himself or out of a culturally imposed guilt that he should Be All You Can Be. Zorba said it was passion; his motive, which Zorba's father could not understand, was what the music did both to and for him. The *santuri* was fun to play, and doing so made Zorba feel good, happy, and contented. It was not about accomplishing anything at all. It was not about learning anything or acquiring a new skill. Kazantzakis, from this moment on, begins to appreciate Zorba in a new way, in part, because Kazantzakis is a productivist (not a consumerist)—an overachiever in today's vernacular. He is a writer committed to his self-expression.

Of course, Zorba calls him a "pen-pusher" and a "bookworm" as he attempts to open up Kazantzakis' heady world to that of passion, everyday life, love, and materialism. But Zorba is not talking about the materialism that Gandhi renounced but the materialism of the sensual world in which we play and rejoice and through which we experience the simple pleasures. Zorba is not suggesting to Kazantzakis that the material world is to be controlled in our effort to maximize our pleasures, nor is he suggesting that materialism means to find pleasure in accumulating as many toys as possible. Materialism, in many respects a materialism that is absent in Gandhi, for Zorba means dancing in the warm sand on the beach, losing himself in his *santuri,* eating outside in the evening air, and making love. This is the materialism of the sensual world, not that of the insatiable improver or limitless consumer. This is the message that Zorba has for Kazantzakis—a simple world of lustful living. This kind of "having fun," of simple pleasure and sensuality is not unknown to us today. The point is to call attention to what we already know about life and what we at some level already appreciate in ourselves and some of those around us. It's the fun that we have without the need to accomplish tasks, improve skills, use toys, or be more. This is what we can carry with us into the Culture of Sustainability.

"Living without accomplishing anything; is this living?" asks Kazantzakis. For a writer and communicator to do so, no doubt, seems ineffectual. If we have defined ourselves as the insatiable improvers, then Zorba's life is hard to comprehend. Ultimately, what impressed Kazantzakis the most was the way that Zorba reacted to their failed mining project. He says:

How can I avoid heartfelt excitement when I recall the words he spoke to me; the dances he danced for me; the santir he played for me on that Cretan shore where we spent six months digging with a mass of laborers; supposedly to find lignite? We both knew full well that this practical aim was dust to mislead the eyes of the world. We waited anxiously for the sun to set and the laborers to stop work, so that the two of us could lay our dinner out on the beach, eat our delicious peasant meal, drink our tart Cretan wine, and begin to talk. (Kazantzakis 1965, 446)

In effect, their endeavor on Crete was not about striking it rich, making money, or improving lives. Kazantzakis adds that "the lignite enterprise went to the devil. Laughing, playing, conversing, Zorba and I did all we could to reach the catastrophe" (446). What Kazantzakis learned from this experience, in which he lost all of his money, was how the goals that we associate with Be All You Can Be are rather shallow in the totality of life. Zorba taught him that. It's not about "success" but about taking care of each other and having fun.

Zorba believed in freedom; at least he accepted its existence. But the freedom that we experience in our Culture of Insatiable Freedom today is not what Zorba meant by the term. Kazantzakis notices that Zorba has a missing finger and asks him about it. Zorba explains that in one of his many jobs (*and Zorba was clearly not a careerist*), he was a potter and threw his pots on a wheel. Zorba says that he loved this art. Why? Because it has that artistic character of starting with nothing, and through imagination and expression, creating something. Zorba comments: "That's what you might call being a man: freedom!" (Kazantzakis 1952, 18). But then the question about his missing finger. Zorba says, "Oh, it got in my way in the wheel. So one day I seized a hatchet." Shocked by this, Kazantzakis asks about the obvious pain. Zorba replies, "I'm not a tree trunk. I'm a man. Of course it hurt me. But it got in my way" (18).

Zorba's notion of freedom? It means creativity, not self-development. It is not the freedom to be always more that counts for Zorba but to create. This is precisely what Bronowski suggests. Creativity may be more our human essence, while improvement is our cultural legacy. And there's Zorba's passion at the potter's wheel. He must have thrown pots with the same abandon that he played the *santuri*. This is not the passion of career-driven self-development but the joy of total immersion in an activity for its own sake, that is, fun.

Yet Zorba's life was not just about having fun. He did believe, like Gandhi, in taking care of each other. He, too, was a fighter for social justice. In 1896 there was a civil war in Crete, and Zorba joined the rebel forces to overthrow the Turks who controlled the island. Zorba would have agreed with Gandhi that violence is not the way but is sometimes necessary if only to avoid being a "vile witness of dishonor" (Mandela 1999). Zorba was troubled by violence but was willing to take up arms if he understood the cause well enough. In the case of Crete, he told Kazantzakis that he did. The cause was Crete's "liberty," said Zorba. For Gandhi, it was India's liberty.

Responsibility? One of our fundamental activities is taking care of each other. For both Gandhi and Zorba this meant fighting for social justice, as those who are victims of oppression and domination, whether from patriarchy, racism, statism, or global capitalism, call to us morally to come to their aid. Gandhi and Zorba responded. They need our help, and we have a responsibility to respond. It's that simple. So taking care of each other means being socially responsible, pulling your weight, and doing the right thing. A Culture of Sustainability requires this. What about Zorba? Kazantzakis says that Zorba faced each day with zeal and enthusiasm as he coordinated the miners' efforts on Crete. He worked harder than any of them. For Kazantzakis, Zorba was an individual "who loved responsibility" (Kazantzakis 1952, 48). It was not power over others that Zorba loved. Responsibility comes, in part, from a feeling of participation and purpose. To the extent that what we do in taking care of each other, whether it is in our jobs and the economy or in our homes and families, if we feel that we have a say along with others, that what we all do is empowering and participatory rather than alienating, then responsibility comes as easily for us as it did for Zorba.

It is being responsible for sharing in the socially necessary labor that any society requires for its reproduction over time. But being responsible is not synonymous with being more. In a Culture of Sustainability nobody is asked to be more but only to be responsible—participate and pull your weight. Kazantzakis says that Zorba loved to go to the mine before the workmen got there and excitedly hack away in search of a new seam of lignite. If he found one? Because he lived in the present moment, he'd "dance for joy" when he discovered it. From the beginning of the mining enterprise, Kazantzakis noticed how "care and responsibility had passed from my hands to his" (Kazantzakis 1952, 49).

Zorba was an individual who could be responsible for his share of the world without resentment, without feeling burdened. He was fun-loving and at peace with the world as it came to him, in a Buddhist sort of way. In fact, Kazantzakis, while on the island with Zorba, was reading some of the Buddha's stories and often reflected on the images that these two personalities presented to him. They were quite different, of course. But at one point, after a number of months with Zorba, Kazantzakis remarked that he admired the "simplicity with which he adapted himself to the world around him, the way his body and soul formed one harmonious whole. I had never seen such a friendly accord between a man and the universe" (Kazantzakis 1952, 132). This is an image of the Satiable Self, not the self who is, like most of us today, driven to be always more tomorrow. Surely, we can live justly and harmoniously by simply taking care of each other and having fun. Both Zorba and Gandhi suggest this.

None of our vision of a sustainable culture requires us to be "better" people than we have ever been (a point made by Daniel Quinn in his novels *Ishmael, Story of B* and *My Ishmael*). Gandhi may be a difficult model to live up to, but that's not his message to us. What is needed is to understand the degree to which we can have a world that works and is sustainable simply by being responsible, getting simple, getting just and fair, and having fun along the way. Our capacity to enjoy the immediacy of the here and now is connected to this. Zorba's passion for life was special, but we all have it within us. Zorba mentioned to Kazantzakis more than once that when he was especially involved in some immediate pleasure, some particular activity of the moment, he tuned the rest of the world out. We all know what this is like.

When Zorba played his *santuri*, danced, or made love, he was able to be totally "present in the moment." This is a notion that is important in Buddhism. Kazantzakis was keenly aware of Zorba's special talent for being present in the moment, in part, because when he lived with Zorba on Crete, he was working on a manuscript about the Buddha. What's the significance of Zorba's ability to be present in the moment? In a Culture of Sustainability, when there are fewer contrived distractions and less commercialization of leisure, having fun can be great, even though we would be minimalists. Why? Because the more we are able to be present in the moment, the more we will be able to have fun, get into our activity, and glean the feeling of joy and pleasure from it, whatever it is.

Zorba went for depth and richness in any experience that he enjoyed. An eminent Buddhist theologian Thich Nhat Hanh says that you can't do this unless you can immerse yourself by being totally present in the moment. We get more out of the activity by being able to immerse ourselves deeply in it. The payoff is that if we can do this, there is every likelihood that we can get more out of simple pleasures and thus have fun without having to be so needy—without having to multiply our stimulation in order to have more fun. It's a case of quality over quantity and doing more with less. Kazantzakis understood Zorba's talent for this. Minimalism, as Gandhi and Zorba both practiced it, doesn't require Gandhi's renunciation of fun, and, in fact, as with Zorba, it is not pleasure, joy, and having fun that would be minimalized in a Culture of Sustainability. The Satiable Self doesn't renounce fun but, like Zorba, gets completely into it.

Ultimately, Kazantzakis' time with Zorba was short. Their lignite mining project was well intentioned but failed completely. They accomplished nothing. But for Zorba, accomplishing tasks, goals, and adding to one's list of achievements was not really living life to the fullest anyway. Acknowledging their failed endeavor, Zorba says, "Let's dance!" He adds, "To hell with paper and ink! To hell with goods and profits!" (Kazantzakis 1952, 290–291). So Zorba dances. But it's his reasons for dancing that are important. He doesn't dance in order to feel better about having failed. He doesn't dance to compensate for the frustration or despair over a goal that's left unfulfilled. Zorba dances because he knows that life is not about accomplishing goals, realizing potential, or achieving more. So he knows that none of what they were doing really mattered, because it's not about accomplishments anyway. That awareness about why Zorba dances grabs Kazantzakis. Kazantzakis makes it clear to us that admiration, love, and respect don't have to be conditioned upon accomplishments.

Kazantzakis learned to appreciate life in a new way by virtue of appreciating Zorba's being-in-the-world. Zorba might have been a Buddhist. But Zorba's Buddhism would have lacked discipline and would have been too much fun to be spiritual. Zorba was a sensualist and a minimalist simultaneously; that is, he understood the need to take care of each other *and* have fun. On the other hand, Kazantzakis was a serious person trying to lighten up. Zorba says that Kazantzakis is tied by a string to his seriousness about life. This keeps him from having fun. What about cutting the string? Zorba says it's hard to break, and one needs "a touch of folly to do that." He suspects that Kazantzakis lives too much in his head—always thinking, always strategizing, always calculating life's tasks and unfinished business. "The head's a careful little shopkeeper; it never breaks the string," Zorba admonishes him. Kazantzakis has it all "except just one thing—folly!" (Kazantzakis 1952, 300–301). A Culture of Sustainability will never happen unless we can link the responsibility of taking care of each other— in the family, in the economy, in politics, and in our global community—to having a lot of fun in the process. Gandhi, by himself, is beyond our capacity, but Zorba is not. Between the two of them or between the two or more people you know who are like this, we can get at least an image of life as a Satiable Self in a sustainable world. Kazantzakis concludes after saying good-bye to Zorba: "I often talked to my friends of this great soul. We admired the proud and confident bearing, deeper than reason, of this untutored man. Spiritual heights, which took us years of painful effort to attain, were attained by Zorba in one bound. And we said: 'Zorba is a great soul!'" (306). Of course, this is what "Mahatma" means in Hindi. Gandhi and Zorba were contemporaries. Mahatma Gandhi's spiritual heights surely exceed Zorba's. But Gandhi's path was more explicitly spiritual and no doubt more of a personal struggle than Zorba's. Still neither one of them told us that truly to be, one must always try to be more.

THE SATIABLE SELF

Most people today would prefer to emulate Zorba's ability to combine taking care of each other with having fun, over Gandhi's fixation on the former. But a bigger issue has to do with the difference between what drives the culture and its economy versus what motivates individuals.

Our *culture* needs to be reformed. *How* these three life activities are institutionalized is the fundamental concern. Clearly, we don't want to prevent each other from the individual pursuit of self-development. If someone seeks a form of self-actualization that is socially and environmentally benign, then so be it. People will continually have skills that they legitimately seek to improve and through which they hope to excel. The point is not to dissuade them from this. But sustainability requires that our culture and economy shift its priorities from number *3* and *2*, to *1* and *2*! Thus, we can create a Culture of Sustainability based upon the Satiable Self with radical reforms of our system and still allow for individuals who so choose to pursue their unique self-development.

Our being is inherently "unlimited." But we have the ability, as well, to control the degree to which we actualize it. As humans we have control over our self-development and self-improvement. We can insatiably develop it or not. We can suspend our self-development for a period of time or not. In other words, we can be as lazy about it or relaxed about it as we choose. By doing so, we don't affect its unlimited or insatiable character. That will always remain integral to our being.

In a Culture of Sustainability there will be, and should be, the freedom to Be All You Can Be as long as to do so doesn't come at the expense of either the environment or the equal freedom for others to do likewise. In this culture, there will obviously be those who are committed to improving their skills in the arts, in athletics, and in all manner of activities, including carpentry, for example, auto mechanics, computer hacking, or fishing. There's no end to the activities that invite such improvement. There will always be people or certain times in all of our lives when we would like to do something better tomorrow than we did today. The freedom for this doesn't have to be an obstacle for global sustainability. It is altogether different when we extend this reasoning to the broader structure of our current culture and economy. You as an individual can feel free to Be All You Can Be, but to have an economy and a culture that compel this or judge people by this is *the* problem. To have Be All You Can Be an imperative and "drive" for us always to be more is what needs to be stopped.

In fact, if we draw again on Marx and Marcuse, we can distinguish between "necessary" and "surplus" self-development. A measure of formal and informal education has been the custom in all economies for hundreds of years. In order for any society to function properly and reproduce itself over time, it has to educate its children. Basic literacy is today essential for "taking care of each other." Much of what is formal education the world over is about skills and knowledge to take care of each other and make the economy and society work effectively. It constitutes self-development. In this regard it is "necessary" self-development. But there can be more self-development if one pursues it through his or her actualization of potential. This would be "surplus" self-development. The point is to have an Economy of Sufficiency in a sustainable culture where the economy is not "driven by improvement" but by "necessary" self-development instead. Actualization of the surplus is up to the individual but must exist within the parameters of sustainability.

Our concern is with the institutional level rather than the personal level. The problem with the insatiable self is that it drives the "system." The priorities inherent in the logic of the system must be changed. We can make allowances for each individual's desire for improvement in his or her skills and self-realization but should do so within a sustainable economy premised upon the Satiable Self. The idea is to transcend the "imperative" character of self-development in today's world and to move beyond a society "driven" by insatiable improvement.

What might this look like? To begin with, there are two levels of reform. One concerns the institutional reforms necessary for a Culture of Sustainability, and here Veblen's notion of sufficiency is important. But first we examine the individual level. For individuals living within the culture of the Satiable Self, security is assured. This was true 2 million years ago and would be the case in the future. Consequently, the "imperative" that drives people to Be All You Can Be would be absent. But this doesn't mean that people can live off the labor of others; nor does it mean that pulling one's weight and being socially responsible are any less necessary.

But the stress of having to perform is reduced. One is not compelled to be more, only to be responsible and virtuous. This allows the individual to get off of the productivism-consumerism treadmill, to relax, and to feel legitimate about not being a "productivist." This is reminiscent of Paul Lafargue's (Karl Marx's son-in-law) article, "The Right to Be Lazy!" What counts is responsibility more than achievement. The current culture measures folks by their accomplishments. With the Satiable Self, what counts is virtue. This was Aristotle's point. People would be motivated not by being more but by being decent people.

Of course, most of our culture is wedded to the sacredness of being more. Folks who don't want to give up the imperative of Be All You Can Be will argue that we might focus our insatiable improvement on taking care of each other. They say that we can always improve here. But this is *not* acceptance of the Satiable Self. The Satiable Self and the cultural consciousness that accompanies it coincide with the "noncareer lifestyle." Today the insatiable self drives us to find careers as a vehicle both to achieve security and to pursue self-development.

Since the career lifestyle in capitalism is a manifestation of the imperative of self-development, failure to be more in the labor market carries a fairly heavy price. The "noncareer lifestyle" is not easy today. The system is not conducive to such alternatives.

But in a Culture of Sustainability, the noncareer lifestyle would be both acceptable and doable. It means that failure to demonstrate the "productivist values" of ambition, achievement, success, and such would be socially acceptable. A noncareer lifestyle in a Culture of Sustainability offers respect, responsibility, security, and a sense of participation as a matter of right, and it has the advantage of being less stressful and still providing the legitimate element of fun. Zorba and Gandhi were not careerists. Gandhi had a cause but not a career (even though trained as a lawyer).

The merit of a noncareer lifestyle would be appreciated in a world of sufficiency, limited wants, and the Satiable Self. Does this mean that a new culture would repress careerism, initiative, and ambition, along with self-improvement? No. The difference is that the "imperatives" to be more would be gone, and policy reforms would assure those who opt off the production treadmill a respectable role as contributing members of society.

It is easy to think of Gandhi and Zorba and what it might be like to live like them in a world of sufficiency and the Satiable Self. The economic, political, and cultural spheres must be molded and shaped into conformity with this. The point is that to get away from the ecological peril created by an economy of have all you can have, we need to let go of Be All You Can Be.

We can examine our improvements from the past and rely on what is sustainable. The cultural context for a sustainable world involves an end to have all you can have. It involves a new *culture* in which it is worthy *not* to Be All You Can Be. One can always be more, if to do so is consistent with the requirements of sustainability. Yet the Satiable Self must become the new cultural norm.

THE ECONOMY OF SUFFICIENCY IS AN ECONOMY OF MAINTENANCE

What about the institutional level of reform? Again, Thorstein Veblen has a contribution to make. *The Theory of the Leisure Class*, now more than 100 years old, has several references to a notion that Veblen never elaborates in the remainder of his works. This is his idea that people have an inherent and intrinsic dislike for "wasted effort." This is largely connected to his discussion of the "instinct of workmanship." But this little-noticed notion is pivotal for our vision of a Culture of Sustainability. The point is that, based upon Veblen's idea, there is a distinguishable difference between the principle of "avoiding wasted effort" and that of both "continuous improvement" and "efficiency."

The guiding principle of an Economy of Sufficiency is to avoid wasted effort and resources. What do we mean by "sufficiency?" Herman Daly and

John Cobb comment in *For the Common Good* (1989) that "if 'needs' includes an automobile for each of 1 billion Chinese, then sustainable development is impossible. *The whole issue of sufficiency can no longer be avoided*" (Daly and Cobb 1989, 76; emphasis added). Following this, sufficiency implies limited needs and the social consensus that it would take to restrain our insatiable appetites. In an Economy of Sufficiency we not only limit our needs and production of commodities but reorganize production itself on a new basis. What capitalism creates as a result of its "driven by improvement" character, that is, its "more is better" character, is an economy of efficiency. "Efficiency" is not about simple avoidance of wasted effort. It is about "getting the most for the least." It's about maximization of profit, more than minimization of costs. According to neo-classical economic theory, particularly the structure of "purely competitive markets," maximizing profits forces firms to minimize their costs. This is supposed to result from the invisible hand of the market, as Adam Smith suggested.

The principle-of-maximization rules, in other words, forces the least-cost-method of production. Of course, all of this has resulted in what Jeremy Rifkin calls "the cult of efficiency." He says:

The modern notion of efficiency emerged in the nineteenth century in the wake of experiments in the new scientific field of thermodynamics. Engineers, experimenting with power-driven machinery, began to use the term "efficiency" to measure energy flows and entropy losses. "Efficiency" came to mean the maximum yield that could be produced in the shortest time, expending the least amount of energy, labor, and capital in the process. The man most responsible for popularizing the notion of efficiency in the economic process was Frederick W. Taylor. His principles of "scientific management," published in 1895, became the standard reference for organizing the workplace—and were soon used to organize much of the rest of society. (Rifkin 1995, 49–50)

Efficiency is about getting the most for the least—but it is not a onetime effort. Efficiency means that we approach all tasks with the assumption that we are never satisfied with the results. We keep a sharp eye on the production process, always looking for ways to "improve performance," always looking for ways to get more for less. Our Culture of Insatiable Freedom is organized around this. In today's Economy of Insatiable Improvers, we continually scrutinize the horizon of production for new ways to improve efficiency.

Veblen had a different take on this. He said that people do instinctively care about their work, that is, what we have to do to keep life going. He called this the "instinct of workmanship." He then said that as we do what's necessary to live, we are conscious of wasting our time and effort in what might turn out to be "futile" attempts at getting the goods produced. He felt that this idea was instinctive with humans. If they know the shortest way to get somewhere or what for them is the easiest way, they generally have an interest in avoiding the long way around. Of course, this assumes that we are talking about a "task" rather than a "process." Clearly, there are times when going the long way or the harder way might be what we desire, because the "process" is what matters at that time. But in production of goods and services, if we know the easiest way, we do it. This, too, assumes that the easiest way is sufficient.

People are doers, says Veblen. They are "agents" in the world, going and coming, working, and engaged in their lives. He doesn't mean that people are always trying to "get ahead" but that they are out there in the world creating, producing, eating, and sleeping. He says that the individual is "seeking in every act the accomplishment of some concrete, objective, impersonal end. By force of his being such an agent he is possessed of a taste for effective work, and a distaste for futile effort" (Veblen [1899] 1945, 33). When we go to sleep, for instance, the point is to be able to "get some sleep." If our goal is to get the vegetables planted in the garden, then we use the tools that are ready-to-hand and do it. If we find that the tool doesn't work very well, then we get frustrated and are aware of the "futility" and "wasted effort" that this might entail, and we do something about it.

What Veblen *doesn't* mean is that when we use a tool, we are constantly thinking in terms of how to improve its efficiency! That's not instinctive but a creation of our capitalist culture. There is a huge difference between an economy that tries to avoid spinning its wheels and one that continuously seeks to improve their traction and speed them up. The former is an Economy of Sufficiency, while the latter is our present system. Veblen says that we have a "sense of the demerit of futility, waste, or incapacity" (Veblen [1899] 1945, 15). In the second chapter of *The Theory of the Leisure Class*, Veblen states that we have a "repugnance to all futility of effort which belong(s) to man by virtue of his character as an agent" (33). He also states that the instinct of workmanship "disposes (us) to deprecate waste of substance or effort" and "expresses itself not so much in insistence on substantial usefulness as in an abiding sense of the odiousness and aesthetic impossibility of what is obviously futile" (93). An economy that is not conscious of wasted effort and resources is the antithesis of sustainability (see Hawken, Lovins, and Lovins 1999).

Although capitalism seeks to maximize profits (or income, sales, revenue, shareholder equity, or whatever it might be), it doesn't always try to minimize costs, and the extent of waste in the system has been well documented (e.g., see the classics of Baran and Sweezy 1966 and Bowles, Gordon, and Weisskopf 1984). As we know from the study of neo-classical microeconomics, firms in "imperfect" markets (where they have some control over prices) actually operate on the declining side of their average cost curves rather than at their minimum. Additionally, their cost curves reflect the waste associated with product differentiation and marketing costs and are therefore higher than they would otherwise be. So waste does exist in today's economy.

But today's firms, regardless of the amount of competition that they face or the degree of price control that they have, definitely are motivated to be "efficient" in the sense of trying to find ways to improve their profitability and ultimately their longevity (unless they are setting up for a "flip" buyout). They are maximizers of one thing or another. They are about "getting ahead."

An Economy of Sufficiency is not like this. Firms would not be "driven" in the sense that they are today. They would have to be careful to avoid wasted effort and wasted resources. They must account for their costs. Instead of driven by improvement, they would be serious about avoiding waste. This amounts to a shift in focus. Incentives must still play a part, and financial rewards and incentives are not going to be forgotten. None of these reforms would imply that firms will operate without budget constraints. The power of the budget must apply. We aren't replacing greed with altruism.

Surely, some of our current dynamism would be absent in the Economy of Sufficiency. There would be new rules that firms have to abide by. All of this is manageable through the reforms that are suggested here, and none of these are novel. But it is true that the "dynamic" or imperative of continuous improvement would be gone in the new economy of sustainability. An example from feudal Europe comes to mind when distinguishing efficiency from sufficiency (avoiding wasted effort). Before the twelfth century the serfs on the manors used oxen in the fields. Because the oxen were difficult to turn around at the end of a plowed row, the rows were extremely long. This allowed for fewer turns and less wasted effort. It was a sufficient technology for getting the food produced. But the manorial system was not about getting ahead or being efficient in today's sense. Serfs did not approach food production or farming with the idea of maximizing yields and productivity as today's farmers do. They did choose to avoid wasted effort but were not focused on getting more for less. Had they been, they would have tried to be more efficient in the fields and would have developed three-crop rotation sooner than they did. Eventually, the crop rotation methods improved fodder crop yields enough to feed a larger stock of horses, which then replaced oxen for field plowing. This was an "improvement." But their feudal economy was not "improvement-driven" like its successor. Our present Economy of Insatiable Improvers is focused on "productivity." An Economy of Sufficiency is less so. Rather than approaching everything with a view to improving productivity, we would think about avoiding wasted effort and resources. Would we be "driven" by this new norm? Probably not!

Would this imply "stagnation"? No, but it would imply a "stationary-state" economy (see Daly 1996). Herman Daly discusses Nobel laureate Frederick Soddy's (1877–1956) contribution to the theory of a stationary-state (or steady-state) economy. Soddy argued that "economic sufficiency is the essential foundation of all national greatness and progress" (187). Adding that "sufficiency means 'enough' and growth beyond 'enough' is just 'seed issuing in seed never in bread'" (187). By approaching the productive process from the perspective of sufficiency, we lose some dynamism, but we don't need more of that. What we need are sustainability and the awareness that we don't want to produce in a manner that wastes our time, resources, or effort.

Instead of an economy devoted to continuous improvement, we would have one dedicated to maintenance. Part of what it means to avoid wasted effort is to understand maintenance. The steady-state economy is one of maintenance. Maintenance and sustainability go hand in hand. A culture of satiability is aware of the importance of maintaining what is. This, in fact, is a very Buddhist concept (e.g., in Robert Pursig's *Zen and the Art of Motorcycle Maintenance*

1974). We have the capability to live well by simply maintaining things well. By maintenance, we mean maintaining our relationships, our means of production, our families, our factories and offices, our health, our neighborhoods and communities, our environment, our earth. We have to think in terms of maintaining what we have rather than getting more of what we either can do or can have. An economy of maintenance is not something that most think about. Of course, it's the case that our efforts to maximize improvement generally fail if there isn't also good maintenance. But today maintenance is supposed to serve the greater purpose of facilitating further improvement. Yet we don't need it to be a means because it is sufficient for maintenance to be an end in itself.

Our capitalist Culture of Insatiable Freedom is organized around maximization of directed effort. Directed effort is intended to go beyond "avoidance of wasted time and energy." It is effort at improvement of anything and everything that we feel is good. If it's good, we want more of it, and if not more of it, then we want it faster, with less effort, and more efficiently. The principle applied today is "efficiency" rather than "sufficiency." Efficiency is maximization- and minimization-related, and it is clearly a product of an "improvement-driven" culture. On the other hand, sufficiency is a corollary of "avoidance of wasted effort." The early hunter-gatherers, in their Culture of Security, organized their lives around the latter concepts, and it worked! So at the policy and institutional level we have to implement reforms that reprioritize within the context of the new Culture of Sustainability.

Clearly, this suggests some serious change. Going beyond the profit-, market-, and growth-driven logic of the global economy is essential. The point is to go beyond the "drivenness" of the current culture. The radical reforms that this implies are ones that progressives have been talking about for years. There is nothing new to add here. Corporate boardrooms must be democratized; Wall Street must take a backseat; full employment legislation is essential; a reorganization of the global economy from the competitive struggle that exists currently to one of negotiated trade is pivotal.

Much of the intent of the reforms falls within what Polanyi would call "reembedding the economy." Polanyi distinguished between "improvement" and "habitation." We know about improvement, but by habitation he meant security. With improvement-driven capitalism, he says, "this formula appears to take for granted the essence of purely economic progress, which is to achieve improvement as the price of social dislocation" (Polanyi [1944] 1957, 34). His comment about the Industrial Revolution applies as well to today's globalized, high-tech revolution: "This time again it was improvement on the grandest scale which wrought unprecedented havoc with the habitation of the common people" (39). He concludes that we have vainly believed for the last century that "all human problems could be resolved given an unlimited amount of material commodities" (40). He suggested fifty years ago that we put habitation ahead of improvement, and the reforms sketched here would do just that. Markets, prices, trade, and profits would still exist but would be subordinated through legislative policy to the requirements of sustainability and security. This isn't so problematic. A host of blueprints that would effectively reduce the economy to a stationary-state condition is well known (e.g., Herman Daly's work).

An Economy of Sufficiency in a Culture of Sustainability would assure security to all, would put democratic decision making in the economy ahead of corporate profitability and Wall Street investors, would redistribute both power and resources to the world's have-nots, and would subordinate the insatiable desire to both have and be more to the need for simplicity, fairness, and equality. The reforms would be "radical" in that, by themselves and considered individually, they are reforms *within* capitalism, but, enacted as a comprehensive package, they would alter the system and culture in a radical fashion, creating a postcapitalist economy. Capitalism can be reformed, but by doing it thoroughly, we can transcend its limitations. It becomes postcapitalist, as David Korten's recent book explains (Korten 1999). There are precedents for this going as far back as Eduard Bernstein's *Evolutionary Socialism* in 1898, one year before Veblen's *The Theory of the Leisure Class* (Bernstein [1898] 1961; Brown 1991a). But in our contemporary literature of reform, Korten's newest book is an excellent sketch of what an Economy of Sufficiency would look like.

Here are some of the basics of radical reform:

- An Economic Bill of Rights that assures access to public health care, the right to a decent job, and a "say" on the job through union, participatory, and empowerment legislation. Bowles and Gintis suggested such a bill in the early 1980's (Bowles, Gordon, and Weisskopf 1984).
- A federally funded environmental and social/urban redevelopment jobs program targeted for youth.
- Democratization of corporate boardrooms and corporate decision making by mandating seats for workers, community members, women, and so on.
- Imposition of green taxes to reduce purchases of environmental "bads."
- Public investment in urban revitalization, mass transit, and the environment, paid for, in part, by defense spending reductions.
- Disinvestment in the automobile and its infrastructure.
- Increase corporate profit taxes and capital gains taxes to at least their 1950 levels.
- Impose a tax on international currency speculation.
- Cancel all Third World debt.
- Democratize the World Trade Organization, the International Monetary Fund, and the World Bank by mandating voting membership to Third World nations, unionized workers, and so on.
- Increase income taxes on the richest 20 percent in the U.S.
- Impose a consumption tax.
- Implement flexible wage and price controls, for example, a "tax-based incomes policy."
- Raise the minimum wage to fifteen dollars/hour.

- Implement an industrial policy that brings together government and industry leaders to shift investment from private to public needs.
- Create a public banking system to foster green and low-income lending.
- Legislate a full employment act (like the Humphrey-Hawkins precedent in the 1970s) that assures a decent-paying job to everyone through both the nonprofit sector and the public sector.
- Create a United Nations fund for sustainable development programs in the have-not nations financed by the richest 20 percent of the member nations.
- Pass Fair Trade Agreements between nations that assure livable wages and decent environmental constraints.
- Renegotiate all free trade agreements to assure fair, labor-centered, environmentally sound trade.

This is not an exhaustive list of reforms. It communicates a message, however. All of these reforms have been specified and suggested by others over the past half century. None of them are novel, and most of them have been either advocated or actually implemented in other parts of the world, like Japan and the social democratic nations of Europe. The mixed economy matrix (Figure 5.2) illustrates this. All of these reforms together would alter the national and global playing field. They would reduce the profitability of the global system, redistribute income, create a more egalitarian world, and subordinate profits to the social and environmental needs of the people. They would strengthen the social safety net and make jobs, education, and health care *the* priorities over the dictates of Wall Street, investment bankers, and shareholders. Investment funds need to shift to the Third World in an effort to create their own sustainable, self-reliant, bioregional economies. They must be democratized as a condition for receipt of these funds. Alternative agriculture (permaculture), education, birth control access, and sustainable development programs are essential.

Many of us have read year after year the literature of reform. Books by David Korten, Paul Hawken, Amory and Hunter Lovins, William Greider, Robert Kuttner, Herman Daly, Jeremy Rifkin, and others are only the tip of the iceberg. The literature that both critiques and suggests solutions is absolutely enormous. My economics courses use *Natural Capitalism* (Hawken, Lovins, and Lovins 1999) among other titles with similar themes. In fact the *Wall Street Journal* named Amory Lovins one of the twenty-eight people most likely to "change the course of business" in the 1990s, and much of the blueprint for these changes is in the 1997 book *Factor Four: Doubling Wealth; Halving Resource Use* (Hertsgaard 1998, 300). The themes are always this: the system can be changed with a commitment to reform. Corporations will not go out of their way to initiate this but can be pressed into it, especially if it is the wave of the future. Some corporations already are on board. Some corporate leaders are more progressive than others.

It is clear that a set of radical reforms will change the corporate and business landscape tremendously. The competition for profits and power will have to go and be replaced with a cooperative approach. Getting rich in the bullish stock market, like that of the 1990s, will end. An industrial policy that assembles all major corporate leaders, industry by industry, to begin negotiating their market shares and their security is essential. We can change the rules for all business players such that all must comply with increased taxes, paying higher wages, green production, and environmental codes. Their profits will be less. They must disclose all of their financial records to everyone, including their communities, workers, the government, and others in the industry. If they all have to play by the same rules, all will be impacted in an equally negative way. These rules have to be negotiated at the global level, as well. Negotiated trade will have to replace free trade. Determination of secure market shares and investment planning with price fixing will be needed. In the U.S. our closest experience with this was the brief National Industrial Recovery Act of 1933. But it was declared unconstitutional because it reduced the competitive reliance that the U.S. had come to accept as "natural" for capitalism to work. We have professed a blind faith in a competitive and profit-driven system for 200 years of American capitalism. But we can change this.

It is clearly hard for many to comprehend an economy that is not driven by competition and insatiable improvement. My experiences in higher education suggest that nonprofits can work. Many disagree, of course. But consider what it is and how many of us in the capitalist industrial nations have experience with well-functioning economic enterprises that are *not* profit-motivated, privately owned, and market-based. One example is my state university—we are a business; we run on budgets; we cater to our customers; we work hard; and we try to provide a good product. It has worked. America's education system, for all of its faults, has created a level of broad-based, mass education that has built both the technologies and competent labor force to grow and improve us all the way to the brink of environmental exhaustion. How can we explain these "successes"? It's *responsible* business activity in the nonprofit sector. The Salvation Army was featured in an issue of *Forbes* magazine in which the famous management expert Peter Drucker commented that the Salvation Army is "by far the most effective organization in the U.S. No one even comes close to it in respect to clarity of mission, ability to innovate, measurable results, dedication and putting money to maximum use" (Lenzner and Ebeling 1997, 97). The point is that good business practices can happen in a noncompetitive, nonprofit, but *responsible* fashion in a different culture. It's already being done by nonprofits and NGOs the world over. David Korten says that "although the longer-term goal is to eliminate the for-profit, publicly traded corporation as we know it, the interim objective is to restore the doctrine that a corporation enjoys only those privileges specified in its charter to facilitate the conduct of a business in the public interest and that these privileges are subject to a periodic public review and withdrawal" (Korten 1999, 191).

Corporations resist changes of this sort, because their motive has been greed and insatiable expansion. But they have been successfully pressured to change their ways in the past and to accept a different climate from what they would have preferred. For instance, in Europe, the business class has been more conciliatory in the last century, acquiescing to much of the social democratic drift of the people. They have accepted more of the welfare state, higher taxes, and higher wages than their American counterparts. So they have submitted. The American corporate class will do likewise if the Congress, the local governments, and the people push them. Both during the Depression and in the late 1960s the U.S. corporate class bent with the wind and accepted Social Security, unemployment compensation, minimum wage, and public assistance, and then in the late 1960s they accepted the Occupational Safety and Health Administration (OSHA), the Clean Air and Water Act, Equal Employment Opportunity Commission, the Environmental Protection Agency (EPA), and the Civil Rights Act. They had to be pushed, but they acquiesced, nonetheless.

Subordinating Wall Street and the profit motive is a qualitative leap from what corporations have been asked to do before now, and this is so, in part, because there is in these reforms a commitment to equality, redistribution from the rich to the poor, and democratization of decision making in the economy (what has historically been called industrial and economic democracy or worker self-management). But we are justifying these demands for an entirely new reason: global sustainability of humankind. As Hertsgaard cautions, the market can be an effective vehicle but only if "backed by relentless pressures on corporations to do the right thing; the carrot works best when combined with the stick" (Hertsgaard 1998, 279).

The problem of social, cultural, and economic change is exacerbated by the fact that many people in the U.S. and around the advanced capitalist world are getting very rich in the new global economy. In 1996 *Forbes* magazine said that the wealth of the 447 billionaires, whose wealth is claimed by these people to be a result of "enterprising" activity, equals the combined annual income of the poorest *half* of humanity. Yet in 1991, only five years before, there were only 274 billionaires (Korten 1999, 80). There are now so many new billionaires that *Forbes* has quit counting them. These people are not going to favor radical reforms.

But there's a good chance, if the progressive alternatives are made clearer over the next half century, that as much as two-thirds of humanity will be ready. Those getting rich in the new high-tech world are still a minuscule number compared to those who are losing ground in it. In a 1996 op-ed article in the *International Herald Tribune* Klaus Schwab and Claude Smadja, who head the World Economic Forum—a global corporate association of the 1,000 largest multinationals—said that "although conventional wisdom says that technological change and increases in productivity translate into more jobs and higher wages, in the last few years technology has eliminated more jobs than it has created" (Korten 1999, 201). The new wealth at one end of the global system is creating more insecurity at the other, and employment insecurity is only increasing each year. As Schwab and Smadja also add, "Globalization tends to delink the fate of the corporation from the fate of its employees" (Korten 1999, 201). In other words, we need the corporations more than they need us—exactly what Marx said 100 years ago.

The journal *Yes! A Journal of Positive Futures* has published work by Paul Ray that surveys the attitudes of Americans about a cultural transformation. His surveys show that 68 percent of Americans "want us to return to a simpler way of life with less emphasis on consumption and wealth" (Korten 1999, 217). Korten mentions a Merck Family Fund survey that asks respondents to rate the things that would make them more satisfied with their lives. Fifty-six percent chose "if there was less stress in my life" as their top priority, and 62 percent agreed that they would like to simplify their lives (218). The point is that there is interest in an Economy of Sufficiency and a Culture of Sustainability. Korten says that "to create a just, sustainable, and compassionate post-corporate world we must face up to the need to create a new core culture, a new political center, and a new economic mainstream" (261).

It won't happen overnight. It doesn't need to—Yet! It will take a much clearer understanding that what people will get for letting go of the Be All You Can Be and have-all-you-can-have world that we've come to see as "eternal," "natural," and "universal" is a feeling of safety, security, relaxation, and fun. It will take the creation of participatory and democratic work, so that, on the job, people will feel a sense of belonging, being needed, and having their work "meaningful," if not "pleasurable." Not all work can be made pleasurable or fun, but by democratizing it and empowering the worker, all work can be made meaningful. If this happens, then, we are all more likely to accept social change in return for fewer goods. After World War I, American and European workers were led to accept alienated, meaningless labor for the "goods life" that higher incomes would buy. That was, in part, what Henry Ford was intending with his five-dollar-day wage. From the worker's perspective, and many today have had this experience, it is that, "I'll accept the meaninglessness of this job if the pay is good. At least with the money, I can buy the things I want to compensate for the drudgery of the job." One of the biggest selling points for an Economy of Sufficiency is that work will be made more meaningful and less stressful, the inequalities will be reduced, and the system will feel fairer. Security will be assured. But our purpose is not to create an economic blueprint in itself. The purpose is more about what it means to live in a sustainable culture that is not based upon continuous improvement and the insatiable self.

Most people have little sense for what it means to live in a world in which Be All You Can Be is *not* the guiding principle of life and in which "continuous improvement" is *not* the essence of being human. All blueprints that have been published assume that, although "having more" is not sustainable, "being more" is. It's not true. In terms of social priorities, a shift to the Culture of Sustainability implies that "improvements" would be consciously chosen in a democratic and collective process. This would not be a culture without capacity for improvement but one in which decisions about how to produce and allocate the economic surplus would be subject to democratic social decision making.

The agenda for improvements and the prioritizing of them would involve public policy and the democratic process that is now in place (notwithstanding much-needed campaign finance reform, checks on private interest lobbying, and a visible presence in Congress for leftist views). The extent of democratic accountability needs to be widened and deepened in our political as well as economic sphere so that the range and type of decisions about priorities would be greater in scope than today. Health care, the search for medical cures for disease and illness, and public and private investment in the environment would be part of the list to be debated. Clearly, all of the quality-of-life issues and social justice concerns would be essential to the agenda for "improvements."

The debate about opportunity costs and trade-offs would be more vigorous, too. We would choose our improvements carefully and not be driven by the assumption that more is necessarily better. It's important to make the statement that in this new culture, there is room for improvements, but they would be subordinated to the cultural norm of sustainability, security, and the Satiable Self.

What constitutes an "improvement"? It's hard to debate which improvements come first, that is, to prioritize them, unless we have a consensus regarding the legitimate range of parameters. Many improvements can be left to individual firms at the office or shop-floor level. Workers have always been able to examine their work and describe ways that their jobs might be better done, in either a safer, easier, or more meaningful fashion. At the industry level these kinds of improvements can be discussed, their cost effect to the economy can be measured, and the extent to which these various changes can be implemented in the least bureaucratic and most decentralized way can be clarified. There are improvements that can be made at the neighborhood and community level, also implemented out of local tax revenues and decentralized. There are improvements that can be funded and implemented in a decentralized way and that therefore require no national debate.

Other social and global kinds of improvements do necessitate broad policy debate. It is logical to consider improvements at these broader levels to concern one fundamental issue: the elimination, reduction, and prevention of human suffering. This is perhaps the single criterion for constituting an improvement. In other words, if the economy is no longer "driven" by insatiable improvement, and yet we know that improvements can take place, what criterion do we use to compare them? Who's to say that his or her particular improvement should be preempted by another's? Democratic debate is how we do this now, and it will continue at the local, state, and national level, both in the legislative political sphere and in the streets through mass demonstrations and such.

Can there be any improvement that is of a higher priority than that related to reducing human suffering? There are improvements that add to happiness, play, having fun, the use of child and adult "toys," better running shoes, wrinkle-free clothes, better fishing reels, easier-to-use snow shovels. Many of these can be decentralized decisions, but if they involve major expenditures, they have to submit to the criterion of reducing suffering. Many won't measure up.

If an Economy of Sufficiency (and Maintenance) isn't fundamentally about reducing suffering, then it won't work. There are only three types of human suffering that we have to distinguish between:

1. Needless Suffering
2. Accidental Suffering
3. Existential Suffering

Of course, needless suffering is the most essential to address when we evaluate investment in social improvements. Needless suffering is just that: needless and preventable. The suffering that results from global inequality, the social injustice that puts the rich ahead of the poor, that allows the richer folks to live beyond their share of resources—this is needless suffering and economic hardship due to social injustice. It may be the result, therefore, of racism, sexism, classism, or nationalism. It's suffering that can be eliminated through democratization and redistribution of power and resources. It is suffering that results from economic exploitation in the Third World sweatshops of multinational corporations. When we examine the list of improvements that need to be undertaken, the top priority should be to those projects that reduce and eliminate needless suffering.

Then there is accidental suffering. Some of the obvious cases are those due to natural disasters and weather. Hurricanes, earthquakes, droughts, severe storms, floods, and fires are among this type. Some of the associated human suffering can be eliminated and is, in fact, needless. For example, with recent earthquakes, although the quake itself can't be prevented, because many poor people in affected Third World nations are reduced to living on marginalized land in substandard housing, they are more severely impacted by the quake than they otherwise should be. But the suffering caused by such calamities is not always controllable. They are accidents. We can prepare for them and ready ourselves for intervention when needed. This is done today in a variety of ways from crop insurance to the declaration by governments and leaders of "national disasters" qualifying for financial relief.

What about diseases, illness, and injury? This is critical. Some diseases are needless, and their suffering is due to the inequality that keeps people poor and without adequate health care. Smallpox, typhoid, malaria (especially the new strain of this in Africa) are diseases of poverty that are needless. Others are accidental. There's the suffering that is visited upon those who experience an injury that is debilitating and irreparable. It may well be an accident that just happens. It is suffering for the victim and friends and family, to be sure. But it is not of the "needless" category. There are injuries like car accidents and those from power tools or even guns. Are they needless? Clearly, many are. Too many cars, too much congestion, not enough mass transit, too many guns, too much violence—much of it is needless. A fall on a bicycle or an amputation from a power tool can be bad luck. We have to accept that these kinds of suffering will always be with us. There are diseases like cancer, AIDS, and heart conditions for which we have as yet no cure. To what extent is it an accident that any one of us gets cancer? If it's due to polluted drinking water or occupational hazards, then it's needless, of course. Some of it may be accidental. Some may be preventable through improved diet or preventive health care itself.

The diseases that now confront us like AIDS, cancer, and heart failure are not all "diseases of civilization." If they are, then we can continue to fight for their amelioration by investing in improvements that will reduce such suffering. There are diseases and illnesses of old age, as well. How needless are these? Many are not and shouldn't command our attention. We have to accept death. In general, the medical cause of death for the aged is identifiable. For some who die sooner, the cause might be accidental or even needless, for example, from Alzheimer's disease. As yet there is no cure, and prevention is negligible. For most victims, it's accidental suffering. But if a cure can be found, some suffering can be reduced. We can try to prevent accidents and likewise the suffering that they induce. But accidental suffering will always exist and is of a different genre from that of needless suffering.

Finally, there is existential suffering. It is part of life, part of our existence. It is not preventable and can't be eliminated. If you lose a loved one in a horrific tornado, it was an accident. You suffer. The best we can do, beyond taking the necessary precautions to prevent tornado damage, is provide support, human understanding, and the love, compassion, and sympathy that those who grieve deserve. Death is a case of existential suffering. It is suffering for the survivors that can't be eliminated and is part of life itself. It is existential—part of our sentient being. There are "losses" in life, tragedies, and bad luck that will never be overcome. The suffering that results is existential. The best we can do socially in a Culture of Sustainability is provide the compassion, care, and kindness that the victims deserve.

An economy that is no longer driven by the insatiable desire to be more or have more, or by the logic of insecurity and competition, or by insatiable improvement is an economy that will require us to prioritize our improvements on the basis of how much suffering they reduce. It's not that we won't have or be more or that we can't achieve more. But the culture and economy won't be driven by it.

How do we get there? With respect to the cultural type of change that we are proposing, the process will unfold, if it does, in an organic and evolutionary manner. But the key ingredient is to build the "movement of movements" through a series of coalitions of progressive groups. Again, there is little that is new here. There are activists worldwide doing this now. The Third World Network, a global organization of progressive social and environmental groups, has over 200 member groups today. There will be more Earth Summits with more participants. As Mark Dowie, author of *Losing Ground: American Environmentalism at the Close of the Twentieth Century* (1995), told Hertsgaard in a recent interview: "The international listing of environmental NGOs is thicker than the Manhattan phone book. So the infrastructure is there, and the popular consciousness exists, it's just a matter of putting them together" (Hertsgaard 1998, 309). In fact, this is beginning to happen. Small local groups that have formed to fight for single issues in their locality are organizing, thanks to the Internet, into larger, thematic nonprofit organizations (NPOs) and networks.

The one thing that all progressive movements have in common is that they care more about quality of relationships than anything else. This is significant. By quality of relationships we mean social justice, relations between workers and employers, those within the family and community, and those between men and women. There are others as well. But these movements, including the environmental movement, the women's movement, the labor movement, gay and lesbian rights movement, peace movement, and human rights movement, all assume one thing: that the self is social. The Satiable Self cannot be satisfied with anything less than humanized and democratized social relationships.

On the other hand, the insatiable self has pursued forms of self-development aimed at compensating for alienated relations in many aspects of life. This would no longer be necessary. The variety of social movements will have to grope their way toward a shared vision in which each understands that "quality of relationships" is vital. This is their commonality that has to be built upon. The goal is to bring these groups together so that there is eventually a majoritarian global movement that can press for the needed radical reforms. In the pre-Neolithic world people didn't have much that we consider essential today. But they had two dimensions to their lives that must be restored: (1) meaning and (2) justice. It is not hard to think of living without many of the goods and services that we have today. But for the Satiable Self to find life "sufficient," there surely needs to be an awareness that life makes sense and that it is fair.

Fairness and meaning are key features in this vision. The rest of it is a matter of what gratifications are sustainable and which ones are not. Basic needs can be agreed upon, as suggested here:

> How little,
> From the resources unrenewable
> By Man, cost the things of
> Greatest value –
> Wild beauty, peace, health and love,
> Music and all testaments of spirit!
> How simple our basic needs –
> A little food, sun, air, water, shelter, warmth and sleep!
> (Adams and Newhall 1968, 92)

What the individual gets out of this is a less stressful life of equal simplicity.

Some will want to improve themselves. So be it. Others who don't care won't be penalized. The Culture of Sustainability has a tolerance for "doing nothing with your life" beyond being socially responsible. The dynamism that drives capitalism today would be gone. We would have to choose our improvements carefully and thoughtfully. We would drive them rather than be driven by them! Perhaps there are peace and comfort in stagnation, and we return to features of the Culture of Security in which improvements occur either by accident or by intentional choice.

In an important respect, Aristotle was correct. The self as we understand it in all of its multiple dimensions is capable of behaving insatiably, but this isn't the way to happiness or sustainability. Existentially and as a result of the reflexivity of consciousness, people are transcendent, becoming beings. The argument is not about this. People will always be those beings who can conceive themselves beyond what they are at any given time. Clearly, Martin Heidegger's philosophy in *Being and Time* (1962) clarified this. In fact, phenomenology makes this point, and even Jean-Paul Sartre's analysis in *Being and Nothingness*

(1953) validates it as well. The history of philosophy is merely the working out of what it means to be a becoming being.

But this also makes us capable of limiting ourselves in ways that are sustainable. Our freedom is insatiable, but it also allows us to choose our essence, to choose our becoming, and to direct our intentionality. Sustainability requires us to become but to become satiable, not just in having but in being, too. We accept that we are becoming beings, without being driven by it.

The question for a satiable culture is this, What does it mean to have the Satiable Self with "limitless being"? Is this an oxymoron? Not at all. The Buddhist philosopher and spiritual leader Thich Nhat Hanh has addressed this. His "New Century" message on the eve of the new millennium was inspirational and yet consistent with the Buddhist notion of limited living *through* the acceptance of our insatiable potentiality. In many respects it is true that only by *accepting* that we *don't have to be more* are we going to be able to live meaningful, just, and simple lives with less. We don't have to continuously be more. We don't have to be less. But only by truly coming to terms with forgoing the actualization of our capacity to be more and accepting this, are we going to be content just being in the present—with being who we are. By always wanting to be more, we are implicitly expressing our discontent with who we are. This makes us today creatures of permanent discontent. We have to get comfortable with who we are, and this requires creating the just, simple, and equal world of sustainability. In part, our ability to do this is a function of letting go of the drive always to be more. To live well in a Culture of Sustainability, we have to let go of our discontent with who we are, because this creates the inner need to insatiably improve.

Thich Nhat Hanh said that "if the 20th century was the century of humans conquering Nature, the 21st century should be one in which we conquer the root causes of the suffering in human beings—our fears, ego, hatred, greed, etc. If the 20th century was characterized by individualism and consumption, the 21st century can be characterized by the insights of interbeing. In the 21st century, humans can live together in true harmony with each other and with nature; as bees live together in their bee hive or as cells live together in the same body, all in a real spirit of democracy and equality" (Thich Nhat Hanh 1999). In other words, he suggests that we need to focus on ending needless suffering and making "quality of relationships" (interbeing) a source of satiable meaning and contentment.

Our being is limitless, but this doesn't require a culture or economy that pushes us to the max. We don't need continuous improvement. We need sustainability, and we can get that now through redistribution, justice, simplicity, equality, and compassion. So far, continuous improvement has not solved any of the major problems facing humans. It won't because it will always put the solutions out there beyond our reach. Daniel Quinn is correct: we don't need to be "better" people. In his vernacular, what we need is to give up being a "taker" culture which he contends began with settled civilization 10,000 years ago. The expansive logic of "more" that really began at that time makes us a "taker" world. When that happened, we viewed many of the resulting social problems of conflict, violence, and inequality as being solvable only by either our ability to be "better" people or salvation through a higher power. We don't have to be "better" people, because we are not actually "fallen" sinners anyway. We just got off on the wrong track—the "taker" track of more is better. We evolved on this track to a Culture of Insatiable Freedom and an Economy of Insatiable Improvers. It's time, if we want to get sustainable, to let our unlimited being be!

The point is to create a Culture of Sustainability in which becoming more is not an imperative. We are the becoming beings who can choose consciously to limit our becoming to the requirements of sustainability. Personal growth books, self-help actualization manuals, self-realization seminars—these popularized icons of the present Insatiable Freedom Culture would no doubt have their place. But the cultural context in which they would appear in the future would not be the same. These would be helpful guides for individuals but would not be expressions of permanent discontent or the insatiable desire to Be All You Can Be.

If the Culture Time Line (Figure 3.1) could be completed with the creation of a twenty-first-century Culture of Sustainability, our history might look like Figure 6.1.

Figure 6.1
The Culture Time Line: An Extension

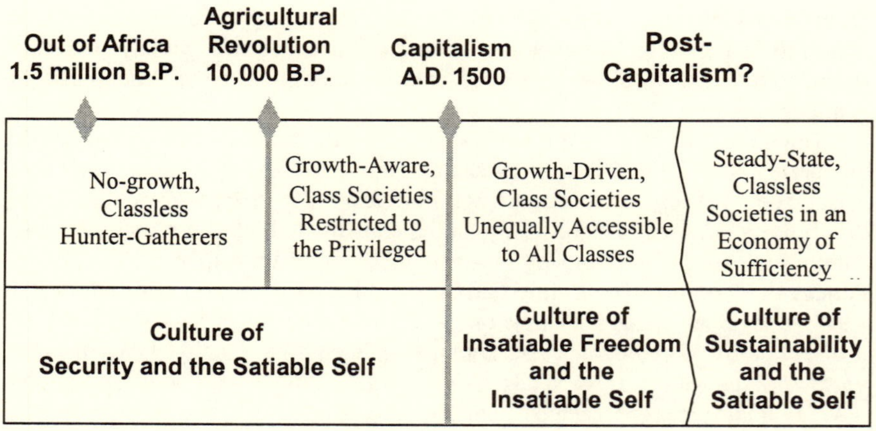

Out of Africa 1.5 million B.P.	Agricultural Revolution 10,000 B.P.	Capitalism A.D. 1500	Post- Capitalism?
No-growth, Classless Hunter-Gatherers	Growth-Aware, Class Societies Restricted to the Privileged	Growth-Driven, Class Societies Unequally Accessible to All Classes	Steady-State, Classless Societies in an Economy of Sufficiency
Culture of Security and the Satiable Self		Culture of Insatiable Freedom and the Insatiable Self	Culture of Sustainability and the Satiable Self

Conclusion: A Sustainable Economy or Postmodern Feudalism?

Whatever happens over the next century has a lot do with the trajectory of the globalization process. Whether or not we weather this storm, there is more and more evidence that the *direction* is wrong. We might get through this without changing directions, but the probability of increased human suffering along the way is very great. We can't predict the outcome, but we can examine the *direction* of today's globalized capitalism and its high-tech revolution.

Here's an example. In 1999, the Fiat auto company in Italy celebrated its centennial. Its CEO, Paolo Cantarella, announced its plans to build 4 million new cars a year over the next decade, exceeding the previous year's 2.66 million. Fiat is the world's sixth largest automaker and Italy's largest industrial group. Cantarella said that "Fiat is finding new opportunities for growth in manufacturing parts and in targeting special product niches. He cited as an example the recently announced contract with Mitsubishi Motors Corp. to develop and build a four-wheel-drive sport utility vehicle in 2001. Europe is Fiat's primary market but officials say they want to boost production and sales in the emerging markets of Asia, Eastern Europe and South America. One part of that strategy is the New Punto subcompact. Fiat plans to produce 600,000 to 700,000 New Puntos a year at three Italian plants and plans to sell at least half outside Italy" ("Fiat Marks Centennial," 1999, 3A). Fiat's CEO is excited about its growth prospects, of course. But the *direction* of "more cars" in the world is not sustainable. We know this, yet this is precisely the *direction* of globalization. Hertsgaard adds that because present levels of production and consumption are not likely to be sustainable, and much of our social legislation is ineffective for both workers and the environment, the prospect of more globalization simply suggests a "form of planetary suicide" (Hertsgaard 1998, 308). Planetary suicide is not likely to occur. But Fiat and every other corporation are driven by more growth, more profits, and ultimately "more is better." Cantarella may feel that there are already too many cars in the world, but he excuses his excitement about more by stating that it is a "compete or die" world that Fiat must accept. He would no doubt add that if Fiat is going to continue creating the payroll for thousands of Italian workers, then it is imperative that it survives this global, competitive struggle. To do this, it must continually improve its performance and Be All You Can Be. Finally, like all those who speak for this imperative, he would conclude that he and Fiat cannot do anything about the *direction* of the global economy. In effect, the system rules. This is true, and it is why we have to change both the system and the rules so that corporations begin working together, agreeing on market shares, and planning their investment with each other and with those who are affected by their decisions. The Economy of Sufficiency requires that we replace do-or-die competition with *collaboration* among corporations, governments, trade organizations, workers, and communities.

When we do examine the direction of globalization, we find that it's not toward simplicity, stable population, less violence, more compassion, biospheric stability, biodiversity, or operative carrying capacity. The direction is toward overuse, more violence, more insensitivity, environmental stress, overpopulation, decreasing biodiversity, global warming, more congestion, and overconsumption.

Lester Brown of the Worldwatch Institute told Hertsgaard in 1990 that what we might need is an "environmental Pearl Harbor" that will shake people out of their lethargy and create the necessary mobilization and activism. "I don't think it's a question of the human species going extinct," he said (Hertsgaard 1998, 296). When people ask Brown whether or not time is running out on the human and environmental clock, his response is, "For whom?" adding that just since 1970, 2 million Ethiopians have starved, thousands of kids in Los Angeles have experienced permanent lung damage from bad air, and 11 percent of Russian infants have been born with birth defects due to the fact that half of Russian drinking water is contaminated (Hertsgaard 1998, 296). For these victims, time has already run out. A likely outcome for continuing in the wrong direction is simply much more needless suffering.

Is capitalism sustainable? Probably. It may not be sustainable without the tragedy of needless suffering, but we have to face the reality that the richest, wealthiest, most privileged, and most protected and comfortable people in the world will be able to shift the burden of suffering, deprivation, and ecological restoration onto those least able to bear this. They will protect themselves at others' expense, as always happens historically. If the poor and underrepresented in the world are uninclined or unable to resist and overcome these odds, then they will suffer. The *wrong direction* will be sustainable. Is humankind sustainable on the basis of capitalism? Probably. But capitalism is a by-product of a cultural evolutionary process, 10,000 years in the making, that has brought us to the point of believing that to be human, one must always try to be more. Capitalism is not the cause of the insatiable desire to have all you can have. It certainly reinforces it, however. But more to the point, *capitalism is the result of a culture based upon the insatiable desire to Be All You Can Be.* This imperative belief is the cause of the *wrong direction*.

There is growing evidence that the world is becoming more dichotomized. A divide is taking place that, if left to the devices of globalization, might well result in "postmodern feudalism." Feudalism as an economic and political system has existed all over the world in a variety of forms. Usually, it has not taken the nation-state form. It has been characterized by warlords or overlords who have armies of conscripted peasants and compete with one another for control over land and resources. Whoever has the biggest army controls. Markets do not drive the system, so tribute and labor services are important. Children are a key element in the armies. There is barter. Disease is usually rampant and allowed to run its course. The evidence pointing toward a new type of feudalism is mounting. Robert Kaplan's article in *The Atlantic Monthly* in 1994, "The Coming Anarchy," is a pioneering piece because it draws our attention to developments that are truly frightening. Since that article was published, the situation has gotten only worse. The developments in the Southern Hemisphere, particularly in Africa, are:

1. the effects of worsening global inequality
2. serious environmental stress in much of the Southern Hemisphere
3. increased militarization of life
4. the breakdown of the nation-state
5. the rise of tribal, ethnic, and religious-based conflicts, none of which follow the geopolitical lines of the post–World War II era
6. the rise of feudal competing warlords
7. increased, but unaddressed, diseases, such as the new malaria strain and AIDS.

Is there such a thing as "postmodern feudalism"? It's not feudalism as we've known it historically, but in Africa it looks like it. Here are some of the facts:

- There are approximately 33 million people in the world that are HIV-positive, and two-thirds of them are in Africa (Kaplan 1994).
- One-third of the world's population is estimated to be carrying tuberculosis (Kaplan 1994).
- Infectious diseases like plague, cholera, and the new malaria are the number one killer in the world and are increasing (Mander 1996, 162; Shell 1997).
- The global incidence of the new malaria has quadrupled in the last five years (Shell 1997, 45).
- Nearly 40 percent of the world's population lives in regions where malaria is endemic (Shell 1997, 45).

- These new infectious diseases are based upon "microbial traffic" and will gravitate to poor populations in Latin America and Africa (Mander 1996, 165–166).
- In sub-Saharan Africa there was a 50 percent decline in investment during the 1980s (Renner 1996, 120).
- "The diamond industry has fueled the war in Sierra Leone, according to a new report by Partnership Africa Canada. For eight years, regional warlords, international companies and neighboring states have greedily traded arms for diamonds with the rebel groups. One of the war's worst atrocities has been mass amputation. Rebel soldiers have hacked off the hands and feet of hundreds of thousands" ("Diamond War," 2000, 6).
- Ninety-five percent of the world's AIDS orphans are in Africa. It is the continent's biggest killer (Muwakkil 1999, 17).
- Due to AIDS, Africa's life expectancy is predicted to fall by twenty years in the next decade (Muwakkil 1999, 7).
- In Zambia 360,000 children have been orphaned by AIDS (Muwakkil 1999, 7).
- The AIDS rate in South Africa's most populous province is 27 percent (Muwakkil 1999, 7).
- The Congo and the nine nations around it constitute one of the world's richest regions in diamonds, oil, uranium, and gold. Yet it is now one of the biggest battlefields in Africa's history and has been called "Africa's first world war." "Six outside states are fighting inside Congo alone, with at least 35, 000 men and boys, battling for a bewildering number of reasons" (Fisher and Onishi 2000, 1).
- Since the Congo war began in 1998 (in part, related to the 1994 genocide in Rwanda) 100,000 people are estimated to have been killed (Fisher and Onishi 2000, 4).
- Kinshasa, Congo's capital, has 6 million people with 10 percent of its mothers and children malnourished (Fisher and Onishi 2000, 5).
- Angola's continuing civil war, since independence from Portugal in 1975, has killed 500,000 people through combat and famine and has left 1 million citizens impoverished and homeless (Salopek 2000, I-3).
- Hundreds have been killed in Nigeria in the uncertain transition to a civilian government where the conflict is largely between Muslims and Christians (Zachary 2000, 10).
- Ethiopian troops have recently overtaken the southwest part of Eritrea, resuming a two-year-old war and triggering a renewed famine (Zachary 2000, 10).
- The clash between Hutus and Tutsis in Burundi since 1993 has killed 200,000 people and created 1.2 million refugees (Zachary 2000, 11).
- In 1992, the UN said that 42 million Africans were at risk of starvation (Hertsgaard 1998, 33).
- Many of the African nations are still feudal in character with a small ruling that class that controls the land, the aid, and the development. The majority are poor sharecroppers (Hertsgaard 1998, 34).

- The Sudanese civil war tragically appears both insatiable and sustainable, "reinforcing the country's reputation as one of the most godforsaken places on earth" (Hertsgaard 1998, 45). Although the war has yet to cease, by 1996 1.5 million Sudanese had been killed, and 85 percent of the southern population consisted of refugees (Hertsgaard 1998, 45).

Unfortunately, these factors add up to a scenario that is far more realistic than our vision of a sustainable world. They point toward a world of haves and have-nots in which the haves of the Northern Hemisphere continue with the globalization of life, economics, and politics. For the haves, the globalization process and the competitive struggle are likely to proceed unabated. For this portion of humanity there will be continued growth, a continued embrace of the magic of the market and consumerism, and a faith that it will all work out. Integration, acceleration, multiculturalism, diversity, and all of the features of the postmodern world will operate. This accords with the cultural mapping by people like Fredric Jameson and David Harvey (Harvey 1989, 1991; Jameson 1991; Brown 1993, 1992a, 1992b, 1991b). The literature on postmodernism is voluminous and likely accurate for this part of the world. Also the critical analyses of writers like Robert Kuttner, William Grieder, and David Korten on the global economy are consistent with the scenarios of the postmodernists. But this may apply *only* to the world of global capitalism populated by the haves.

What about the rest of the world, as exemplified by what's happening in Africa? It's clearly arguable that a totally different pattern may emerge here. With all of the seven developments in the Southern Hemisphere enumerated earlier, these parts of the world may look more feudal than capitalist. Warlords, militarized life, the breakdown of market relations, and disease and environmental pestilence all point to postmodern feudalism.

What's likely? The First World will let it happen. That is, with the host of unmanageable problems that have surfaced, it might be better for the haves to ignore this part of the world and let the pestilence run its course. The advantage to the haves is that by doing so, it might help restore global environmental sustainability without redistribution and without facing hard choices about limiting wants. If there are enough death and decay in some regions of the world, greenhouse gas emissions will be less than otherwise, *global* population growth will be held in check, and resource use will slow down. One part of the world, like Africa, will atrophy so that the advanced capitalist portion can be sustained.

The metaphor is that of agriculture. One long-standing practice in crop rotation is to let part of a field lie fallow while another part is planted. On a global scale this implies that the have-nations of the Northern Hemisphere simply let the overused and abused areas of the world "lie fallow" for as long as it takes to restore some semblance of normality and sustainability. This means to let the warlords rule; let them fight among themselves for control of resources like clean water; let their child armies fight each other; and let disease have its way. Eventually, population would be purged and stabilized, the reduced exploitation of these habitats would bring back ecosystem balance, and restoration of their environments would take place. The fighting, the death, and the destruction, if contained, would be allowed to occur until things finally calm down.

The point for the haves is to cordon off these parts of the world and contain the conflicts and disease. Even though Africa is the most observable example of this today, Latin America, parts of the Middle East, Russia, and the Indian subcontinent perhaps fit this scenario. In the meantime, multinational corporations that need access to resources in these parts of the world would barter with the warlords and provide weapons and provisions in exchange for protected access to the extraction of resources. In effect, there would not be one, unified, and integrated global economy based upon market relations. There would be two worlds—one of postmodern capitalism and the other, more subterranean world of postmodern feudalism. They would be side by side. Images of movies like *Bladerunner, Road Warrior, Water World*, or *The Postman* suggest this scenario. It's speculation, but not without merit. The elements are present today, and the direction is not clearly toward full global integration by markets and business. The evidence of a bifurcated world—a very great divide—does exist. It doesn't have to happen, of course. But it might, and it might as a result of benign neglect by the haves.

There is a process of "acting out" going on in much of the world, and surely it is related to the growing inequality, the insecurity, and the desperation that many feel. Hertsgaard adds that population and per capita consumption are both rising, and this will make the earth's "environmental space" increasingly scarce. Even though we've witnessed a sharp divide between the rich and poor for 10,000 years, "as humanity seeks to create an environmentally sound future, no challenge will be more fundamental, or more difficult, than bridging the ancient gap between rich and poor" (Hertsgaard 1998, 48).

If the climate of terror and insecurity can be contained and isolated by the richer nations, then feudalism of some form will eventually occur in the poorer regions. The rest of the world will carry on. The issue of the environmental impact of trying to grow the have-nots out of their condition would not have to be faced. The population purge will reduce global environmental stress and allow the haves to continue with the Culture of Insatiable Freedom. This is not a prediction, only a possibility. Surely, the creation of a global Culture of Sustainability would mean less needless suffering. Clearly, yet paradoxically, "there is more to life than *more*."

One of the most pressing problems associated with *more* besides being and having more is more people. With over 6 billion people now and with the prospect of 10 billion in the next half century, we have to come to terms with this. Perhaps as long as we are imbued with the insatiable desire to be more, we will continue to believe that having more population is fine. As long as we embrace the Culture of Insatiable Freedom, we will continue to talk about the "right" to have as many children as we want. It's very difficult to imagine controlling and restraining our human population growth when we simultaneously define ourselves as insatiable actualizers of our potential.

The growth in the numbers of our species is more than likely an unconscious by-product of our belief that to be is always to be more, that is, more in self-actualized potential, more in our possessions and living standards, and more in our population. In other words, for much of the world, to Be is to Be More in everything deemed good, and that includes more of our "selves." It's all part of one belief system: the insatiable desire both to be and to have more. Perhaps if this is true, then it will take going beyond today's culture of Be All You Can Be and insatiable improvement if we are to bring population growth rates down to a sustainable level. Many deep ecologists argue that a sustainable world population is about 3 billion people—half our current numbers. This could be accommodated over the next century if we bring birthrates to almost zero. As old age runs its course, then we would eventually see the world's population shrink.

Clearly, an essential part of a program of global redistribution is to provide the means in education, access to birth control, and decent living conditions that would allow the poorest of the world to reduce their population growth rates. For others, there needs to be a broadened public arena to debate the idea that anyone has the "right" to have children. For an Economy of Sufficiency (and Maintenance) to function, we have to get beyond the notion that people have these rights. Rights are not inherent but granted by our human community. If "taking care of each other" is going to be a priority for the future, a case can be made that limiting such rights is necessary for us to truly and effectively take care of each other. Force and coercion won't work, but tax incentives and such might.

Finally, we have to admit that the Culture of Sustainability is fundamentally about security. Security will be assured. Some of our freedoms, like those associated today with corporate "rights" to invest and make profits wherever and however they want and the "right" to have as many children as anyone wants, need to be restrained. With the historical trade-off between freedom and security, the shift needs to go back the other direction—to that of security. It may be that, as Gandhi knew, the "individual" in capitalist society is simply overrated.

But people's belief and acceptance of an economy and social system determine the degree to which it actually works and functions properly. When they challenge a system, whether it is slavery, apartheid, capitalism, or the Soviet model, and they quit believing in it, then it goes into crisis. This happened in the U.S. during the Populist movement in the 1890s depression, again in the 1930s depression, and in the 1960s. When people quit accepting the conditions of an economy, they may hit the streets, act out, slough off on the job, call in sick, and act either angry or apathetic. When this happens, economies don't work very well. This brought down the Soviet system and apartheid. An economic system rises and falls with the degree to which its participants embrace it. They may be quiet about it, and productivity falls; they may be openly hostile and boycott the system, and profits fall. It doesn't matter; the point is that people's enthusiasm for an economic system ultimately determines its performance and longevity. If people get tired of the current performance principle, the productivism-consumerism treadmill, the chronic insecurity they face, and the compete-or-die climate of anxiety, then things might change.

Yet the insecurity (and injustice) that today haunts our culture causes much of the acting out, the anxiety, the violence, and the rage. The desire for a safer, more relaxed, and secure existence might eventually overpower the logic of Be All You Can Be. Then a Culture of Sustainability has a chance. But if people like today's system and are reasonably satisfied with how it works for them, nothing will change. If they acquiesce, nothing will change either; the dominant paradigm will rule. If slaves accept their condition and don't think much about it one way or another, slavery will work and reproduce itself over time. Slavery may be inhuman, but it can be an effective economy and quite efficient as well. It is only when the slaves decide that they don't like it that it begins to crumble. This is the case for feudalism as well.

Likewise, if workers in the sweatshops of the Third World and the fast-food restaurants of the First World feel OK about their lives and livelihoods, then our system will continue. Global capitalism will work well at the systemic level if people believe in it enough to show up for work, accept their pay, and buy their necessities. The environment will continue to decay, and the rich will take the needed precautions to protect themselves. In fact, if workers the world over decide that working is so gratifying that they don't need to be paid much at all, the system would work amazingly well. There would be a major change in the composition of the world's global output from necessities for the mass of people, to luxuries for the elite, but general equilibrium could be achieved. There would be a shift in total income from wages to profit, but as long as spending of profits continued, the system would work, despite what John Maynard Keynes and other Marxists have argued. The point is that people's embrace of *any* economy determines its success. Capitalism is not likely to fall of its own weight or dig its own grave.

But the power and lure of security shouldn't be underestimated. It's safe to say that people actually crave it. Today, security has to be "earned." People may get tired of this and want it assured. If they are willing to be responsible about work and participation, it would work. Quinn talks about security in *My Ishmael* (1997) and says that many people crave it so much that they join cults of various kinds. These are for Quinn the same as "tribes"—what we used for our first million and a half years. He says that people are:

willing to turn over their worldly possessions and to work for nothing in order to *belong*—to have membership and all that comes with membership—food, lodging, clothing, transportation, health care, and so on. Security, in a word. They want to be taken care of *in the tribal way*. They're perfectly willing to give to the cult their total support—in return for *its* total support, which means food, lodging, clothing everything it takes to live as a human. The cult offers them something they deeply want and can't get in the Taker world (our world today). The support-for-support paradigm is more than just a way of staying alive; it's a profoundly satisfying human style. People really *like* living this way. (Quinn 1997, 212)

So if it is the case that an economy and culture function according to how people feel about them, and if people wise up to the environmental and inequality crises and desire security in a more assured way, then an Economy of

Sufficiency will work. If people want it, embrace it, and believe in it, it will work. *If* corporations were to somehow become benevolent, compassionate, caring, and sensitive to who and what are around them, they might get together and collaborate, put people and the environment ahead of shareholder equity, and invite workers and the community to help them decide how to produce— *then it would work.* Chances are that they won't behave this way. But they can be pressured into it. Again, the most basic truth that anyone studying economics can get out of this discipline is that any economy will work if the people in it embrace it. Economies are totally a function of the people who participate in them. They are not governed by any other "laws" of economics or nature. It is not "theories" and "laws" that determine performance but only the people's beliefs. A Culture of Security and an Economy of Sufficiency are doable if the critical mass of supporters can be assembled. This would take something like 80 percent of us rather than the voting majority of 51 percent. But it can and might happen if the lure of security and peace is great enough.

The bottom line is that our culture, based as it is on insatiable improvement, on limitless "getting ahead," is making us crazy. The imperative of Be All You Can Be makes "losers" out of those who don't try to be more; it makes those who try fearful and insecure about "failure" in life; it creates needless stress for those who struggle always to be more; it creates guilt for those who want out of the race. So not only would the Culture of Sustainability and the Satiable Self reduce environmental jeopardy, but they would make our lives simpler and more relaxed. Actualize Your Potential! Mill, Marx, Maslow, and a host of modernist thinkers have been saying this for years. But maybe stagnation is good. Maybe stagnation will save the world. *Don't misunderstand this: the elimination and prevention of needless human suffering are an essential task. We won't compromise this with a steady-state Economy of Sufficiency and Maintenance. They can be reconciled.*

Our human challenge will continue to be in the Culture of Sustainability to eliminate needless human suffering and reduce and prevent accidental suffering. The existential suffering we will have to accept. The loss of loved ones through unpreventable accident and illness and the natural catastrophes that create tremendous suffering—these will continue to demand our attention and diligence. But the elimination of human suffering is different from "improvement for its own sake." The Culture of Sustainability is not a driven culture but is still one in which we must be vigilant about ending suffering, injustice, and alienation. Such an economy and society are not totally stagnant; there will be challenges, and the process of overcoming them is "improvement" and "social progress."

References

Adams, Ansel, and Nancy Newhall. 1968. *This Is the American Earth*. San Francisco: Sierra Club.

Agger, Ben. 1979. *Western Marxism*. Santa Monica, CA: Goodyear.

Albert, M., L. Cagan, N. Chomsky, R. Hahnel, M. King, L. Sargent, and H. Sklar. 1986. *Liberating Theory*. Boston: South End Press.

Aristotle. 1962. *Aristotle Dictionary*. Edited by Thomas P. Kierman. New York: Philosophical Library, 306–307, 334–335.

———. 1982. *Aristotle: Selected Works*. Translated by Hippocrates Apostle and Lloyd Gerson. Grinnell, IA: Peripatetic Press.

Balz, Albert. 1967. *Descartes and the Modern Mind*. Hamden, CT: Archon Books.

Baran, Paul, and Paul Sweezy. 1966. *Monopoly Capital*. New York: Monthly Review Press.

Barnhart, Robert, ed. 1988. *The Barnhart Dictionary of Etymology*. New York: H. W. Wilson.

Baudrillard, Jean. 1975. *The Mirror of Production*. St. Louis: Telos Press.

Bernstein, Eduard. [1898] 1961. *Evolutionary Socialism*. New York: Schocken Books.

Bolles, Richard Nelson. 1994. *What Color Is Your Parachute?* Berkeley, CA: Ten Speed Press.

Bowles, Samuel, and Herbert Gintis. 1986. *Democracy and Capitalism*. New York: Basic Books.

Bowles, Samuel, David Gordon, and Thomas Weisskopf. 1984. *Beyond the Wasteland*. Garden City, NY: Anchor Press.

Braverman, Harry. 1974. *Labor and Monopoly Capital*. New York: Monthly Review Press.

Brinton, Crane. 1967. Enlightenment. *The Encyclopedia of Philosophy*. Vol. 1. Edited by Paul Edwards. New York: Macmillan, 519–525.

Bronowski, Jacob. 1973. *The Ascent of Man*. New York: Little, Brown.

Brower, David. 1998. Interview with David Brower. *Wild Earth*, Spring: 37–38.

Brown, Doug. 1991a. Thorstein Veblen Meets Eduard Bernstein. *Journal of Economic Issues* 25, no. 3: 689–708.

———. 1991b. An Institutionalist Look at Postmodernism. *Journal of Economic Issues* 25, no. 4: 1089–1104.

———. 1992a. Doing Social Economics in a Postmodern World. *Review of Social Economics* 50, no. 4: 383–403.

———. 1992b. Institutionalism and the Postmodern Politics of Social Change. *Journal of Economic Issues* 26, no. 2: 545–552.

———. 1993. The Production of Social Heterogeneity in Postmodern Capitalism. *Current Politics and Economics of the United States* 1, no. 1: 1–14.

———. 1996. East Meets West: Dewey, Gandhi, and Instrumental Equality for the Twenty-First Century. *Inequality: Radical Institutionalist Views on Race, Gender, Class and Nation.* Edited by William Dugger. Westport, CT: Greenwood Press.

Brown, Lester, Christopher Flavin, and Hilary French, eds. *The State of the World 1999: A Worldwatch Institute Report on Progress toward a Sustainable Society.* New York: W. W. Norton.

Brumbaugh, Robert. 1964. *The Philosophers of Greece.* New York: Thomas Y. Crowell.

Collins, Jim. 2000. Built to Flip. *Fast Company*, March: 131–140.

Collins, James, and Jerry Porras. 1994. *Built to Last.* New York: HarperCollins.

Daly, Herman. 1996. *Beyond Growth.* Boston: Beacon Press.

Daly, Herman, and John Cobb. 1989. *For the Common Good.* Boston: Beacon Press.

Davies, Brian. 1992. *The Thought of Thomas Aquinas.* Oxford: Clarendon Press.

Descartes, Rene. 1985. *The Philosophical Writings of Descartes.* Vol. 1. Translated by J. Cottingham, R. Stoothoff, and D. Murdoch. New York: Cambridge University Press.

Diamond War. 2000. *In These Times*, 21 February: 6.

Dominguez, Joe, and Vicki Robin. 1992. *Your Money or Your Life.* New York: Penguin.

Douglas, Mary. 1962. Lele Economy as Compared with the Bushong. *Markets in Africa.* Edited by G. Dalton and P. Bohannan. Evanston, IL: Northwestern University Press, 210–232.

Durning, Alan. 1992. *How Much Is Enough?* New York: W. W. Norton.

Edwards, Richard. 1979. *Contested Terrain.* New York: Basic Books.

Elgin, Duane. 1993. *Voluntary Simplicity.* New York: William Morrow.

Ewen, Stuart. 1976. *Captains of Consciousness.* New York: McGraw-Hill.

Ewen, Stuart, and Elizabeth Ewen. 1982. *Channels of Desire.* New York: McGraw-Hill.

Fiat Marks Centennial. 1999. *Marshalltown Times Republican*, 13 July: A-3.

Fisher, Ian, and Norimitsu Onishi. 2000. Armies Ravage a Rich Land, Creating Africa's "First World War." *New York Times*, 6 February. www.nytimes.com.

Frankena, William. 1965. *Philosophy of Education.* Toronto: Macmillan.

Friedman, Milton. [1962] 1982. *Capitalism and Freedom.* Chicago: University of Chicago Press.

Friedman, Milton, and Rose Friedman. 1981. *Free to Choose.* New York: Avon Books.

Galbraith, John Kenneth. 1958. *The Affluent Society.* Boston: Houghton Mifflin.

Gandhi, M. K. 1938. *Hind Swaraj.* Ahmedabad, India: Navajivan.

———. 1948. *Autobiography: The Story of My Experiments with Truth.* Washington, DC: Public Affairs Press.

———. 1990. *The Essential Writings of Mahatma Gandhi.* Edited by Raghavan Iyer. New York: Oxford University Press.

Gilson, Etienne. 1960. *The Christian Philosophy of Saint Augustine.* Translated by L.E.M. Lynch. New York: Random House.

————. 1986. *The Philosophy of St. Thomas Aquinas*. Edited by G. A. Elrington and translated by Edward Bullough. New York: Dorset Press.

Goldin, Owen, and Patricia Kilroe, eds. 1997. *Human Life and the Natural World*. Orchard Park, NY: Broadview Press.

Gray, Alexander. 1963. *The Socialist Tradition*. London: Longmans.

Greer, Thomas. 1972. *A Brief History of Western Man*. New York: Harcourt Brace Jovanovich.

Gregg, Richard. [1936] 1977. Voluntary Simplicity. *The CoEvolution Quarterly*, Summer: 20–27.

Greider, William. 1997. *One World, Ready or Not*. New York: Simon and Schuster.

Gummere, Richard. 1967. Introduction to *Ad Lucilium Epistulae Morales*, by Seneca. Translated by Richard Gummere. Cambridge: Harvard University Press.

Guthrie, W.K.C. 1967. Pythagoras. *The Encyclopedia of Philosophy*. Vol. 7. Edited by Paul Edwards. New York: Macmillan, 37–39.

Hammonds, Keith. 2000. Grassroots Leadership: Ford Motor Co. *Fast Company*, April: 138–152.

Harvey, David. 1989. *The Postmodern Condition*. Cambridge, MA: Basil Blackwell.

————. 1991. Flexibility: Threat or Opportunity. *Socialist Review* 21, no. 1: 65–78.

Hawken, Paul, Amory Lovins, and L. Hunter Lovins. 1999. *Natural Capitalism*. New York: Little, Brown.

Heidegger, Martin. 1962. *Being and Time*. New York: Harper and Row.

Heilbroner, Robert. [1953] 1972. *The Worldly Philosophers*. New York: Simon and Schuster.

Hertsgaard, Mark. 1998. *Earth Odyssey*. New York: Broadway Books.

Hunnicutt, Benjamin. 1988. *Work without End*. Philadelphia: Temple University Press.

Hunt, E. K. 1990. *Property and Prophets*. New York: Harper and Row.

Jameson, Fredric. 1991. *Postmodernism*. Durham, NC: Duke University Press.

Kahn, Charles. 1967. Anaximander. *The Encyclopedia of Philosophy*. Vol. 1. Edited by Paul Edwards. New York: Macmillan, 117–118.

Kaplan, Robert. 1994. The Coming Anarchy. *The Atlantic Monthly*, February: 45–76.

Kazantzakis, Nicos. 1952. *Zorba the Greek*. New York: Simon and Schuster.

————. 1965. *Report to Greco*. Translated by P. A. Bien. New York: Simon and Schuster.

Korten, David. 1999. *The Post-Corporate World*. West Hartford, CT: Kumarian Press.

Laclau, Ernesto, and Chantal Mouffe. 1985. *Hegemony and Socialist Strategy*. London: Verso.

Lardner, James. 1999. The Urge to Splurge. *U.S. News and World Report*, 24 May: 48–52.

Lee, Richard. 1968. What Hunters Do for a Living, or, How to Make Out on Scarce Resources. *Man the Hunter*. Edited by R. Lee and I. DeVore. Chicago: Aldine, 31–38.

Leiss, William. 1976. *The Limits to Satisfaction*. Toronto: University of Toronto Press.

Lenzner, Robert, and Ashlea Ebeling. 1997. Peter Drucker's Picks. *Forbes*, 11 August: 97–99.

Malloy, Amy, ed. 1999. From the Editor. *Computerworld Careers*. 12, no. 2: 1.

Mandela, Nelson. 1999. The Sacred Warrior. *Time*, 31 December: 94–95.

Mander, Jerry. 1996. Facing the Rising Tide. *The Case against the Global Economy*. Edited by Jerry Mander and Edward Goldsmith. San Francisco: Sierra Club Books, 3–19.

Marcuse, Herbert. [1955] 1962. *Eros and Civilization*. New York: Vintage Books.

Markus, R. A. 1967. St. Augustine. *The Encyclopedia of Philosophy*. Vol. 1. Edited by Paul Edwards. New York: Macmillan, 198–206.

Marx, Karl. 1964. *The Economic and Philosophic Manuscripts of 1844.* Edited by Dirk
    Struik. New York: International.
————. 1973. *Grundrisse.* Translated by Martin Nicolaus. New York: Vintage Books.
————. 1978. *The Marx-Engels Reader.* Edited by Robert Tucker. New York: W. W.
    Norton.
Maslow, Abraham. 1968. *Toward a Psychology of Being.* New York: D. Van Nostrand.
McGeary, Johanna. 1999. Mohandas Gandhi. *Time,* 31 December: 86–91.
McKibben, Bill. 1999. The End of Growth. *Mother Jones,* November/December: 68–95.
McLellan, David. 1979. *Marxism after Marx.* Boston: Houghton Mifflin.
Milbrath, Lester. 1989. *Envisioning a Sustainable Society.* Albany: State University of
    New York Press.
Mill, John Stuart. [1873] 1937. *Autobiography.* New York: P. F. Collier and Son.
————. 1966. *John Stuart Mill: A Selection of His Works.* Edited by John M. Robson.
    New York: Odyssey Press.
————. [1843] 1967. *A System of Logic.* London: Longmans.
————. 1979. *The Collected Works of John Stuart Mill: An Examination of Sir William
    Hamilton's Philosophy.* Vol. 9. Edited by J. M. Robson. Toronto: University of
    Toronto Press.
————. [1859] 1985. *On Liberty.* London: Penguin Books.
Mills, C. Wright. 1951. *White Collar.* New York: Oxford University Press.
Morrow, Glenn. 1960. *Plato's Cretan City.* Princeton, NJ: Princeton University Press.
Munro, Kathryn. 1999. Leadership Forum. College of Business Administration, Northern
    Arizona University. Flagstaff, Arizona.
Muwakkil, Salim. 1999. Africa Is Dying. *In These Times,* 22 August: 17–18.
Novack, George, ed. 1966. *Existentialism versus Marxism.* New York: Delta.
O'Connell, Robert. 1968. *St. Augustine's Early Theory of Man, A.D. 386–391.*
    Cambridge: Harvard University Press.
O'Connor, Martin, ed. 1994. *Is Capitalism Sustainable?* New York: Guilford Press.
Orr, David. 1992. *Ecological Literacy.* Albany: State University of New York Press.
Owens, Joseph. 1963. *The Doctrine of Being in the Aristotelian "Metaphysics."* Toronto:
    Pontifical Institute of Mediaeval Studies.
Piccone, Paul. 1988. The Crisis of American Conservatism. *Telos* 20, no. 4: 3–29.
Plato. 1963. *Plato Dictionary.* Edited by Morris Stockhammer. New York: Philosophical
    Library, 275–276.
Polanyi, Karl. [1944] 1957. *The Great Transformation.* Boston: Beacon Press.
Ponting, Clive. 1991. *A Green History of the World.* New York: St. Martin's Press.
Poster, Mark. 1975. *Existential Marxism in Postwar France.* Princeton, NJ: Princeton
    University Press.
Preteceille, Edmond, and Jean-Pierre Terrail. 1985. *Capitalism, Consumption and Needs.*
    Translated by S. Matthews. New York: Basil Blackwell.
Quinn, Daniel. 1992. *Ishmael.* New York: Bantam Books.
————. 1996. *The Story of B.* New York: Bantam Books.
————. 1997. *My Ishmael.* New York: Bantam Books.
————. 1999. *Beyond Civilization.* New York: Harmony Books.
Ray, Paul. 1995. The Integral Culture Survey: A Study of Values Subcultures and the
    Use of Alternative Health Care in America. A Report to Fetzer Institute and the
    Institute of Noetic Sciences. October.
————. 1996. The Great Divide. *Yes! A Journal of Positive Futures,* Fall: 55–58.
Reich, Charles. 1970. *The Greening of America.* New York: Random House.
Renner, Michael. 1996. *Fighting for Survival.* New York: W. W. Norton.

Rethinking Marxism: A Journal of Economics, Culture, and Society. New York: Guilford
    Publications.
Rifkin, Jeremy. 1991. *Biosphere Politics.* San Francisco: HarperCollins.
———. 1995. *The End of Work.* New York: G. P. Putman's Sons.
Robbins, Lionel. 1932. *An Essay on the Nature and Significance of Economic Science.*
    London: Macmillan.
Rorty, Amelie O., ed. 1980. *Essays on Aristotle's Ethics.* Berkeley: University of
    California Press.
Rosser, J. Barkley, and Marina Rosser. 1996. *Comparative Economics in a Transforming
    World Economy.* Chicago: Irwin.
Roszak, Theodore. 1969. *The Making of a Counter-Culture.* Garden City, NY:
    Doubleday.
Ryan, Alan. 1970. *John Stuart Mill.* New York: Pantheon Books.
Sahlins, Marshall. 1972. *Stone Age Economics.* New York: Aldine.
Salopek, Paul. 2000. Inklings of Peace Intrude in Bereft Angola. *Chicago Tribune,* 14
    January: I-3.
Sartre, Jean-Paul. [1953] 1966. *Being and Nothingness.* New York: Washington Square
    Press.
Schneewind, J. B. 1967. John Stuart Mill. Encyclopedia of Philosophy. Vol. 5. Edited by
    Paul Edwards. New York: Macmillan, 314–322.
Schnitzer, Martin. 2000. *Comparative Economic Systems.* Cincinnati: South-Western.
Schor, Juliet. 1992. *The Overworked American.* New York: Basic Books.
———. 1998. *The Overspent American.* New York: Basic Books.
Schumacher, E.F. 1973. *Small Is Beautiful.* New York: Harper and Row.
Seneca. 1967a. *Ad Lucilium Epistulae Morales.* Vol. 1. Translated by Richard Gummere.
    Cambridge: Harvard University Press.
———. 1967b *Ad Lucilium Epistulae Morales.* Vol. 3. Translated by Richard Gummere.
    Cambridge: Harvard University Press.
Shell, Ellen. 1997. Resurgence of a Deadly Disease. *The Atlantic Monthly,* August: 45–
    60.
Shi, David. 1985. *The Simple Life.* New York: Oxford University Press.
Spencer, Joseph. 1966. *Shifting Cultivation in Southeast Asia.* Berkeley: University of
    California Press.
Stanfield, Ron. 1973. *The Economic Surplus and Neo-Marxism.* Lexington, MA:
    Lexington Books.
Stromberg, Roland. 1968. *European Intellectual History since 1789.* New York:
    Meredith.
Sullivan, Roger. 1977. *Morality and the Good Life.* Memphis: Memphis State University
    Press.
Telos: A Quarterly Journal of Critical Thought. New York: Telos Press Ltd.
Theobald, Robert. 1997. *Reworking Success.* Gabriola Island, Canada: New Society.
Thich Nhat Hanh. 1999. New Century Message from Thich Nhat Hanh. Duplicated.
Trapped in the Theology of Work. 1989. *The Arizona Republic,* 6 September: A7.
Ulich, Robert. 1945. *History of Educational Thought.* New York: American Book.
———. 1965. *Education in Western Culture.* New York: Harcourt, Brace, and World.
———. 1967. John Amos Comenius. *Encyclopedia of Philosophy.* Vol. 1. Edited by Paul
    Edwards. New York: Macmillan, 146–147.
———, ed. 1964. *Education and the Idea of Mankind.* New York: Harcourt, Brace, and
    World.
United Nations Development Program. 1998. *Human Development Report.* New York:
    Oxford University Press.

Vajda, Mihaly. 1981. *The State and Socialism*. London: Allison and Busby.

Veblen, Thorstein. [1899] 1945. *The Theory of the Leisure Class*. New York: Viking Press.

Wachtel, Paul. 1989. *The Poverty of Affluence*. Philadelphia: New Society.

Wallerstein, Immanuel. 1974. *The Modern World-System*. Vol. 1. New York: Academic Press.

————. 1980. *The Modern World-System*. Vol. 2. New York: Academic Press.

Walzer, Michael. 1983. *Spheres of Justice*. New York: Basic Books.

Ward, Leo. 1963. *Philosophy of Education*. Chicago: Henry Regnery.

World Bank. 2000. *Entering the 21st Century: World Development Report 1999/2000*. New York: Oxford University Press.

Wright, James. 1967. Seneca. *The Encyclopedia of Philosophy*. Vol. 7. Edited by Paul Edwards. New York: Macmillan, 406–407.

Wyse, Elizabeth, and Barry Winkleman, eds. [1988] 1997. *Past Worlds: Atlas of Archaeology*. London: HarperCollins.

Zachary, G. Pascal. 2000. Africa in Agony. *In These Times*, 26 June: 10–13.

Index

About the Author

DOUG BROWN is Professor of Economics in the College of Business at Northern Arizona University. His areas of research focus on institutional economics, comparative economic systems, the globalization of capitalism, and human and environmental sustainability. His books include *The Economic Status of Women Under Capitalism* (1994), co-edited with Janice Peterson, and *Thorstein Veblen in the Twenty-first Century* (1998). He is active in the Association for Institutional Economics and the Association for Evolutionary Economics.